disput

essays on
psychoanalysis,

subjects

politics and
philosophy

disputed

essays on

psychoanalysis,

subjects

politics and

philosophy

**JANE
FLAX**

Routledge · New York & London

Published in 1993 by

Routledge
29 West 35th Street
New York, NY 10001

Published in Great Britain by
Routledge
11 New Fetter Lane
London EC4P 4EE

Copy © 1993 by Routledge

Printed in the United States of America on acid-free paper.

Library of Congress Cataloging-in-Publication Data

Flax, Jane.
    Disputed subjects : essays on psychoanalysis, politics, and
philosophy / Jane Flax.
      p. cm.
    Includes bibliographical references and index.
    ISBN 0-415-90789-6. — ISBN 0-415-90790-X (pbk.)
    1. Feminist theory.   2. Psychoanalysis and feminism.
    3. Postmodernism.   4. Philosophy, Modern — 20th century.   I. Title.
HQ1190.F59   1993
305.42'01—dc20   93-15321
                                              CIP

British Library Cataloguing-in-Publication Data also available.

This book is dedicated to the memories of Audre Lorde and Dorothy Dinnerstein, in gratitude for their hard lessons and unrelenting integrity; and to Gabe and Fred for simple gifts, the most difficult to receive.

CONTENTS

EPIGRAPHS

There are times in life when the question of knowing if one can think differently than one thinks and perceive differently than one sees is absolutely necessary if one is to go on looking and reflecting at all.

People will say, perhaps, that these games with oneself need only go on behind the scenes; that they are, at best, part of those labors of preparation that efface themselves when they have had their effects. But what, then, is philosophy today—philosophical activity, I mean—if not the critical labor of thought upon itself? And if it does not consist, in place of legitimating what one already knows, in undertaking to know how, and up to what limit, it would be possible to think differently?"

Michel Foucault

The further one goes, the more possibilities there are, if you keep your eyes open and your mind not fixed—the mind that so often says, 'Well, that shouldn't be.'

Merce Cunningham

We do not know, when a man dies, what has come to pass. We know only: he has left us. We depend upon his works, but we know that the works do not need us. They are what the one who dies leaves in the world—the world that was there before he came and which remains when he has gone. What will become of them depends on the way of the world. But the simple fact that these books were once a lived life, this fact does not go directly into the world or remain safe from forgetfulness. That about a man which is most impermanent and also perhaps most great, his spoken word and his unique comportment, that dies with him and thus needs us; needs us who think of him. Such thinking brings us to a relationship with the dead one, out of which, then conversation about him springs and sounds again in the world. A relationship with the dead one—this must be learned . . .

Hannah Arendt

PREFACE

The essays in this volume were written in response to questions about my last book, *Thinking Fragments*.[1] In that book I created conversations between psycho-analytic, feminist, and postmodernist theorizing. There were several purposes for these conversations. I wanted to illuminate the strengths and weaknesses of a variety of theories and to show what each alone and conversations between them could contribute to understanding contemporary Western cultures. I also intend-ed to explore and practice alternatives to the classic truth-enunciating mode of Western philosophy.

These conversations introduced as many questions as answers. I have not acquired any better answers, but I can offer some new contributions to my old conversation topics. These topics include knowledge, power, subjectivity, gender, justice, and responsibility. I continue to track the connections and conflicts within and among these topics and to pursue discourses that elucidate their meanings.

The previous conversations also generated many responses. Readers have chal-lenged me with several claims. These include: postmodernists are necessarily politically irresponsible nihilists; they can make no contributions to useful notions of subjectivity; psychoanalysts must maintain allegiance to a unitary notion of a core self; and successful struggles against male dominance require a solid, empirical, and collective sense of female subjectivity. As my responses here indicate, I have not yet been convinced by these arguments. They appear to rely on unproductively flawed assumptions about subjectivity, knowledge, gender, justice, and responsibility.

In the first essay, "Minerva's Owl," I analyze my continuing obsession with these topics. This essay works on at least two levels. It is an exercise in contingent autobiography—a narrative that is resistant to and critical of assumptions that traditionally inform its genre. However, it is also an attempt to place my intellectual moves in personal, theoretical, and political contexts and to reflect upon the empowering and constricting aspects of these contexts and moves. I think about paths that appear to be irrevocably barred and others whose seductions are a recurrent danger. A commentator on an earlier version correctly pointed out its pervasive sense of nostalgia. It is full of nostalgia in Milos Kundera's sense—a mixture of regret, longing, and desire for objects irretrievably lost but powerfully present in their absence.[2]

In the second essay, "Final Analysis," I struggle again with psychoanalysis, one of my enabling and constricting discourses. Making use of one of my favorite intellectual objects, Michel Foucault, I analyze analysis as a discursive formation. This approach in part is meant to disrupt dominant conversations about psychoanalysis. Too often discourse about it is carried out within the question of its (actual or potential) scientific status. This approach is a symptom of some of its (and our) problems; it is not conducive to very interesting or fruitful conversations.

The recurrence of this question reflects the ambivalent location of psychoanalysis and other Western discourses—both in and outside Enlightenment metanarratives. In these metanarratives an idealized version of science serves as the exemplar of and locus of hope for the possibility of objective, mirroring knowledge of reality. However, for psychoanalysis at least, this ambivalence is no longer constructive. It enables analysts to rationalize some of their own dangerous innocence concerning the politics of their knowledge and practices. It also impedes development of an essential process in all discursive formations: the constitution of discourse-specific rules regulating the production of truth and the justification and legitimation of power. Lacking such rules practitioners within a discourse cannot be responsible to each other. Under these conditions productive negotiations or conversations with others outside their own discursive practices are unlikely.

Despite their many discourse-specific problems I still find psychoanalytic ideas and strategies essential. One issue I frequently revisit in my clinical and theoretical work is the relationships between mothers and daughters. I am particularly interested in fantasies associated with these relationships and how they recur in theorizing as well as in personal interactions. In "Forgotten Forms of Close Combat," I move from an analysis of an interaction between a female patient and myself to tracking fantasies about the maternal through feminist discourses. I discuss some of the purposes such fantasies serve, especially absolving white women of their complicity in relations of domination such as race.

The valorization of maternal images within contemporary feminist theorizing and the splitting of (good) maternity and (bad) sexuality are extremely problematic. They indicate that despite their powerful critiques of patriarchal thinking, traces of it circulate within feminist discourses. These fantasies are also enlisted to protect men and women from knowledge we already possess—that the powers humans may have are far exceeded by the extent of our powerlessness, our mortality, and the frequent lack of coincidence between desire, intentions, and outcome. Full responsibility for our actions (despite imperfect conditions) can be disavowed as long as we are waiting for some more powerful person or force to take care of us.

One of the still-powerful hopes of Enlightenment is that knowledge could serve as a simultaneously neutral and beneficial force. It will empower us to act rationally and in so acting we could perfect humans and their institutions. Reason, truth, knowledge, and power interact to generate rational and therefore legitimate authority. Such authority reflects and ensures our freedom; in obeying it we confirm our sovereignty and escape from domination.

Some contemporary theorists, including Jürgen Habermas, argue that it is still possible for us to redeem the emancipatory promises of Enlightenment. I am quite skeptical about such claims as are other writers, including Michel Foucault. Unlike Foucault, much of my skepticism reflects an awareness of the gendered qualities of narratives and promises of Enlightenment. Like many feminist theorists I do not think these qualities are accidental or extrinsic to the coherence or plausibility of the narratives.

To pursue the question of the emancipatory potential of Enlightenment, I return to one of its founding texts, Immanuel Kant's essay, "What is Enlightenment?" The constituting roles and effects of male dominant gender relations and a gendered division of labor and human qualities are unveiled in my deconstruction of this text. Along with writers like Julia Kristeva and Luce Irigaray, I argue that modernity's promise is not redemption but the simultaneous generation and devaluation of differences. A rich, satisfying political life will require something else than more of the same.

What kinds of subjectivity resist domination and struggle for something else? Unlike Kant, Habermas, John Rawls, or some contemporary feminists I argue that a subject in whom rationality is the privileged quality cannot sustain emancipatory struggles. In "Multiples," I explore the possibilities of fluid, multiple subjectivities whose desires for differences will impel them toward resisting (inner or external) relations of domination.

Our abilities to imagine such subjectivities are impeded by the positing of false alternatives. Some postmodernists confine all talk about subjectivity to critiques of the split Cartesian rationalistic subject or of the unitary, authentic "true self." On the other hand, critics of postmodernism and some postmodernists reduce all descriptions of a decentered subject to a fragmented one that lacks any agency or organization. None of these constructs are appealing or plausible. Their juxtaposition and the limits of the arguments demonstrate how difficult it is to imagine subjectivity outside Enlightenment ideas of it. The unitary self and the fragmented one are simply mirror images; neither represents an alternative to the subjects Enlightenment discourses construct.

What practices of justice would multiple subjects desire and sustain? I take up this question in "The Play of Justice." This essay also has multiple purposes. I want to show by example that there is no inherent contradiction between postmodernist commitments to the play of differences and ethical ones. Quite the contrary, full commitment to the play of differences requires resistance to relations of domination and development of new theories and practices of justice.

Postmodernism does not entail a belief that all differences are equal or reconcilable. The number of forms of life that can coexist peacefully is necessarily limited. Conflict and power (in its generative and constraining modes) are intrinsic to all social relations, including politics. However, postmodernists recognize the unavailability of any transcendental trump or universal measure of the good. They forsake the hope there could be transdiscourse rules or neutral procedures to resolve disagreements. Rules are discourse specific and have limited and heterogeneous effects. The possibility always exists that some conflicts cannot be resolved peacefully or to the satisfaction of all disputants. The pursuit of one's own mode of life may necessitate harm to others. An ethics of injustice would thus be a constituent element of any practice of justice.

In "The Play of Justice," I critique recent attempts to construct rationalistic theories of justice. Drawing on the work of D. W. Winnicott, especially his idea of transitional spaces, I outline an alternate notion of justice as processes. These processes simultaneously contribute to the construction and sustenance of fluid subjectivities. I argue that talk about justice cannot be deontological, that is, it cannot occur outside consideration of the good(s) we desire. It also requires conversations about who its practitioners wish to be; about how our subjectivities are to be constructed and sustained.

The problem with rationalistic theories of justice is not that they require and depend on a notion of subjectivity but that this subject is self-destructive. The construction and maintenance of such subjectivity require excessive internal and external relations of domination. This subject's attempts at justice result in self-defeat and the destruction of many differences required for rich transitional spaces or political lives. I do not imagine that such spaces will be free from tragedy, disappointments, or frustration. However, they will be more generative of and satisfying to complex subjectivities. They will evoke and support more responsible modes of life.

The writers I feel drawn to—Machiavelli, Weber, Freud, Winnicott, and Foucault among them—struggle with responsibility under conditions of disenchantment, disorder, and imperfection. None of them have any hope or expectation humans will be redeemed from engagement in this struggle, although they all imagine better and worse ways to live it. Machiavelli placed Fortuna, the goddess of chance, as the central force in political life. Fortuna controls only half our actions but we can never know when she will choose to intervene or leave us to exercise our own creativity. Machiavelli traces (as will Winnicott later) the simultaneity of and connections between creativity and destruction, order and will, and power and powerlessness. We are responsible for and suffer the consequences of our actions, even if their outcomes differ greatly from our intentions.

"The End of Innocence" grapples with the meanings, possibilities, and consequences of disenchantment. Hope for redemption from such conditions is a dangerous illusion. In the twentieth century it has served as a warrant for the most terrible human actions. Humans have developed godlike weapons of destruction and strategies of annihilation, but not omniscience or universal beneficence. The viability, justice, and pleasures of our postmodern worlds depend on developing and practicing ethics of limits and complicity. Like Jean-Francois Lyotard I have a profound distrust of metanarratives or grand theorizing. Full disenchantment would not be nearly as dangerous or as paralyzing as is the inability of the modern unhappy consciousness to abandon its hope. This hope is that the monsters and gods it now recognizes as its own flawed and powerless creations will finally and nevertheless carry out the projects assigned to them.

I intend these essays to contribute to ongoing processes of disillusionment and to discussions about the development of more realistic hopes. What should or could replace the grand totalizing dreams of Western modernity? These dilemmas and questions are context specific. I cannot imagine speaking for or about the dreams of persons in locations other than my own as a well-off, white Western intellectual woman. However I recognize my obligation to grapple with complicity in generating some nightmares for many unlike me. From this and other similarly determined and determining positions conversations ensue.

ACKNOWLEDGMENTS

Each of these essays was initially written and subsequently revised in response to invitations to present a paper. Some have already been published, but all have been substantially revised for this book. I want to thank the following programs and institutions for providing me with hospitable and challenging contexts for conversations: The Mellon Foundation "Works in Progress" Series and the Women's Studies Program at Emory University; The European University Institute, Florence; Haverford College; Babson College; The Harland Fund and the Women's Studies Program at Duke University; The American Council of Learned Societies Travel Grant; The Office of the Dean of Social Sciences, University of Southern California; The Essex Symposia, University of Essex; The Division of Philosophy at the University of Bielefeld; The Berkeley Psychotherapy Institute; The University of Richmond; Institute for the Humanities, Department of Psychology and Women's Studies Program, University of Michigan at Ann Arbor; Postdoctoral Program in Psychology at New York University; The 350th Anniversary Committee of the University of Utrecht; The Advanced Program in Women's Studies at the University of Utrecht; Grinnell College; The Gender and Politics Lecture Series, University of Maryland College Park; Division 39 of the American Psychological Association; Willamette University; The Sixtieth Anniversary Conference Committee of the

Chicago Institute for Psychoanalysis; and the Rockefeller Foundation for its Conference on Rural Women and Feminist Issues at the University of Iowa.

I have been fortunate to interact with people who made my travels pleasant and interesting. In particular I would like to thank the following people for their discussions and caretaking: Mary Price, Eliza Woodford, Arlene Saxonhouse, Bob Fajardo, Barbara Fajardo, Elizabeth Fox-Genovese, Jean O'Barr, Fritz Fleischmann, Steven Collins, Sally McConnell-Ginet, Bob Hatcher, Kim Leary, Sally Markowitz, Rosi Braidotti, Valeria Russo, Janneke van Mens-Verhulst, Miriam King, Suzanne Jones, Michael Dear, Maggie Iverson, Margery Wolf, Caroline Sachs, Randy Milden, Cynthia McSwain, Elisabeth Young-Bruehl, and Polly Young-Eisendrath.

I am also indebted to a network of friends who keep me honest and unsettled: Elizabeth Abel, Irene Fast, Nancy Hartsock, Sandra Harding, Mervat Hatem, Peter Lyman, JoAnn Reiss and Barrie Thorne. My son Gabe Frankel's sense of humor is especially helpful in moments of despair or grandiosity.

Two people are especially important to the production of this book. Maureen MacGrogan, my editor, cajoled and encouraged it into print. Rick Seltzer introduced me to the joys of computing and rescued me from some of its perils. Howard University provided sabbatical leave for me to complete this project.

Finally, I am unable to adequately express my gratitude to Gisela Bock for my little room in Berlin, to Janet Adelman for talks in Berkeley, and to Kirsten Dahl for her steadfast love and continuity. Although geographically dispersed they are lovingly present and appreciated. To Fred Risser, best friend extraordinaire, my heartfelt love.

ONE

OVERVIEW/REFLECTIONS

I

Minerva's Owl

FRAGMENTS OF A THINKING LIFE

When philosophy paints its grey in grey, then has a shape of life grown old. By
philosophy's grey in grey it cannot be be rejuvenated but only understood. The owl
of Minerva spreads its wings only with the falling of the dusk.

G.W.F. Hegel,
Philosophy of Right

Oh, I was so much older then;
I'm younger than that now.

Bob Dylan

MINERVA'S OWL?

Surprisingly, the prospect of reflecting upon my writing fills me with melancholy. Perhaps the unconscious effects of a still-powerful, though disavowed,
Enlightenment wish contribute to this mood. It would be pleasant to chart a
straightforward and progressive course: from error to truth, from uncertainty to
clarity, from confusion to complex simplicity, from relative poverty to the accumulation of theoretical excess. Instead, I feel compelled to tell a more ambiguous story whose content mixes personal history and theoretical reflection.

I do not assume any straightforward relationships between theorizing and
experience. Instead, I will stress the contingency and discontinuities of my theoretical moves. I do not think experience validates theory or determines choices
among theories, or even that experience directly informs theory (or the reverse).
My years in psychoanalysis (and postmodernism) make me painfully aware of the
constructed nature of any narrative. I know the telling of the tale is constrained
and shaped by the narrative and theoretical conventions available. These con-

struct and reconstruct "me" as I fabricate it. Much material must also elude my awareness, including the excluded content of and unconscious motivations for my story.

I want to explore the politics of my writing, its dependence on and complicity with various forms of power, its relations to my political history and commitments. None of these relationships are direct, determining, or unambiguous. Sometimes the relationships between theorizing and practical political activity are highly mediated and circuitous. My immediate motives for theorizing vary; not all of them are determined by political utility. Aesthetic pleasure, play, and intellectual curiosity are sometimes equally or more important. My theorizing provides me with no privileged insight into political matters, nor does it directly determine or ground my political commitments. As I will discuss below, my suspicions about knowledge and reason immediately complicate my understanding of the political status and activities of any intellectual, including myself.

My understanding of theorizing is a pragmatic one. Theorizing comprises a variety of practices, and no one mode can meet all our needs. Theorizing includes contextual puzzle solving as well as metalevel thinking about thinking. Each theoretical practice has its own purposes, limits, appropriate domain, tools, and rules. The most persuasive basis for adopting or criticizing one is to take these seriously.

Sometimes theorizing is exclusively defined as abstract metalevel work, but this is incorrect. Such theorizing is not a higher-order or more comprehensive form of thinking. In many contexts metalevel theorizing is utterly irrelevant; in others it may be necessary to understand political or intellectual stalemates. Like all theoretical practices, it serves distinctive and limited purposes, such as identifying implicit assumptions about method, truth, or knowledge. It may also provide a satisfying form of intellectual play for some people.

One of my main motives for theorizing is "to be of use," and context determines utility. A Marge Piercy poem expresses my own feelings:

> . . . I love people who harness themselves, an ox to a heavy cart,
> who pull like water buffalo, with massive patience,
> who strain in the mud and muck to move things forward,
> who do what has to be done, again and again.[1]

To be useful requires communities. Writing may overtake and surprise me. However, I cannot write without an (at least imaginary) audience—a community. Communities provide one with puzzles to address; theoretical frames to appropriate; purposes to evaluate, adopt, or reject; conversation partners to engage; multiple senses of identity; loyalties that can moor and enrich one's sense of place; and a sharp brake against one's narcissism and grandiosity. In defining their boundaries and identities, communities name and constitute outsiders and enemies whom it is necessary and correct to attack. They also provide one with reasons to continue to slog through the mud, especially when the intrinsic satisfaction of the task appears slight. One can at least have the fantasy that one is acting on behalf of something larger and more important than oneself.

Another component of my melancholy may be that writing this essay forces me to confront my discouragement about certain trends in contemporary academic feminist (and other) politics. Ever since I entered graduate school in 1969, activist and academic feminisms have been primary communities for me. Yet I find aspects of contemporary academic feminisms increasingly troubling. One concern is the increasing disparity between the complexity of academic feminist theorizing and the virulent simplicity of the antifeminist and racist backlash, so evident, for example, in the recent Republican convention in Houston. Solutions to this disparity cannot include providing crudely empiricist feminist analyses or prescriptions or writing "antitheory" papers. Writing, thinking, and acting in the world all entail theorizing. Furthermore, any possible feminist futures will require more rather than less appreciation for complexity, limits, and ambiguity in political life. We need to cultivate the capacity to assign and take responsibility without turning others into monstrous villains or heroes. These qualities are essential to nurture political creativity, or even to sustain survival, in our multicultural, postmodern world. Yet, effective means to develop them are elusive.

Additional facets of the current politics of feminist discourse are disturbing as well. The tendency to berate others for their political/theoretical errors while failing to subject one's own ideas to the same critique is especially objectionable. This tendency often pervades the contemporary rush to accuse other writers of failing to pay adequate attention to the current holy trinity of "difference": race/class/gender. Motives other than the putative one—political correctness —can engender such moves. A strange appropriation of "the other" sometimes occurs in which the voices remain curiously the same.[2]

White women may deploy "race" against other white women to evoke shame, monopolize conversation, or paralyze potential speakers. The author often deploys such criticism to cover her own, quite different desire—to position her-self as the singular authority able to correct the errors of the others. While the author continues to maneuver behind the mantle of objectivity and intellectual correctness, any detailed attention to the trinity (especially to race as a constitut-ing relation for white women) remains absent.

In parts of white feminist discourse, women of color may now be appropri-ated as "tokens" in a new manner. Some white women attempt to use the "oth-ers" as pieces in our own wars. We compete among ourselves to criticize the absence of women of color in our writings and politics. Sometimes we define the problem as a failure to include or represent everyone's experience. The excluded must be let into existing structures. This definition recapitulates the rhetoric of early integrationist strategies, and it generates and reflects the problems of those approaches. Women of color remain marked as the only raced group; race as a constituting element in contemporary gender relations is inadequately articu-lated. The assumption that there is one relatively harmonious and homogeneous reality available for a singular mode of representation rests undisturbed.

The destabilizing effects of race on the categories of women and gender are even less adequately thought through. Certain absences are noted and deplored, but much writing on women and gender continues as if this very noting then per-mits us to ignore or renders neutral our elision of the internal differentiation of these categories. Once again, the naming of the marginalized serves to legitimate the discourse that continues to locate them at the margins. Despite all the talk about difference, it seems much harder for many of us to imagine it as an internal and potentially discordant heterogeneity within and across complexly related ele-ments.[3] Perhaps it is more comfortable to treat difference as variations between fairly homogeneous and unrelated blocks. Then one can deny complicity in con-structing and being constructed by the difference of the others.

Equally discouraging is the tendency in feminist writing for an author to reduce the complexity of another person's ideas to one simple position or creed. The intolerance of ambiguity, change, and development found in "mainstream" American politics sometimes marks its "marginalized" others as well—including feminist discourses. In reading feminist criticism, for example, one can some-times detect a sense of relief when the commentator believes she has successfully located an author in one exclusionary political-theoretical slot. She may do this simply to show how wrong the ideas are, in contrast to her superior ones. Even worse is the tendency for feminists to demonize others. Some recent criticism creates the impression that adherents to often-misconstrued but disliked positions—whether "individualism" or "postmodernism"—represent a greater danger to feminist aims than those with the power, for example, to outlaw abortion.

A PASSION FOR JUSTICE

These developments in feminist communities complicate my efforts to maintain a fragile intellectual balance. One of the paradoxical qualities of my more than fifteen-year writing history[4] is the continual search for a comfortable intellectual community, coupled with an apparently congenital inability to reside too long anywhere. I try to operate in good faith within a set of theoretical and practical loyalties while resisting the pull to become a dogmatic prisoner or advocate of them. Different discourses provoke and enable me to ask particular questions. In pursuing these questions I become perhaps too quickly aware of the limits of the discourse itself and the inadequacy of the originally posed question.[5]

The longer I write, the more uncertain I become about any aspect of my theorizing. Besides my intensifying quandaries about audiences and purposes, even the most basic tools I use, categories such as woman/women; man/men; gender; class; self; sexuality; experience; race; politics; knowledge; emancipation; and practice, appear increasingly unstable and suspect. On the other hand, I have never disregarded and am still deeply attached to certain visceral beliefs about justice and how people should be treated. These are so emotionally loaded that a better term for them is feeling-thoughts.

Many of my political passions have persisted despite and through numerous theoretical transformations. Such persistence through change has taught me much about the highly contingent relations of theorizing and practice, reason and commitment. Reflection on my own theoretical practice shows that changes in thinking are heavily dependent on the availability of alternatives. I cannot imagine any author, including myself, as an isolated Prometheus, creating something new out of nothing. Hence the postmodernist view of the "author" as an effect of discourse does not surprise me, nor does it seem to be a denial of the possibility of creativity—quite the contrary.

I have also never understood the postmodernist claim that meaning and action depend upon power, preexisting discourses, and resistances to them to entail the necessary absence of emancipatory possibility. It has always seemed rather a question of which discourses are available and what sorts of resistances exist.

The content of both depends in part on power and chance. However new or transformative they may feel in the moment, the discursive frames through which we name and process information are determined by the available set and prior choices among them. Our theoretical commitments are motivated and sustained in part by complex, idiosyncratic psychological desires, temperament, and family dramas as well as by reason, group loyalties and identities, the set of language games available and contingencies of historical events and locations.

My own history is a complex artifact of the interplay of contingency, overdetermination, and the available, narrative conventions. As a child of Berkeley in the 1960s I was predisposed to deploy political discourses to make sense of my world. Participation in civil rights, student, and antiwar movements reinforced my inclination to understand events in certain political ways. Yet, it was pure luck from my individual point of view that the women's movement emerged when it did. What would have happened had I been ten years older?

Why people belittle, attack, kill, abuse, constrain, or hate others for a condition that is highly contingent (although it may be constructed and presented as "natural" and hence unchangeable) is one of the puzzles that drive my work. Such behavior violates the ethical tenets that pervaded my early family and public education. My schools were homogeneous in race and class: almost totally white and well off. The existence and rightness of equality appeared indubitable. As an undergraduate at Berkeley I was fortunate to study with superb political theorists who were passionate about justice. The struggle to put these commitments into practice, through political participation and in our daily lives, seemed like a normal part of everyday life.

My attachment to justice deepened when I went to Yale for graduate school in 1969. Unfortunately, like many other whites in the civil rights movement, I thought racism was black people's problem. We (whites) were just helping "them" out. The Vietnam War was also a somewhat impersonal injustice; I did not want my male friends to be drafted or the Vietnamese to be destroyed. As a resident of Berkeley in those years, I did not particularly feel like an "American" (much less like the occupant of an overdeveloped country whose comfort depended in part on the misery of others). American troops occupied our own city in the spring of 1969. To the extent I did identify myself as an American citizen, I felt shame at what "the government" was doing in my name. Knowledge of the Holocaust certainly would have given me a sense of ontological insecurity. However, no one at home or in school discussed it. This was not an unusual situation for those growing up in the wealthy white suburbs in the 1950s.

THE PROBLEM WITH NO NAME

At Yale, politics became personal as they had not been before. My good Jewish father raised me to believe that my intelligence occluded the dreadful marks of femininity. It was quite startling to become, or to realize one always was in certain ways, devalued, if not hated, because one was not a white, preferably Protestant, male. It was shocking to discover that being smart was not enough to save me from inscription as an inferior within the male/female asymmetric binary. No doubt this discovery continues to generate some of the emotive force of my skepticism about the Enlightenment metanarrative of emancipation through reason.

My sense of urgency about injustice intensified as I simultaneously began to realize the pervasive devaluation of women and to encounter new vocabularies to name it and movements to resist it. I do not know how I would have made sense of some of my experiences at Yale, or perhaps even persisted in school despite them, had not women's movements surged forth.[6] On the other hand, if had I not acquiesced in my father's wish for me to infiltrate Yale, which he perceived as a WASP citadel, and attended Brandeis instead (where I would have felt more at home culturally and intellectually), would my feminist feelings run as deep?

Like many others of my generation, I became a feminist theorist as I participated in feminist politics. In my formal education no one discussed existing feminist writings or the history of protests against male dominance. Feminists initially assembled the rudiments of our theoretical discourses as necessary aspects of feminist activity.

In graduate school, the outlines of many of the other questions that continue to drive me also emerged. These questions concern the relationships between politics and knowledge and between "inner" fantasy worlds and "outer" consensual reality and between all of these and relationships of domination. When I was a student, the question of whether political science could be (or already was) an empirical science dominated its discourses. One might think this was an odd question to convulse a discipline whose charge is to study politics, especially at a time when cities were burning and domestic and international politics were particularly chaotic. Even then, though, I had an intimation that knowledge claims and politics were interdependent. A discipline must acquire authority before it can enter into and affect political discourse. In the modern world scientific status is a necessary warrant for such authority claims. Hence in a time of chaos, the status of one's epistemological foundations is especially important.

DIALECTICS OF ENLIGHTENMENT

I would not have been able to develop these intuitions without another fortu-itous circumstance. At a conference for Danforth Fellows, I met a group of stu-dents who were working with Herbert Marcuse. Some of them had been to Germany to study in Frankfurt with Theodor Adorno. They introduced me to "critical theory," my first intellectual home.[7] Several aspects of critical theory are particularly appealing and helpful. First, it is an enabling model of intellectual inquiry. The work of Adorno, Horkheimer, and Marcuse (my primary focus) has an extraordinary breadth, especially by American academic standards. In their writing these authors range freely through and incorporate art, music, philoso-phy, psychoanalysis, the family, history, politics, economics, sociology, and popu-lar culture. One could take a single sentence of a book like *Dialectic of Enlightenment*[8] and spend hours decoding its implicit references to Kant, Schiller, Marx, Weber, and so on. Furthermore, although these authors often write at a high level of abstraction, one can always sense the emotional force of their engagement with the texts and issues discussed. The generative power of their political/ethical commitments is also evident.[9]

Another helpful aspect of critical theory is its attempt to relocate epistemol-ogy within the terrain of social relations. They reconceptualize the meaning and purposes of epistemological inquiry. Questions about truth, the adequacy of knowledge, and so on are not solvable through the formulation of abstract rules or a suprahistorical logic. The critical theorists reframe these problems pragmati-cally. The ultimate test of a theory is its political consequences; history, not logic, is the final judge.

They argue knowledge is a social practice. It both reflects the social relations from which it arises and can contribute to their transformation. Particularly important for my later purposes is their claim that knowledge arises out of and reflects social conflict. To understand how and why people put forward certain truth claims and why particular ones prevail, we must analyze their social-histori-cal context. A general logic of discovery or universal decision procedure cannot solve such questions.[10] However, perhaps because of their dislike of "identity the-ory" (in which idea and thing become one), Horkheimer, Adorno, and Marcuse are generally able to avoid the reductionism of many Marxist writers. Their interest in psychoanalysis and their aesthetic sensibilities diminish the appeal of any crude (material) base/(ideological) superstructure theorizing. They rarely treat ideas as a "simple reflex" of class (or any other) social relation.

Horkheimer, Marcuse, and Adorno claim the European working class "failed" to make a revolution in the 1920s and 1930s. As they attempt to account for this "failure," their criticism of Marxism intensifies. They also undertake a more serious consideration of psychoanalysis. Psychoanalysis illuminates some of the deficiencies and failures of Marxism. From a psychoanalyst's perspective, Marxist accounts of human subjectivity and intersubjectivity appear particularly thin and impoverished. Psychoanalysts investigate the importance of fantasy, desire, families, and sexuality in the constitution of individual subjectivity, in the behavior of persons in the "outside" world, and in the structure of social institutions such as the state. Once one begins to identify the effects of unconscious processes class conflict forfeits its privileged (or exclusive) role as *the* dynamic force in human history.

NEGATIVE DIALECTICS

This exploration of psychoanalysis, especially within the context of philosophic and political concerns, was enormously influential on my work. Despite tremendous political pressure in the late 1960s to mid-1970s, I never felt at home within most Marxist theorizing or many Marxist-informed practices. As my interest in psychoanalysis intensified, my disaffection increased. I found the absence from Marxism of sexuality, fantasy, and childhood more disturbing. My long, mostly internal quarrel with Marxist theorizing grew more complex. It may seem odd after the collapse of the Soviet Union, but until recently hopes for a better society in the United States and in many parts of the third world were often represented by various strands of Marxism. The question of its status as an emancipatory theory and practice was unavoidable.

I deeply appreciate Marx's attention to social relations and to the concealed or denied aspects of the circulation of power. His discussion of the fetishism of commodities is particularly inspiring.[11] Similarly, other theorists such as Lukacs and Gramsci are helpful in relocating philosophical issues such as consciousness within more practical terrains.[12] Yet I remain suspicious about the universalizing and causal forms Marxist claims about history and social relations tend to take.

Marxist theories illuminate and describe some of the features of capitalist society in a different vocabulary. This shift of vocabulary makes it more evident that political commitments enter into and partially generate any description of or claim about capitalism. We ought to subject all such descriptions, claims, and commitments (including Marxist ones) to critical scrutiny.

Claims to neutrality or knowledge of objective scientific laws violate Marx's own accounts of the historical and social constitution of knowledge. Their plausibility eventually relies on a transcendental trump. Marxist theorists employ such trumps as positing mental access to the "iron laws of history" or the ontological and epistemological privilege of a particular sort of "labor" (or of the class that engages in it). Alternatively, one is required to make a leap of faith that "in the last instance" certain (economic) factors will be determinative.

Long before I came across postmodernist writers like Foucault or Lyotard, I studied contemporary debates in the philosophy of science and social science. Immersion in these debates left me deeply skeptical about the plausibility of "grand theories" and determinist or causal accounts of human activities.[13] Radical critics of mainstream political science argued that social scientists made claims of neutrality and science to forward or protect claims to power. Even at the time it seemed to me that if it was true, the same might be said about Marxists. One consequence of my many encounters with members of "revolutionary vanguards" in the late 1960s and early 1970s is an intense apprehension about how people motivated by a belief in any "objective" position tend to act toward others who do not share their views. Everyone might be better off if we acknowledge we are all operating on the terrain of power and not truth or objectivity. What counts as "better knowledge" depends in part on its utility for particular political ends.

I also read enough classical political theory to suspect that Marx's promotion of sensuous practical activity (or labor defined as the production of use values) as *the* human essence reflects rather than provides a thorough critique of capitalist societies. It is obvious to me (as it has been to political theorists since Plato) that the social distribution of surplus, the production of material goods, and access to and control over such production has enormous social effects and consequences. Any adequate political theory should prescribe social arrangements to guarantee just production and provision of material needs.

Theorists will evaluate these arrangements according to the ethical, psychological, and political commitments that pervade and motivate their work. While such arrangements are necessary they may not always be considered the definitive human activity. "Materialist" accounts of history may appear more appealing to us precisely because we live in capitalist cultures in which other vocabularies and ways of life, for example, ones based in civic virtue, kinship, faith, or aesthetics, are marginalized.[14] After all, why should Marxism be less marked by the social determination of thought than any other theory?

Questions posed by my students at Howard increased my awareness of and discomfort with the Eurocentric qualities of Marxism. Marxist theorists seem unable to capture the complexities of precolonial, colonial, and postcolonial societies. In many of these societies, some of the relations most absent in Marxist accounts of history—for example, kinship, religion, race, and gender—are determining forces. Marxist theories of development frequently lack any alternative ethical models of social arrangements. Many theorists at least tacitly promote the empty overdevelopment of the West as a stage of progress other countries must achieve.

One could treat Marxism as a theory that is useful only within Western capitalist societies. However, then it is even more significant that important features of these societies, such as racism and male domination, are missing from its explanatory vocabularies and concrete histories. Neo-Marxist attempts to account for racism as a ruse to divide the working class or maximize profit are too thin. They do not provide adequate accounts of dominant groups' investment in and rewards from racism. These accounts also do not do justice to the injuries racism continually inflicts upon dominated groups or to the ingenious forms of resistance the oppressed exercise.

Feminist work makes the gendered qualities of Marxist theorizing more evident and troubling. Initially I focused on the weaknesses of Engels' attempt to explain the oppression of women.[15] Eventually, like many others, I came to believe the gender biases in Marxist theories are foundational, necessary, and disabling. Especially important are the gendered character of its constituting ideas such as labor, class, and history. None of these ideas seem to account for or include the effects of male-dominant gender systems or many of the activities historically performed by women.[16]

Although socialist theorists offer a variety of strategies to "save the theory," the potential political or theoretical payoff for their efforts appears increasingly dubious and insignificant. I have come to believe that these omissions are necessary to the coherence of Marxist theories. Attempts to include gender and race relations and the unconscious will result in the theories' implosion even if we limit Marxism's domain to Western capitalist states.

However, I recognize that one can never give a completely rational or coherent account of one's disillusionment with a theory. My belief that Marxist theorizing is fatally flawed, rather than usefully imperfect, undoubtedly has many irrational, aesthetic, and idiosyncratic determinants. It is certainly possible to arrive at a different position from the same set of "facts."

Freud cannot provide an account of intersubjectivity 'cos his theories are drive-based.

MIMESIS AND DISENCHANTMENT

I found aspects of critical theory very enabling. As I grew more comfortable within it, I also began to confront its political and intellectual limitations. As I became more involved in feminist activities, my sensitivity to its gender biases increased. It was increasingly impossible to ignore how the defense of a certain kind of reason leads the critical theorists to an ambivalent defense of bourgeois culture, especially the patriarchal family. Later, my exposure to postmodernism and the development of more sophisticated feminist philosophies only increased my distance from and deepened my critique of such beliefs. An intensifying interest in psychoanalysis—which my study of critical theory and my feminist activities lead me to pursue—further spurred my disillusionment. My discovery of object relations theories, especially the writings of D. W. Winnicott, transformed and continues to have profound effects on my clinical and theoretical work.

The original critical theorists tend to rely on Freudian structural and drive theories. There is no space for or account of intersubjectivity in these approaches. Despite compelling clinical accounts of the permeability of inner and outer worlds, conceptually the two remain radically other and distinct. The only bases for object relations or the interaction of inner and outer worlds are the imposition of force from the outside or impersonal demand from the inside.

In these theories the ego and superego are secondary mental structures. They develop under the pressure of the instinct of self-preservation and the need for drive gratification. The id is the locus of the drives, but it has no capacity for reality testing. Hence, the ego develops. Reason and rationality are located in and are attributes of the ego. The ego can engage in reality testing and broker compromises between the demands of the id, the superego, and the outside world. The superego develops through the Oedipus crisis, in which the (boy) child renounces his desire for his mother. Under threat of castration he internalizes through identification the authority of the father. The father also represents the ethical demands of the culture. Through this renunciation/identification the boy acquires a masculine identity, a conscience, a sense of his place within and his obligations to preexisting social (and gendered) systems, and a capacity for ethical action. None of these developments, however, transform the id. It remains a somatic/natural/fantasy (primary process) substrate within each person's psyche.

reality principle.

Drives seek satisfaction without concern for their objects or the consequences. To some extent therefore conflict between the demands of the drives for satisfaction and those of culture for productive work, social cooperation, and suitable behavior is unavoidable. Humans will continue to need, be frustrated by, and suffer from civil order. However, for Marcuse at least, this conflict is also a source of hope. Our need for pleasure may motivate us to revolt against "surplus repression" and the oppressive regimes that impose it.[17]

Despite their immersion in this form of psychoanalysis, the critical theorists also could not abandon a Kantian notion of reason. As the possibility of any humane socialist society appears increasingly remote, the theorists relocate their remaining hope for a better future in the emancipatory possibilities of reason. They claim reason has certain innate attributes, including the will to freedom, autonomy, and self-actualization. Freedom is the ability to determine self-consciously the course of one's life in conjunction with other similarly autonomous selves. Horkheimer claims, "Reason's intuition of itself, regarded by philosophy in former times as the highest degree of happiness, is transformed in modern philosophy into the materialist concept of a free, self-determining society."[18]

My immediate problems with this argument arose out of a psychoanalytically informed skepticism that such a reason could exist. Freud's later structural theories undermine the plausibility of Kantian accounts of reason.[19] Freud argues the ego is initially a bodily one. It arises out of and retains its permeable and dynamic relations to the id. The boundaries between the ego and the superego are also not stable or impenetrable. The superego transmits some of the effects of existing authority and ethical relations to the ego. Parts of the ego itself can be dynamically repressed. Given this constantly shifting and conflict-ridden system, what space or ground is there for an undetermined or self-governing (autonomous) reason?

I also could not ignore Horkheimer and Adorno's arguments that the development of such reason requires a bourgeois patriarchal family. A defining characteristic of these families is their gender-based division of labor. The bourgeois family incorporates love and authority. The mother contributes love, nurturance, and gratification. The mother's warmth and love are partially dependent on her disengagement from the cold instrumentality of capitalist work relations. Her love makes it possible for the family to provide a "haven" from the outside world. To a large extent her love *is* this haven. The father is less emotionally expressive. He exercises a more impersonal authority that is reinforced by his status as the representative of the outside world of work and culture.

Winicott's "Transitional Space"

A strong superego can develop only with the successful resolution of the oedi-pal crisis. The superego will not develop properly unless the (boy) child has a strong, authoritative and autonomous father against whom he can rebel and then with whom he can identify. If development unfolds correctly, the superego will be strong but not punitive. The superego and ego can then ally to resist irra-tional authority. The ego can consult and gain comfort from its conscience and its memories of childhood gratification. The superego will also combat the demands of the id, providing a space within which the ego can act freely.[20]

Horkheimer and Adorno do acknowledge that women are oppressed in such arrangements. However, they tend to stress the positive aspects of them. Such arrangements are necessary for the development of people who can resist the pressures of mass culture and authoritarian regimes. Their arguments obscure the probability that at best this could be true only for a certain group of men, since women will continue to be oppressed. What is more important, they occlude the damaging effects of familial hierarchies on the psychological develop-ment of women and men. Horkheimer and Adorno minimize the destructive impact these might have on reason and on potentially emancipatory desires.[21]

PSYCHOANALYSIS AND ITS DISCONTENTS

The psychoanalytic claim that humans live simultaneously in multiple, hetero-geneous, and conflicting worlds has been central to much of my own work.[22] Like the critical theorists, I believe psychoanalysis is an enormously enabling and circumscribed intellectual home. I have devoted much effort to appraising what is useful and harmful about its stories.[23]

I value the complexity of psychoanalytic theorizing, the idea of the uncon-scious and Freud's insistence on the noncoincidence of sexuality with acceptable social norms and practices (heterosexuality, marriage, or love). My thinking about epistemology and subjectivity has been stimulated by psychoanalytic atten-tion to family relations as central forces in social and psychic life.

Winnicott's idea of transitional space and his and other object relations theo-rists' accounts of how important relations with others are in the constitution of subjectivity continue to provide me with rich material for theorizing.[24] Klein's and Winnicott's accounts of the psyche-soma and the intra- and intersubjective bases of the desire for knowledge have been enormously helpful to me in thinking about the deficiencies of Cartesian and Kantian epistemologies.[25] Their accounts also provide promising avenues for developing different approaches to knowledge.

Winnicott's apparently straightforward language tempts the reader to ignore the complexity of his ideas and the multiple meanings of many of his terms. All too often, writers attack his notion of the "true self" as if it were simply another version of the humanist myth. His idea of the "good enough" mother and her importance in the early life of the infant can become the basis of mother blaming or mother glorification.[26]

Contrary to these readings Winnicott regards "human nature" as intrinsically and irreducibly conflicted. He insists we live simultaneously in three radically distinct worlds (inner, outer, transitional). Relations between these worlds and the worlds themselves are unstable and subject to frequent and unpredictable change. His notion of a "true self" has almost nothing in common with the unitary, stable, unconflicted one pop psychology promises. His account of object relations is quite dissimilar to socialization theories. Winnicott's story of our relations with others is marked by his distinctive emphasis on fantasy and aggression and the disjunction between the object the child or adult makes (and continually remakes) and the person "out there." I have found no other theoretical perspective that impels me to complicate constantly my understandings of subjectivity. None are equally compatible with the increasingly complex accounts of politics and knowledge I wish to develop. I try to keep in my mind's eye psychoanalysts' view of humans as embodied, desiring, thinking, and social creatures.[27] They portray humans as inhabitants of consensual and idiosyncratic realities, continually engaged in polyphonic inner and outer conversations. Humans can benefit from a relatively stable cohering of some of these pieces and from social relations that generate productive grids along which the forces can run. Our social construction, especially along axis of domination, can also cause us great misery. We suffer when bits cohere to produce painful states or rigid, fearfully held organizations.

However, each of the most compelling versions of psychoanalysis—Freudian, object relations, and Lacanian—is also deeply and productively imperfect. The constitution of each is marked by and probably depends for its coherence on profoundly problematic assumptions about gender, subjectivity, and knowledge. The modal person whose development is so complexly traced is clearly a white, heterosexual, modern Western European male. The story of female development in

"Socialisation models"

its Freudian and Lacanian versions is one of deficiency, envy, absence (of a penis and of an adequate conscience due to weak superego formation), and excess (of desire outside the law).

Freudian psychoanalysis graphically conveys the deformations required to assume the position of "normal" femininity. However, it does not provide much to work with in constructing alternatives. Furthermore, as Freud himself concedes, while he might make important contributions to understanding fathers and sons, the relations of mothers to their sons and daughters and female development remain dark continents. Freud became more willing to acknowledge the importance of preoedipal mother-daughter relations in female development. However, this acknowledgment also serves defensive purposes. It enables him to screen a particularly potent source of male anxiety, the relations of mothers and sons.

AN UNCONSCIOUS OF HER OWN

Paradoxically, my interest in doing long-term psychoanalytic therapy developed during and because of my involvement in feminist antipsychiatry activities. A group of New Haven feminists established a women's crisis center. The initial purpose of the center was to provide support and counseling for women in crisis—for example, battered women or people who felt guilty about ending unhappy marriages or putting their children in daycare. We also hoped to politicize and reframe the descriptions of and explanations for these crises. Rather than thinking of them as instances of (typical but) individual female pathology, we sought to analyze and treat them as effects of a pathological set of social arrangements—male dominance or patriarchy.

However, after working at the center for three years, I came to believe that this approach was too simple, as is the exclusive focus on the pathological individual/female. The life histories of participants in the center and their responses to our interventions varied enormously. Socialization models, even with feminist commitments, in which political forces shape personality and determine individual outcomes are not adequate to explain the variations in our participants' lives. They are also demeaning, since they cannot do justice to the creativity and dignity that these women sometimes exemplified in their struggles. Observing such variation over time stimulated my curiosity about the interactions between people's inner worlds, their temperaments, social circumstances, kinship and support networks, and their ways of making sense of the world and how political forces shape and are shaped by all of these.

A politically sensitive psychoanalysis should be helpful in tracking and developing accounts of these interactions. I turned my attention to psychoanalytic theory and continued training in psychoanalytic psychotherapy. However, my exposure to alternative possibilities and the expansion of my practice as a therapist (both in volume and approach) intensified and clarified my dissatisfactions with "orthodox" analysis. Fortunately three feminist works that profoundly affected my thinking were published at this time—Gayle Rubin's "The Traffic in Women," Nancy Chodorow's *The Reproduction of Mothering* and Dorothy Dinnerstein's *The Mermaid and the Minotaur*.[28] These books suggest possible feminist appropriations of psychoanalysis. Chodorow's and Dinnerstein's emphasis on the importance of mother-child relations helped to clarify many puzzling aspects of my patients' lives and their interactions with me.

Since these books were published, feminists have continued to reconstruct psychoanalysis, including the work of object relations or Lacanian theorists. We have used research and clinical experience to elaborate different theories of feminine development and new methodologies to study it. Feminists make use of knowledge gained through consciousness-raising and other forms of political activity. By reading literature in new ways, and studying the histories of everyday life and the practices of other cultures, we have uncovered different aspects of femininity. Feminist writers have contributed much to mapping out the previously "dark" spaces of female subjectivity.[29] Recent reconstructions of the centrality of mothers and our relations with them—not only in individual childhoods but throughout our personal and collective histories—are very important. The revaluation of many of the traits "maternal" practices and relations between parent and child can require and display—intersubjectivity, respect for the other, responsibility, a practical ethics of care and nurturance—is still unfinished.

THE RETURN OF THE REPRESSED

Contemporary psychological theories may be less androcentric. A number of discourses display a greater willingness to acknowledge the importance of social relations and intersubjectivity in the constitution and practice of subjectivity.

People are more willing to look at the benefits of stereotypical female traits and the deficiencies of male ones. While I deeply appreciate this feminist work, I could not limit myself to applying feminist insights to critique many aspects of psychoanalysis. I also began to use my theoretical tools and practice as a psychotherapist to analyze wishes and fantasies that often circulate so uncritically through some analytically informed feminist writing.[30]

I was operating on an assumption that only became explicit later with further developments in feminist theorizing: women as well as men play out unconscious anxieties (about race and gender among other issues) in the ways we think, do research, and put forth knowledge claims. Like men, women have powerful wishes to acknowledge only some of our forms of subjectivity to ourselves and others. We ought to investigate and be suspicious of all such representations. The specific content of each (privileged or marginalized) form is overdetermined by cultural, political, racial, and class contexts as well as inner fantasies, sexuality, and relations with others, past and present.

I can no longer read any "description" of women's "difference," female development, mother-daughter relations, maternal practices, or subjectivity without wondering about the unconscious and political factors that motivate the putting into play of certain claims and not others. I do not think there is one true account of subjectivity or any definitive reading of a writer. However, the influence of deeply held unconscious wishes can press one to avoid uncomfortable aspects of complex phenomena.

I am increasingly uncomfortable with certain feminist discourses, especially ones that appropriate object relations theory and my own work in particular ways. The foregrounding and valorization of certain modes of "relational" thinking or social interaction in accounts of female development and subjectivity especially concerns me.[31] The mapping of women's difference in and through particular metaphors or accounts of maternity makes me deeply suspicious. I worry about what is left out or marginalized in such accounts and about why particular stories are so popular now among certain audiences (feminist and others).

For example, many feminist writers claim to use an object relations–based account of mother-child (especially daughter) relations as a model for alternative theories of subjectivity. However, often these writers do not take into account the central roles of hate and ambivalence for both mother and child in this relation.[32] They also fail to confront the implications of an "inner world" that is highly idiosyncratic (and not particularly intersubjective) and our need for access to such spaces to feel alive. These narratives of subjectivity tend to disregard attention to its multiple determinants, including temperament and somatic influences. They ignore the aspects of development that are incomplete, nonlinear, conflicted, and provisional.

I also find reductive readings of my own work quite puzzling. Interpretations of my writings have certainly made me receptive to the postmodernist claim that discourse has little to do with authorial intent or even with the meanings of the text. Rather, texts often become markers of or locations for political arguments and claims to power. Like all writing, my own must have political and unconscious motives and meanings exceeding my intent. So do the various readings and appropriations of it.

Nonetheless, it does surprise me how often the complexity I at least believe is there is read out. I certainly do not advocate mothering as a privileged or unproblematic trope for the representation or analysis of femininity. From my earliest paper on mothers and daughters, I have tried to explore and emphasize the ambivalence and conflicts that mark contemporary women's inner worlds and their relations with others. I stress the costs of these relations and the repression of numerous desires that accompany daughters' identification with and (sometimes) closeness to mothers. The desire to repress aspects of psychic life or to deny wishes or impulses affects women as profoundly as men. Like all other qualities, "relatedness" is an ambiguous virtue. Its origins, expressions, and consequences are not necessarily benign.

GENDER, POWER, AND THE WOMAN PROBLEM

I have argued recently that these stories may have particular appeal among some white women now because they construct "woman" as a homogeneous category. This category incorporates certain characteristics for which some white women have traditionally been valued but excludes other more problematic ones. Sexuality, aggression, and relations of domination among women are especially noticeable for their absence.

Throughout U.S. history, sexuality and aggression have traditionally been attributed to "other" lesser women—African-Americans, "ethnics," poor women, and servants. Thus, while I used to think about "difference" discourses primarily as a necessary "transvaluation of values," now I believe a more thorough

deconstruction of them is necessary. Race and the circulation of power, especially the interplay of theoretical claims and the generation and legitimation of
positions of authority, would be central subjects of this deconstruction.[33] The
"nature" of woman and which discourses best represent her are put into question
in and as politics among women. These moves are not merely effects of male-
dominated games.

I recognize some of the subjective and political motivations for my own discursive moves. One is an acute sensitivity to relations of domination among
women. As a therapist, I often confront the power of the wish to control others
in patients and myself. I observe some of the ways in which women exercise this
wish as mothers, lovers, workers, and friends. Women as a group are no less
aggressive than men in expressing our wish to control others. We may express
this aggression differently in response to cultural and intrapersonal sanctions and
norms.

Probably more influential than my clinical practice in fixating my attention on
relations of domination, however, is my work (since 1978) as teacher of political
theory at Howard, a historically black university. This work has certainly cured
me of any tendency to romanticize the oppressed, since I have seen many
instances of poor treatment by blacks against others. Howard is no more free
than any other university or institution of gender bias and male domination.
Oppression in one aspect of one's life does not necessarily impel one to avoid
oppressing others, or to empathize or ally with others similarly or differently
oppressed. Of course, these observations apply to white women as well. No
particular set of beliefs or behavior necessarily follows from the experience of
oppression (or any other experience, for that matter). Any such set is a highly
contingent construct, dependent on many subjective, intersubjective, discursive,
historical, and simply random factors.

Despite (or because of) some disillusionment, I feel a deep gratitude to
Howard for providing a context in which I can think through and constantly confront the matter of being raced. The circumstance of being a "triple minority"
(white, Jewish, and female) has been enormously productive for my thinking,
both about "mainstream" philosophies and feminist theorizing. I am intensely
grateful to my students, whose personal generosity, intellectual courage, willingness to engage me in challenging conversation, and sheer bravery in the face of
often hideous discouragement continually impel me to avoid the temptation of
coming to rest anywhere.

ONE IS NOT BORN A WOMAN

A lack of home, like any location, has ambiguous consequences. I have acquired a deep skepticism about any "standpoint" epistemology, whether grounded in race (Afro-centricity), gender (feminist standpoints), or class (the standpoint of the proletariat). Standpoint theories require one to believe a position that is highly contingent and constructed (eg. race, gender, or feminist consciousness) results in or can be the basis of a not just different but objectively better, less biased, and more inclusive grasp of "reality."[34] They logically entail the assumption that there is a relatively stable, similarly determined unit of experience that can and should be represented through a singular category. Emancipation depends upon locating or constructing such a unity and speaking in its name.

My disagreements with both standpoint theories and the epistemological assumptions on which they depend have many philosophical and political determinants. I will discuss two of the most important ones here—my shift from thinking about "women" to analyzing gendering and my ongoing disillusionment with certain epistemological beliefs.[35] The language in this section will slip all over the place and is confusing. I have chosen not to disguise this confusion or impose order prematurely. All my attempts to discuss social processes like race, sexuality, and gender are highly inadequate and frustrating. The term "gendering" is my latest, still-unsatisfactory attempt to do justice to the idea that gender is not a fixed or simple identity or set of social relations. I am trying to think of it as a plural verb rather than a single noun. Gendering is constituted by complex, overdetermined, and multiple processes. These processes are historically and socially variable and are often internally contradictory. The processes of gendering are provisional and must be reproduced and reworked throughout our lives. In future work, I hope to improve my thinking about other identities such as race or sexuality by treating them as verbs as well.

My own thinking about gendering is strictly limited and contextual. It arises out of a desire to understand particular social relations within contemporary Western societies. Its utility is probably limited to analyses of these societies. I intend everything that follows to apply only within this discrete domain.

Simone de Beauvior's assertion, one is not born a woman (and Monique Wittig's reworking of it),[36] is one of the most radical ever made within feminist theorizing. We are still coming to grips with its vast meanings and unsettling

implications. Her statement suggests many questions. How and why is the category "woman" produced and reproduced? How do its meanings and effects
change over time? What are its relations to and effects on concrete women,
located in particular social spaces? How do specific women participate in (or get
excluded from) presenting and representing "woman"? How and why is a vast
and always changing array of human characteristics organized around and then
explained through this category? Could woman exist outside her production as
and location in the binary pair of man/woman? Are or could there be societies
in which gender is not a constituting social relation?

I have become increasingly dissatisfied with the focus on "women," because it
appears to require acceptance of a category—Woman—that is clearly a product
of the very social relations that are so problematic. The existence and meanings
of this category are partially determined by relations of domination. Power is
required to produce the categories of gendering such as male, female, and difference. These categories are not present in "nature" waiting for us to stumble
upon them. They are not consequences of neutral empirical observation. We are
not simply forced to acknowledge their existence through our investigations of
other "natural objects" such as human bodies.[37]   Raced and gendered categories
cannot be destabilized if we insist on their necessity as a foundation for "emancipatory" knowledge. Thinking about feminist theorizing as discourses about gendering, and gendering as relations of domination, makes it is easier to discuss differences among women. The complex circulation of power among women is
more evident once we disaggregate the class "woman." It is more difficult to
assume the existence of a homogeneous group—women—who are all the
oppressed "same." White women can no longer see ourselves as innocent of the
domination of others due to our oppression by men. If for no other reason, this
realization should make race a matter of urgency for all those interested in gendering.

I do not deny that gender-based power relations (or male dominance) affect
many women in similar, awful ways. However, thinking about race makes it evident that women (and men) do not all have one gender. Thinking about gendering makes it equally clear that African-Americans (and other racial groups) do
not all have one race.[38] Race and gender are both internally differentiated social
relations; they are not a stable or homogeneous cluster of unitary characteristics.

Analyses of gendering require tracking power relations, specific historical constructions and representations of man/woman and their relations to the concrete

lives of different men and women. The relationships between the constructed categories man/woman and the lived circumstances of men and women are simultaneously highly contingent and determinant. Race is a constituting relation for white women as well as the "others." Gender is a constituting relation for all men, although its effects are race-differentiated.

Both men and women are implicated in the production and circulation of these categories and in the social relation in which they are embedded. Both sexes simultaneously resist and permit the existence of race/gender categories as social "realities." This lack of identity between race/gender categories and actual men and women provides the space for resistance and struggle over their meanings. However, race/gender systems also endlessly attempt to stabilize their intrinsically unstable foundational categories. Such attempts require the relentless circulation of power and the production and contentious renewal of regulatory practices (for example, struggles over abortion) to fix the unfixable.

Representations of race/gender are put into play for many political purposes. For example, certain representations of white femininity and black masculinity have been put into play in power struggles between black and white men, between black men and black women, and between white women and black men and women. Gender relations and representations are important in organizing relations among men and in ordering and legitimating racial formations, political authority, and the law.[39]

Women also struggle among ourselves for the privilege of representing "woman," and we use race/gender discourses to legitimate exercises of power over other women. Some women, for example, have allied with the patriarchal state to participate in the regulation of other women's sexuality. Such activists may claim to seek protection for others (like prostitutes or workers in porn industries) or even for the honor of Womankind. Through such activities they simultaneously replicate and validate discourses that construct some women as "pure" over and against the lesser "fallen" ones. They also, however unintentionally, locate themselves on the privileged "pure" side of the binary pair.[40]

My discursive shift to racially differentiated gender analysis also reflects my wish to implicate men, not simply as dominators but as deeply constituted by race/gendering. Dominant groups are often portrayed as unaffected by the systems they control. White people tend to be represented as unmarked by race; men are represented as unmarked by gendering. Focusing on race/gender systems does not imply that men are just as oppressed as women. One can be constituted by occupying a dominant position as much as by an inferior one. Potential access to dominant positions is also unequally distributed; the complex interactions of race/gender, class, sexual identities, and other social relations confound any unitary location of power. Nevertheless, neither dominance nor its constituted and constituting character should disappear. Although both man and woman are effects of race/gendering systems, it does not follow that the oppressive effects of a system fall equally on everyone within it. Privilege can be as contingent and as determinative as oppression. That one did not volunteer for one's superior position does not mean one is innocent of or untouched by its effects and privileges.

A focus on race/gendering does not require the disappearance of women. It also does not imply that race and gendering ought to be collapsed into one grand unitary concept. Neither may be the most salient or determining relation in a particular social context. I do not assume that race and gendering are the effects of exactly the same set of social relations, only that the two may be complexly related in some situations. The relationships and degree of interdependence between them will vary by context and event.

Contrary to the claims (or fears) of some, I do not believe the possibility of effective feminist politics requires the ability to represent a unitary woman or even a singular multiple category of women.[41] A number of assumptions and wishes motivate this hankering for a universal. It is a trace of the continuing operation of Enlightenment belief systems and the absence of useful alternatives to them.

One characteristic Enlightenment belief is articulated by Kant, Rousseau, and others (for example, our contemporaries Rawls and Habermas). These authors assert that a moral claim can possess force or legitimacy only if it is made in the name of all (mankind).[42] These approaches share a fundamental problem—such a unitary voice requires the suppressing of many differences. The masking of this suppression makes the appearance of universality, universal consent (or pragmatics), or a general will more convincing. No one has proposed a plausible solution to this problem. Incorporation into the "universal" seems to require that despite or underneath the mask of neutrality, some people's moral commitments and ways of life are privileged. Other persons' entrance or incorporation into the general can occur only on the condition that they sacrifice their modes of life and mimic those of others. They must pretend that the particular is the universal, and the ways of others have become their own.[43]

As I have already indicated, I also believe this hankering for a unitary representation is motivated by a wish to deny or avoid the many conflicts among women. It sometimes reflects a nostalgia for an originary unity that is possible only with the exclusion of many differences and the privileged position of a few. For example, some white women are reluctant to acknowledge that women are situated differently to men. For women of color, men of one's own race may be allies rather than enemies. The construction of the homogeneous and binary category—man-as-oppressor/woman-as-victim—depends for its coherence on a writing out of the complex relations of race. It necessarily marginalizes the voices of many women and obscures the raced qualities of gendering systems.

A unitary construction of woman may also have the paradoxical effects of simultaneously obscuring, condemning, and privileging heterosexuality. How do we account for the fact that some women express a desire for and pleasure in "sleeping with the enemy"? Feminist theorizing has had much difficulty doing justice to the simultaneously constructed yet undetermined qualities of desire. Some writers avoid the problem altogether, focusing instead on the more socially acceptable maternal representations of woman. Others deal with the problem by declaring sexuality politically incorrect. In discourses like MacKinnon's the apparent existence of heterosexual desire among some women has to be dismissed as false consciousness or as a mark of oppression so that a potentially undifferentiated category of woman-as-victim can be saved.[44]

The radical feminist insistence on the intertwining of sexuality and domination has usefully complicated feminist discourses on sexuality. Foucault's critique of the "repressive hypothesis"[45] and feminist understandings of the centrality of the construction and regulation of "sexuality" to race/gender systems undermine a central hope of earlier sex radicals. Their claim that resistance to previous sexual prohibitions will necessarily increase our freedom or pleasure is less persuasive. Foucauldian discourses also alert us to the ambivalent genealogies and consequences of the construction of subjectivity partially through and as "sexual identity." The implications of these realizations for feminist theorizing and practices, whether gay or straight, are unsettling and represent major challenges for future work.

Part of the problem with gender analysis is its failures so far to deal with the man problem. Women have certainly not disappeared, but all too often men are still invisible. Although gender analysis has become trendy in certain academic circles, its predominant content still seems to be the study of woman and her difference. Representations of masculinity are rarely treated as problematic, histor-ically contingent, and effects of power.[46] Perhaps how men have or continue to represent women should be of less interest than how they have and continue to represent themselves.

How these representations result or enter into social relations and institutions that profoundly *affect* concrete women and men (differently) can be crucial femi-nist concerns. I would like, for example, to write about representations and practices of late-twentieth-century African-American masculinity. Judith Butler's "performative" concept of gender could be fruitfully applied here.[47] However, I would pay special attention to what happens to representations and practices when, due to their social locations, some men lack the power to bring off the roles they and others expect them to perform. How in turn are these "failures" then represented and incorporated into other political discourses and practices, for example, public policy (the crisis of "the" family or of crime)? How do men struggle among themselves for the privilege of representing mas-culinity, and how do they use constructions of femininity in their battles? How and why do black and white men end up blaming black women for the "crises" of the contemporary African-American community? Why haven't white women intervened more vigorously in these debates?

My current understanding of race/gender is a dynamic, disorderly, yet sys-temic one. Everyone is marked within and by race/gender systems (although dif-ferently). Gender and race categories, practices, and concrete historical beings are in multiple, unstable, contingent, and deeply determining relations with one another. In one sense, race/gender systems are like quilts. Many kinds of materi-als accumulated over time from many different sources are stitched together to create an object that is simultaneously durable and fragile. No one knows which squares will prove to be essential to the survival, destruction, or more pleasing arrangements of the quilt.

THE ANGEL OF HISTORY

> To articulate the past historically does not mean to recognize it "the way it really was" (Ranke). It means to seize hold of a memory as it flashes up at a moment of danger.[48]

Throughout this narrative a theme recurs. A process similar to falling in love and then experiencing a certain amount of disillusionment pervades my intellectual history. As the initial delusion of passion and fantasy begins to fade, one notices the distinctive qualities and limits of one's lover. No person can perfectly approximate one's ideal form or even satisfy one's most immediately pressing desires, although some may come closer than others. How to deal with such disappointments is a continual struggle. There are many temptations when disappointment surfaces. These include: making the other all bad; feeling victimized or betrayed; cynicism; or withdrawal from engagement with others. Others are: assigning total failure to the other so one's own fantasy of omnipotence can be sustained; trying to manipulate, blame, or shame the other; denying one ever cared about, was involved with, or wanted anything from the other.

Psychoanalytic theorists such as Mahler or Winnicott claim that we initially experience this process of blind love and disillusionment in early childhood and then again in adolescence. The child has a magical belief in the omnipotence of herself and her intimate caretakers. Security in this belief allows one eventually to bear one's disillusionment. Gradually one learns that, while people may have unequal access to power and different capacities to exercise it in a variety of locations, no one has absolute power or control over oneself or the outer world.

While this is frightening, it is also a relief; whoever has absolute power has, at least potentially, absolute control. Struggles between humans become zero-sum games in which one person's loss is necessarily someone else's gain. There is only one alternative to absolute control or power—absolute chaos or total submission to an other. Even winning a struggle is frightening since it would require the annihilation of the other. Such beliefs make one averse to risk. A mistake would signal utter failure, total loss of agency, and the final extinction of the fantasy of omnipotence. Victory entails destruction of the very object of one's desire. Lacking a sense of the limits of oneself and others, one cannot attain any realistic sense of responsibility. Hence one suffers from a feeling of total guilt or a need to see oneself as a victim, simply the object of another's power.

My relationships with the theories I have adopted follow the same pattern of absolute acceptance and then disillusionment. I have tried not to give in to the various temptations of disillusionment. In this struggle, I have found psychoanalysis, first as a patient and now as a therapist, very helpful. Freud and subsequent psychoanalysts stress the importance of the ability to tolerate ambivalence to psychic well-being. Psychoanalysis encourages us to live with rather than foreclose contradictory impulses. It shows us the benefits of treating humorously the impossibility of many of our desires.

I have also found postmodernism a particularly powerful antidote to political and philosophical despair. My reading of postmodernism differs from those who see it as a form of neoconservativism, nihilism, or "cynical reason."[49] The most important postmodernist writings for me—Richard Rorty's *Philosophy and the Mirror of Nature*, Jean-Francois Lyotard's *The Postmodern Condition*, and almost all of Michel Foucault's work—offer me a way out of the despair of the *Dialectic of Enlightenment*.[50] These writers help me to understand that absolute despair is the necessary opposite of absolute belief.

The salient faith here is the cluster of beliefs I clump too simply under the rubric of the "Enlightenment." Postmodernists insist that contemporary white Westerners are still under the influence of this faith. Our increasingly desperate attempts to preserve belief are a source of some of the unhappiness, paralysis, and ugliness in our public life. Westerners suffer from what Hegel calls the "unhappy consciousness"—consciousness recognizes the error of its ideas but is equally unable to abandon them.

I do not read postmodernism as a narrative about the identity crises of a few, relatively privileged contemporary Western white men. Despite our marginalization by them, white Western feminists are not situated completely outside the belief systems postmodernists question. How we could be, since it is a dominant strand in contemporary Western cultures? However marginalized we may be by and within these cultures, white women are also beneficiaries and products of them. There are many ways in which white feminist discourses are dependent upon and participate in maintaining Enlightenment hopes.[51]

Enlightenment tenets can be quite seductive. Many of us find quite appealing its promise of the existence of a neutral yet emancipatory reason, an undetermined subject, and a progressive and ultimately benign logic to history. The possibilities that the exercise of authority could be innocent of domination and that political life can be a rational and harmonious coordination of autonomous self- and other-regarding beings have tremendous appeal. I would like to believe them myself.

However, I cannot. Following Foucault, I feel compelled to inquire into the genealogies of the wishes that animate Enlightenment beliefs and their implications in and complicity with relations of power, productive or resistant. I do not wish to reject utterly some of the animating wishes of this faith. Any just society would include respect for individuals, space for self-government and collective autonomy, some control over the economic and political structures that determine one's life, protection from the arbitrary exercise of authority and violence, and a sphere of privacy within which one can pursue one's own pleasures and fantasies. I would want to add the socialist insistence for a reasonable degree of material security and many more playful and aesthetic qualities as well.[52]

I fall away from the faith, however, since I can sustain little hope that knowledge or reason will make foundational contributions to creating or maintaining such societies. I do not believe such societies are progressive in the sense that they represent an absolute leap forward in the total sum of human happiness or perfection. As a child of the Holocaust, I cannot believe in a linear, progressive, or teleological view of history in which all suffering has a purpose and time only moves in one direction, toward the redemption of us all.

I also cannot believe in the natural goodness or necessity of any ethical commitments or moral vocabulary, or that each does not also entail costs that may be as great as their benefits. I cannot anticipate that such costs will be equally distributed among the participants of even the best states, or that there is an authority that can represent and tend to the good of the whole. I do not believe a neutral form of authority is possible or that we can design a set of rules or a decision procedure that will not favor some views of the good life over others.[53]

There are no transhistorical or neutral justifications of the views a particular social arrangement favors. No epistemological procedures exist that can cleanse our knowledge of its multiple origins, or prohibit the effects that escape our intentions and think us as we think we are mastering them. Any form of knowledge is a product and reflection of human wishes and practices, including the will to power. The availability of certain kinds of knowledge is as much a matter of contingency, the available struggles for power, and the history of past and present practices as it is of the triumph of truth over error.

The temporary privilege of some views over others will be a consequence of a variety of factors, including power struggles and the wielding of truth claims. The truth content of a knowledge will not necessarily determine its reception or its triumph over others. We adopt the knowledge that fits our uses. Humans are very good at creating rational reasons for rejecting knowledge that does not fit our purposes or would make us doubt them. Cultures develop stories that present these outcomes as legitimate and morally binding. The stories will retain their persuasive magic as long as culturally specific moral vocabularies retain their force (in both senses of the word).

Any society will have costs particular to it. Every society will privilege some forms of life and some persons over others. Each will necessarily marginalize other, perhaps equally desirable, potential forms of subjectivity and knowledge through exercises of power. It does not follow that all arrangements are equally good. Quite the contrary, since we cannot fall back on any universal trump, we must take responsibility for our beliefs and try to persuade others of their utility. However, in doing so we must make use of culturally intelligible vocabularies. The persuasiveness of our claims will depend on struggles for power, the qualities of our social relations, and the utility of such claims to our practices, not their truth content.

As a therapist I cannot believe in the purity of reason or that it should occupy a privileged place within our subjectivity or political hopes. Just treatment of others depends on many qualities other than reason. These include empathy, self-respect, and containing one's own envy and grandiosity. I am wary of the capacity of reason to rationalize and to find persuasive ways to justify its harm to others. I can see the power of the wish to believe in some suprahuman force, whatever form it may take: reason, law, history. . . . As we realize the limits of our own powers and the frequency with which outcomes of our actions do not coincide with our intentions the strength of this wish intensifies.

I have also become profoundly frightened by the consequences of appeals to non-contingent beliefs and the refusal to see oneself as necessarily and deeply embedded in various relations of power. Rather than abandon such grandiose beliefs, we are tempted to find others whom we can absolutely control and onto whom we can project our finite and flawed humanity. I believe four of the greatest tragedies of modern Europe—slavery, the oppression of women, Nazism, and Stalinism—were potentiated by our collective wish that innocent and universal positions are possible and desirable.

I am drawn to writers such as Lyotard and Foucault, because I imagine them staring unrelentingly at aspects of our recent history (Nazism and Stalinism) without searching for another to blame. They might not say with Adorno that the guilt of the Holocaust alone is what compels them to philosophize.[54] I think they would agree that it and the other tragedies of modern European cultures should compel us to suspect ourselves and to continue the process of disillusionment and the struggle with its temptations. Neither the great refusal nor absolute hope will help us cope with the messy contingency of everyday life.

WINGS OF DESIRE (ANGELS OVER BERLIN)

Recently I visited Berlin for the second time since the Wall was torn down. On the previous trip, I had made a special effort to visit many of the remaining sites of pre-Holocaust Jewish life in Berlin. The city provides a map with which one can organize such a tour. What is more important, I had the company of my friend, Gisela Bock, who has devoted part of her scholarly career in Germany to studying Nazism and German history. On my recent trip, restoration of one of the largest synagogues in Berlin, which I had previously seen in its burned and bombed out state, was almost complete. One can stand in the center of the city, on a bridge over the Spree near Alexanderplatz, and see its large golden dome. There it was, an unavoidable and integral part of the city. It could not have been burned, as it was on Kristallnacht, without the knowledge of many Berliners. They had plenty of reasons to know what was happening.

There I was, staring at an empty synagogue in the presence of a loved German friend. I could not help wondering what the "restoration" of this synagogue or other such sites could possibly mean. What motivated such acts? Can we simply knit up history and move on? What representations of contemporary Germany and its history are being put into play? What I most impossibly, desperately, and desolately want to understand though, is: where are the Jews? The dead are everywhere, some of my own relations among them. How can so many people simultaneously be absolutely absent, yet pervasively present? Am I part of German history or not? Are Germans my enemy? How can I love my friend?

My German family were early advocates of reform Judaism. A small volume, written in Hebrew and English, stands on one of my bookshelves at home: *The Form of Daily Prayers According to the Custom of the German and Polish Jews*. The English was quite literally translated from German by Joseph Guns. The book, published in Vienna in 1857, was quickly exported to New York for use among the German Jews who settled there. My dead father, like his ancestors, had believed deeply in the power of reason, the goodness of knowledge, the privilege of intelligence, and the permanence of its products when all else may be destroyed. To me, now, listening to the melodies of this faith is like the sirens' song for Ulysses—almost unbearably seductive, yet undeniably fatal. Unlike Ulysses, there is no crew to tie me to the mast; my own struggles and conversations with others must continually retie the ropes.

TWO

PSYCHOANALYSIS

TWO

2

FINAL ANALYSIS
CAN PSYCHOANALYSIS SURVIVE
IN THE POSTMODERN WEST?

If—which may sound fantastic today— one had to found a college of psycho-analysis, much would have to be taught in it which is also taught by the medical faculty: along-side of depth-psychology, which would always remain the principal subject, there would be an introduction to biology, as much as possible of the science of sexual life, and familiarity with the symptomatology of psychiatry. On the other hand, analytic instruction would include branches of knowledge which are remote from medicine and which the doctor does not come across in his practice: the history of civilization, mythology, the psychology of religion and the science of literature. Unless he is well at home in these subjects, an analyst can make nothing of a large amount of his material. By way of compensation, the great mass of what is taught in medical schools is of no use to him for his purposes.

Sigmund Freud,
The Question of Lay Analysis

FINAL ANALYSIS?

Can psychoanalysis survive in the postmodern West? To address this question, I will first define psychoanalysis. Discussion of the meaning or status of psychoanalysis is too often dominated by the question of whether it is or could be a science. I will argue below that if we seek a better understanding of the psychoanalytic enterprise, this is the wrong question to ask. The dominance of this question is a symptom of profound difficulties within psychoanalysis itself. Continuing to pursue it will be no more productive for theory or practice than it has been.[1]

I will propose an alternative way of thinking about psychoanalysis based on the work of Michel Foucault. He invents the term "discursive formation" to capture some of the complexities of modern social practices in which knowledge and power circulate, congeal, and generate resistance. After I define this term more fully, I will discuss some of the distinguishing features of the discursive formation of psychoanalysis. I will delineate three of its components: theory and the pro-

duction of truth, clinical treatment, and disciplinary organization and its production of legitimated experts.

Next I will discuss the larger philosophical and political contexts in which the
discourse of psychoanalysis is located. Radical transformations in these contexts
undermine its truth and power claims. Philosophically, postmodernists and feminists (among others) call into question the universality and privilege of the
modal object (and practitioner) of psychoanalysis: the white, well-off masculine
Western subject. They also pose profound challenges to the epistemological
underpinnings of psychoanalytic truth claims.

The decentering of Western power and cultural privilege and challenges to
what Foucault calls "biopower" create serious political problems for psychoanalysis. Biopower (which I will define in more detail below) is one of the unique
forms in which modern Western states exercise control and generate legitimacy.
Psychoanalysis is simultaneously a beneficiary and consequence of this form of
power. It is also potentially one of its most subversive expressions.

Finally, I will discuss how favorably psychoanalysis is located in these profound
political and philosophic transformations. Some psychoanalytic philosophies of
mind and clinical practices are compatible with and even exemplary instances of
postmodern and feminist practices. However, what I consider the strengths of
psychoanalysis are sometimes treated by others as temporary weaknesses that
should be overcome. If psychoanalysis is to survive in the twenty-first century, it
will have to abandon its obsession with its status as a science. Instead it will have
to generate discourse-specific epistemologies. It must become more conscious of
and self-reflective about the politics of its theories, clinical practices, and its relations to other forms of power and knowledge. Within its own disciplinary practices it will have to find new ways to develop and highlight the qualities psychoanalysts recommend to their patients. These include a tolerance for ambiguity,
ambivalence, and difference and the ability to flourish within an increasingly
multiple and contradictory external world.

DISCURSIVE FORMATIONS AND
THE POWER OF KNOWLEDGE

One of Foucault's most important contributions is to extend epistemology
beyond its traditional concern with such matters as internal coherence, evidence,

truth, logic, and the relationship between subject and object. Marxists and other practitioners of the critique of ideology also expand the practice of epistemology. However, Foucault is unusual, because he does not assume *a priori* the privilege of any particular power relation in the constitution of knowledge. He also does not collapse knowledge and power or make one the ultimate determinant of the other, unlike, for example, some Marxists who treat knowledge as a reflex of class relations.

Foucault also expands the definition of power. He argues that the traditional view of power as the exercise of force in and through which one person's will dominates another is insufficient. Power, especially in the modern world, takes other forms. Repression or domination (power over others; power from the top down) is not its only or even most important modern expression. Power is a productive force; discursive formations could not operate without it. It does not "only weigh upon us as a force that says no but traverses and produces things, it induces pleasure, forms knowledge, produces discourse."[2]

Foucault highlights three facets of discursive formations. They are historically contingent, dynamic, and conflict ridden. Discursive formations develop through a gradual cohering of initially disparate and unrelated elements. We can only perform what Foucault calls a genealogy after a formation evolves. A genealogy is a history motivated by particular contemporary interests. It reconstructs a practice or an institution that now appears inevitable, internally coherent, or homogeneous. The appearance of inevitability is an effect of relations of power. It is not a consequence of a practice's intrinsic truth or conformity to "nature." Tracing the history of a practice may recover its contingent and disparate elements and loosen its spell of inevitability or naturalness.

Discursive formations are also dynamic and productive systems. They produce knowledge, power, and experts. These elements are mutually constituting and interdependent. Foucault argues knowledge claims cannot exist or be understood unless they are situated within complex networks of disciplinary practices through which power circulates. These networks are also the loci of the legitimation of and resistance to power.

Discursive formations include rules that enable members to identify some statements as true or false. These generally tacit rules enable practitioners to construct a map, model, or classification system to organize knowledge claims. Rules are necessary for the formation of meaningful statements and the production of truth. These rules also necessarily and simultaneously exclude other participants, prohibit other operations and confine both within delimited systems. Conformity to the necessarily restricted set of discursive rules determines the validity of statements and truth claims within the discourse.

The will to knowledge cannot be separated from the will to power even though, as presently constituted in our culture, "the fact of power [is] invariably excluded from knowledge."[3] Knowledge produced within a discursive system legitimates power and experts. Discursive formations identify and authorize truth speakers. They produce experts who attain such status due to the discourse-specific knowledge they have acquired. Certification as an expert entails access to and control over certain kinds of power. These include the power to adjudicate truth claims, train and certify others as experts, and establish and work through institutions. These institutions name, regulate, and control behavior according to a legitimated, discourse-specific vocabulary.

Discourses are conflict ridden and unstable. They produce their own internal resistances to knowledge, power, and experts. Discourses are also unstable because boundaries between them are shifting and contested. They often compete with other discourses for the same potential terrain. Since truth is discourse specific, the rules that determine what counts as truth in one domain may not apply in another. A discourse as a whole cannot be true or false, because truth is always contextual and rule dependent. No master rules or decision procedures are available that could govern all discourses or resolve conflicts among or choices between them. Hence, truth claims may be incommensurate across discourses. What will decide the outcome of such contests is not greater truth content but power.

This inevitable instability within and across discourses leads them to seek an appearance of normality and objectivity. One of the effects of power within and among discourses is to produce the appearance of an objective or neutral resolution of competing truth claims. Power can produce this effect by eliminating, ruling out, or effacing certain truth claims. Discursive practices situate some voices as authoritative and worthy of attention and respect and marginalize or silence others. The historical contingency of their foundings and the past is obscured. Present resistances to them are masked, marginalized, or labeled as the behavior of deviants or inferiors. Such behavior is presented by some within a discourse as evidence of the need for its further expansion and intensified surveillance.

Psychoanalysis is embedded in the structures of modern Western societies. Foucault's concept of a discursive formation improves our understanding of some of these societies' distinctive traits, especially their processes of legitimation. Contemporary discourses like postmodernism and psychoanalysis undermine many of the foundations of this mode of legitimation. However, no alternative has successfully dislodged it.

A mode of legitimation is a set of practices and beliefs in and through which people come to believe their rulers have the right to exercise power over them. Each society has its own mode.[4]   Although most regimes originate in acts of violence and require force to sustain them, legitimate rule is deemed the opposite of domination. People's habitual participation in its replication enables power to circulate. When a mode of legitimation is successfully in force, its adherents are not even aware of its effects. Obedience to a form of rule or conformity to a set of institutional demands is an unquestioned habit. This is the most effective method of exercising power, since it requires the least wielding of overt force.

Typically, a mode of legitimation is characterized by one privileged set of practices that are foundational and determinative of it. Religion occupies this place in some societies; in others kinship or tradition does. The ruler rules because God has decreed it (the divine right of kings), or because he is the oldest male (patriarchy), or because it has always been this way (tradition).

Modern Western societies have a distinctive mode of legitimation, one Weber calls technical-rational and Foucault calls the regime of truth. This mode incorporates and is grounded in a particular set of beliefs. In our culture we must produce the truth. There can be no exercise of power without its concomitant production of truth. Legitimate power requires grounding in and justification by a set of rational rules. Since the universe is governed by rational laws, the more rational our social rules are, the higher their truth content will be. The converse is also true—the more access to truth we have, the more rational social arrangements will be. The truth value of the rules can be tested by the exercise of reason. These rules ought to be accessible to and comprehensible by any rational person.

In this mode of legitimation a special kind of knowledge, power, social institutions, and status are interdependent. Modern societies are characterized by the rule of experts. These experts generate and control clients or subjects. They

themselves are empowered and constrained by complex and increasingly pervasive systems of bureaucratic regulation. Technical expertise, that is, access to and
mastery of particular kinds of knowledge, is a predominant basis for and justification of the exercise of power.

Claims to scientific status are particularly desirable in establishing expertise
and legitimacy. The practice of science is defined as the exemplar of a rational,
neutral logic of discovery that governs a disinterested community of inquirers.
Scientists share open access to knowledge and transmit it freely. These characteristics legitimate the status of science as a privileged practice within modern
knowledge/power systems.

Citizens obey because they believe technical-rational rule conforms to and
is grounded in truth. Modern Westerners are taught to believe we are free and
sovereign when governed by laws that conform to our reason. The rational
is universally true and binding. Hence, rational rule can be simultaneously
neutral and beneficial. We presume if governance is rooted in rational knowledge and exercised through public procedure and law, rule must be other than
domination.

PSYCHOANALYSIS AS A DISCURSIVE FORMATION

At least three, not necessarily compatible, projects exist within the discursive
formation of psychoanalysis. These are: perpetuating and constructing theories
or positing truth claims, providing clinical treatment, and conserving a profes-
sion with particular practical and disciplinary interests. Dissimilar people in
divergent intellectual and practical locations may pursue these projects. The
audience, purposes, and modes of legitimation for and within each may also vary.
While my primary interest here is in the character and status of the first (theoretical) project, I will briefly discuss the others as well.

I. Theory

Like all discursive formations, psychoanalysis marks out a domain within
which it claims authoritative or privileged knowledge (or the means to obtain

and judge it). Authorities put forward and deploy various theoretical positions. They claim these hold true not only within the domain of psychoanalysis but outside it as well. The domain claimed by psychoanalysis includes the nature of subjectivity, the appropriate methods to investigate it, and the most accurate or useful theoretical languages to interpret or represent it. Psychoanalysts vigorously contest such claims among themselves. Nonetheless, there is probably a broad area of consensus among analysts about which claims are false, irrelevant, or unworthy of attention.

There is less consensus among analysts about the most desirable location of their discursive practices and who their external audiences are, should be, or could be. One of the contemporary paradoxes confronting American psychoanalysis is the lack of reciprocity in its allegiance to and identification with the medical model. These have not been particularly fruitful, either theoretically or practically. Devaluation of psychoanalysis pervades much of scientific writing on the topic. Psychoanalysis is all but invisible within its traditionally desired discursive location—the institutions and practices of medicine and biomedical research. However, interest in and writing on psychoanalysis is widespread, lively, and diverse within the humanities and social sciences and in professions such as psychology and social work. None of these discourses, however, have the status or privilege that medicine enjoys within the knowledge/power systems of the United States. This discursive rejection, loss of status, and boundary confusion have had and will continue to have profound effects on all three aspects of psychoanalysis.

The discursive domain claimed by psychoanalysis overlaps with terrain shared and contested by others, for example, philosophers, neurologists, sociologists, and anthropologists. For a variety of political and philosophical reasons, some of which I will discuss below, subjectivity is one of the most salient and contested issues within contemporary postmodern culture. Therefore, analysts ought to expect fierce battles for territory and control to continue indefinitely.

The other contestants have no particular reason to cede privilege to the analyst when he or she makes claims about subjectivity. At minimum they will await acknowledgment that their own claims exist and have implications for the analysts' projects. More likely, they will expect the analyst to follow their own discursive practices and norms concerning knowledge claims. If, for example, an analyst claims to put forward a general "science of mind," the neurologist will expect him or her to follow the rules of science as practiced by neurology. Within the neurologist's discursive frame, the analyst's claims will probably seem meaningless unless translated into the language of neurology and tested by its methods. The analyst, of course, can ask what authorizes or legitimates the neurologist's judgments. Since there is no neutral decision procedure both share, argument is likely to reach an impasse.

2. Clinical Treatment

The second aspect of psychoanalysis, clinical treatment, is also controversial. Analytic practices and justifications/legitimations vary, even among practitioners authorized by widely acknowledged, official agencies such as the International Psychoanalytic Association. In addition, the number of people who are not graduates of official training institutes yet claim to practice psychoanalysis continues to increase. Simultaneously, psychoanalysts have little influence or control over those with the discursive legitimacy to question the clinical efficacy of analysis. Medical researchers and public officials who evaluate health care to determine if it is effective (and reimbursable) are increasingly skeptical about its worth.

From Freud on, analysts have relied upon certain truth claims to legitimate analytic practices as a source of knowledge and as a form of treatment. Freud's own accounts of the mind undermine many of the assumptions upon which these ideas depend. However, many psychoanalysts perpetuate and refuse to abandon them. Claims about the relationship between facts and theories and about the nature of science have had an especially foundational role within psychoanalysis.[5] These claims are grounded in a curious mixture of assumptions. The mixture includes empiricist beliefs about the nature of "observation" and the relationships between theory and data. It also incorporates Enlightenment ideas about the neutral yet beneficial character of reason and science.

Reason is privileged as the unique means of access to and voice of the Real, and science is identified as the ideal form of knowledge. In science, rationality manifests itself in the origination of a "logic of discovery." This logic is universal and binding on all scientific practitioners. It is neutral in that it affects neither the subject/investigator nor the object/data. Science's "successes" (discoveries) are due to the adherence to this logic by its practitioners. The "scientific method" enables all those who use it to dis-cover (not construct) the truths of its objects. Science can reveal bits of the Real that exist independent of the scientist and the scientific modes of investigation.[6]   Many analysts from Freud on would probably agree with statements like these: "by testing thoughts against reality, science helps liberate inquiry from bias, prejudice, and just plain muddleheadedness."[7]

Some analysts rely on this set of beliefs to provide accounts of the location, meaning, and epistemic value of the clinical situation. Even today, analysts present clinical vignettes as if these can support or demonstrate the validity of an analytic idea or theory. The analyst gathers bits of "data" from the object/patient and gradually assembles these into more general ideas that constitute a theory. He or she then "tests" the validity of these ideas or theories in subsequent analytic encounters. If the analyst complies with the analytic rules, treatment can be epistemologically and politically neutral. Analytic procedure or the social/political context in which both participants and process are embedded will not contaminate the patient's treatment or the data generated by it.

3. Discipline, Training, and the Production of Expertise

These assumptions about knowledge and authority underwrite the disciplinary practices of psychoanalysis, including training and legitimation. Like any discursive formation, psychoanalysis seeks a monopoly over the production of certain sorts of experts and practices. It also attempts to normalize its construction of and control over certain domains. The legitimacy of analytic institutes requires a belief among both candidates and training analysts in the doctrine taught. Members of institutes generally do not question the truth value of analysis as a method of acquiring knowledge about oneself and others. They do not challenge the right of particular organizations to mark out and regulate their domain and their authority to train and evaluate others. Successful normalization obscures the power/knowledge practices through which this occurs. Power can then flow more freely and productively.

However, monopoly and normalization are necessarily unstable. Certain kinds of questions are particularly dangerous to discursive formations. Most perilous are questions concerning the validity of their production of knowledge and its truth, their control over a domain, and their right to train, regulate, and produce expert practitioners. Generally these three aspects are interdependent and reinforcing; a challenge to one eventually endangers the entire formation.

Challenges to either theory or monopoly control produce crises of power and legitimation. Internal challenges, especially by those already recognized as experts, are most immediately threatening. If serious enough, the challengers may face expulsion (withdrawal of authority) or excommunication (declarations of heresy).[8] Contestants from outside the discourse are often less threatening to those within it. They lack the discourse-specific power/knowledge to speak. Challenges by these others can undermine a discourse when it lacks economic autonomy or if its capacity to generate prestige or produce truth is compromised.

Within certain cultural contexts, psychoanalytic discourse has been remarkably successful in achieving normalization. For example, imagine a situation in which a white, middle-class sixteen-year-old is not attending school. What description and treatment would this person encounter? First, the sixteen-year-old would receive the classification of an "adolescent"—a "life stage" unknown one hundred and fifty years ago. The psychological and sociological discourses that produce this "stage" also create the experts who investigate and treat it. Second, authoritative people will define the situation as a problem. No one is likely to question whether this person should attend school. Third, experts may categorize this now-established problem as a "psychological" one, probably "school refusal," and as a possible symptom of a more serious "mental illness."

The description/diagnosis determines the treatment. In white, middle-class culture, experts generally characterize "psychological" problems as individual attributes and as consequences or symptoms of people's subjective states. The appropriate experts should examine the "inner" or subjective workings of this person. This expert will "specialize" in "adolescence," and one of his or her prerogatives is to determine if the person is deficient or deviant (according to the standards generated by experts' discourse). The discourse stipulates who should "treat" the problem and how. The expert must "help" the person to alter the problematic subjective state or at least her or his behavior.

It is easy to see how this process recreates and reaffirms the knowledge and expertise it assumes. The process creates the object/pathology that then becomes its legitimation. In other social contexts, one would describe this situation differently. Alternative possibilities include: (1) a moral failure by someone who must be held accountable for his or her actions by religious authorities; (2) a failure of the school to hold a student's interest and hence a problem for educators to investigate; (3) a refusal by the individual to uphold his or her obligation to the community and hence a matter for legal intervention; (4) a mark of shame on the family that requires action by the appropriate kinship group; (5) a failure of the community to find the proper place for the person about which proper political deliberation must occur.

PSYCHOANALYSIS AND WESTERN LEGITIMATION CRISES

Psychoanalytic discourse has attained considerable success in normalizing its domain. However, challenges to its legitimacy are strengthening. Lacan's questioning of the authority of the analyst, the training and legitimation procedures within psychoanalysis, and the status of its knowledge is no longer unusual. Psychoanalytic theory, clinical treatment, and disciplinary practices all face strong intra- and extra-discursive challenges. The social-political context of psychoanalysis compounds its difficulties. Profound crises of cultural identity, subjectivity, meaning, authority, and status pervade the postmodern world. Contemporary political and intellectual developments are especially disruptive to the white, relatively rich Westerner's sense of identity and confidence. These persons have been the primary subjects/objects of psychoanalytic discourse.

Until recently, the United States was the dominant location of psychoanalysis. White, well-off Americans, the primary practitioners and clientele of psychoanalysis, are facing a particular sort of disillusionment. The fantasy that our social history is exempt from the disorder and tragedy experienced by others is disintegrating. The long string of events beginning with the assassinations of (among others) President Kennedy, Robert F. Kennedy, Martin Luther King, and Malcom X, urban uprisings, the war in Vietnam, Watergate, and the resignation of President Nixon continue to affect us. The accelerating decay of civility and urban life also disrupts this fantasized sense of immunity and intensifies our sense of inefficacy. The United States no longer appears as the "land of promise" free from the suffering and mistakes of other cultures.

These disruptions occur within the context of global ones. The Holocaust, contests for power within the West and between it and Japan, the collapse of the Soviet system, anticolonialist revolts, and challenges to racism and male-dominance continue to undermine expectations of order, continuity, and stability. These political shifts alter the circulation of knowledge and power in many ways. The meanings—or even existence—of Enlightenment ideas (reason, history, science, progress, power, gender, and the inherent superiority of Western culture), including those upon which psychoanalysis depends, are subject to increasingly corrosive attacks.

Internal dissent has further disrupted the epistemological security of Western thinkers. Postmodernists and feminists undermine the foundations of Western thought. They expose the essential contestibility of its constituting notions. This exposure creates a legitimation crisis, since these notions then appear as mere humanly created artifacts for whose effects and consequences we alone are responsible. If knowledge is an effect of discrete, historical human action, it can no longer underwrite or guarantee political neutrality. Its relation to any larger truth or transcendental Reality appears at best highly contingent, contestable, and underdetermined. The circuits of power and their relations with the production of truth are more evident.

As we will see, these philosophic and political developments pose profound challenges to some of the most cherished and legitimating psychoanalytic ideas. Two foundational notions now appear particularly problematic. One notion is the belief that psychoanalysis is an empirical science because it can rely on clinical "data" to validate theory. The other is that analytic treatment (or its legitimating theories) can be politically neutral.

I. Postmodernism and the Powers of Knowledge

Postmodernists challenge Enlightenment ideas about truth, knowledge, power, history, self, and language still predominant in the West.[9] The power of reason to apprehend the truth is a central theme in Enlightenment stories about knowledge. One of the most important and definitive abilities of reason is its intrinsic capacity to recognize truth. Truth emerges out of a properly conducted relation between subject and object. Any rational subject apprehending or operating properly on the same object would arrive at the identical truth about it. The philosophy of knowledge can identify the optimum methods and rules for conducting this relation. It can provide accounts of how truth is generated and general standards by which truth claims can be more effectively produced and evaluated.[10]

Postmodernists' stories about truth do not focus on reason, method, and the relationships between subject and object. They treat truth as an effect of multiple and various discursive practices, including the circulation of power. They also question the ideas of mind, language, and the Real that underlie and ground any transcendental, empirical or foundational claims.[11] Intrinsic to either transcendental or empirical epistemologies is the belief that the mind can register data or ideas accurately. Our theoretical assumptions, methods, and mental processes need not in principle obscure the mind's reception of information about reality. For example, an empiricist analyst would claim that in listening to the patient's free associations, she or he is directly observing bits of the patient's unconscious processes. Unless countertransference intervenes, reliable information accumulates over time. The analyst can increase the sum of our accurate knowledge about the unconscious by reporting data gleaned from the analytic situation. Particular tenets of psychoanalytic theory can be tested against this data. Our theories can then be brought into line with the data, thereby increasing their accuracy and truth content.

A postmodernist would claim that the empiricist's view rests on fundamentally mistaken ideas. Postmodernists stress the dependence of thought on language and the epistemological consequences of this reliance. Language, a primary medium of psychoanalysis, cannot be a transparent, passive, or neutral instrument. Language is not a simple matter of putting the appropriate labels on objects. Each of us is born into an ongoing set of language games. We must learn these games to be understood by and to understand others. In acquiring linguistic skills we take on a way of life and enter into specific circuits of power. This emphasis on power distinguishes postmodernists from hermeneutic thinkers. The hermeneutic approach does not locate linguistic practices within discrete discursive formations in which knowledge and power are interdependent. Hermeneutic philosophers also believe that a text has a deep meaning (or meanings) against which particular interpretations can be evaluated. Postmodernists reject this idea and claim the *meanings* of a text are multiple and indeterminant.[12]

Language partially constructs our personhood including the structure, categories, and content of thought. The dependence of thought on language means that it and the mind itself are partially socially and historically (pre-)constituted. Language necessarily affects the *meanings* of our experiences and understandings of them, including interpretations of clinical data and analyses of it. To speak of experience near knowledge is mistaken, since without language we can neither conceptualize an event as experience nor communicate it to another. The linguistic constitution of experience is simultaneously a social and theoretical organization of it. Experience cannot speak for itself or directly to us. Language speaks us as much as we speak it. Its effects are often hidden and inaccessible to us.

Postmodernists also deny the possibility that an ahistorical or transcendental standpoint could exist. How could we acquire and maintain universal, transcendental, or a priori mental categories or ideas? The human mind is not homogeneous, unitary, lawful, or internally consistent in or over time. Attaining a transcendental standpoint would require cleansing the mind of all its social and linguistic determinants and acquiring a "god's-eye" view. What mental agency could carry out such a cleansing? All the sense data, ideas, intentions, or perceptions we have are already constituted. They only occur in and reflect linguistically and socially determined practices.

Lacking such a standpoint, even if the Real existed, we could never immediately apprehend or directly report it. Even if we could attain a god's eye view, what use would it be in making sense of our messy, contingent lives? Rather than mourn the inaccessibility of the Real, postmodernists investigate the sources of desire for it. They regard wishes for order or an eternal, homogeneous real with suspicion. Unity is an effect of domination, repression, and the temporary success of particular rhetorical strategies. They hope to open up possibilities and create spaces in which multiple differences can flourish.

However, it would be incorrect to assume that postmodernism is a form of relativism. Relativism has meaning only as the partner of its binary opposite—universalism. The relativist assumes the lack of an absolute standard is significant. If there is no one thing against which to measure all claims, then "everything is relative." If the hankering for a universal standard disappears, "relativism" would lose its meaning. We could turn our attention to the limits and possibilities of local productions of truth. The god's-eye view will be displaced by admittedly partial and fragmentary multiples of one.[13]

2. Feminism and the Instabilities of Gender

Feminists define gender as a changeable set of social relations that pervade many aspects of human experience from the constitution of the "inner self" and family life to the "public worlds" of the state, the economy, and knowledge production. Gender is not a consequence or effect of "natural sexual differences." It cannot be explained by reference to anatomical or biological attributes, although the relations of gender to embodiment are an interesting and controversial question. Gender is an indispensable category in the analysis of current Western cultures.[14]

Definitions of gender in feminist accounts often differ from psychoanalytic ones. Feminists stress the role of relations of domination in the production and maintenance of gender. They analyze gender as complex, historically contingent and determinative relations in and through which both masculinity and femininity are constituted. Gender is not the same as the "woman problem." It cannot be understood nor its problems addressed solely by studying the psychology of women. This approach does not relieve women of their positions as deviant others. Incorporation of more material about women into existing discourses is insufficient and may be counterproductive. Such incorporation allows the operation of gendered claims within existing discourses to remain undisturbed.

Feminists claim that neither men nor women within contemporary Western cultures exist outside gender systems. One of their effects is the constitution of masculinity/femininity as exclusionary and unequal opposites. Power and domination partially constitute and maintain these relations. In relations of domination, no subject can simply or voluntarily switch sides. We receive certain privileges or suffer certain injuries depending on our structural positions, no matter what our subjective intent or purposes may be. Men can no more easily resign from masculinity and its effects than I can from being a white woman. Gender and race relations mark both men and women, although in different and unequal ways.

By situating men as well as women within gender relations, we remove their purity/privilege. The social production of reason and knowledge production becomes more evident. Rather than insisting that women's reason can be as "pure" as men's, it is more productive to question the purity of reason itself and the claim that no valuable or truthful knowledge can arise from the activities traditionally associated with women or the passions.

We can also investigate the motives for insisting on such splits and this hierarchical ordering of human qualities. The insights derived from feminist object relations psychoanalysis are especially helpful in this investigation.[15] Children develop in and through the contexts of relations with others. Given the current sexual division of labor, the subjectivities of both men and women initially evolve partially through interactions with a woman—a mother and/or other female relations. The predominant role women must assume in our early caretaking and in our fantasies generates problems for both genders. To some extent, male identity emerges out of oppositional moves.[16] Men must become not-female as they acquire masculinity. In a culture where gender is an asymmetric binary relation, men must guard against the return of the repressed—their identification with mother and those "female" qualities within them. This provides a powerful unconscious incentive for identifying with and overvaluing the abstract and the impersonal. It is a strong motive for reinforcing gender segregation, including within intellectual work, to ensure that women will never again have power over men.

IMPLICATIONS FOR PSYCHOANALYSIS

I. Theory

Psychoanalysis' relation to recent intellectual and political developments in the postmodern West is profoundly ambivalent. Freud and some contemporary analysts remain powerfully attracted to Enlightenment notions of knowledge. They share its belief in the emancipatory potential of science and rational thought. Nonetheless, Freud and subsequent analysts such as Winnicott and Klein contribute to the undermining of confidence in the integrity and powers of reason. Freud's post-1920s writings on the structure of the mind as intrinsically conflicted and simultaneously psychic and somatic are especially important. Winnicott's notions of the psyche-soma and the transitional space as the locus of culture suggest many alternatives to rationalism. Klein's positing of an epistemophiliac instinct also hints at directions worth pursuing.[17]

Within psychoanalytic accounts, psychic structures and processes appear increasingly fragmented, multidetermined, fluid, and subject to complex and often unconscious alterations. Unlike many philosophers, analysts such as Freud, Klein, and Winnicott conceptualize the mind as fully embodied,[18] inherently conflict ridden, dynamic, heterogeneous, and constituted in and through processes that are intrinsically discordant. These processes cannot be synthesized or organized into a permanent, hierarchical organization of functions or control. The equation of mind and conscious thought or reason or the psychical and consciousness becomes untenable.

Their ideas subvert the dualisms such as mind/body, subject/object, thought/passion, and rational/irrational that pervade some forms of modern philosophy and science and impede the success of their own projects.

Psychoanalysts also challenge Enlightenment ontological premises by positing various forms of desire (for objects, drive satisfaction, mirroring, or the Other) rather than reason as the definitive and motivating core of our being.

Psychoanalytic theories of mind also contradict and challenge many contemporary epistemologies. Both the rationalist's faith in the powers of reason and the empiricist's belief in the reliability of sense perception and observation are grounded in and depend upon assumptions about the mind. It must have the capacity to be at least partially undetermined by the effects of the body, passions, and social authority or convention. However, psychoanalysis throws into doubt all epistemologies that rely on the possibility of accurate self-observation and direct, reliable access to and control over the mind and its activities.

Psychoanalysis identifies forces whose effects and boundaries can never be transparent to us. These forces, which include bodily experience, libidinal wishes, authority relations, and cultural conventions perpetually affect thought. Insight into the mind's operations will remain incomplete and provisional, because even aspects of the observing ego are repressed.

We cannot not "control for" bias if its source is in the dynamically unconscious repressed material to which the conscious mind lacks direct access. The agency of our knowing is contaminated by the influence of these unconscious forces, including desire and authority. Being able to give reasons for one's choice of action or definition of self-interest is not straightforward evidence of rationality or freedom from the unconscious. A "rational reconstruction" of the reasons for a choice or belief may be an elaborate rationalization of or reparation for an irrational wish or fear.

This complicated view also challenges those who portray mental life as the epiphenomena of a relatively simple series of electrochemical processes and networks. The subjective meanings of, say, delusions will never be captured within the discourse of neural firing. However, the rich content of such phenomena is clearly important in understanding the intricacies of subjectivity.

While psychoanalysts have much to contribute to conversations about subjectivity, they are vulnerable to challenges to the validity of their truth claims. Analysts cannot solve this dilemma by claiming that psychoanalysis is or could (given certain specified conditions) be a science. In my view, this approach is profoundly erroneous for several reasons. It undermines the confidence of others, including philosophers and practitioners of the natural sciences, in psychoanalysis. Such claims merely generate endless and unproductive debates about the scientific status of psychoanalysis. Instead, we should question the beliefs behind the assumption that this is a crucial matter. What could this status mean, and what would it add to the content or usefulness of psychoanalytic theory?

Obsession with this topic repeats rather than interprets Freud's own fixation on Enlightenment thinking. "Real" knowledge and science are still equated. Such arguments arise out of outmoded and inaccurate views of what science is and how it produces its own truth claims. Most importantly, it obscures, avoids, and retards addressing a problem faced by all discursive formations—how to generate discourse-specific means and tests for the production of knowledge. For psychoanalysis, this project will require better accounts of the knowledge that clinical experience generates and of the qualities of clinical relations and treatment. Psychoanalysts could contribute much more to epistemology, philosophies of mind, and to stories of human development, subjectivity, and the importance of human relations within them if they could provide better accounts of psychoanalytic processes.

2. Clinical Treatment

Psychoanalytic thinkers such as Freud and Lacan also undermine the Enlightenment belief in the intrinsic or necessary relationships between reason, self-determination, and freedom or emancipation. Contrary to the great hope of Enlightenment, use of one's own reason will not necessarily make us free. If the conscious/rational self is "not even master in its own house, but must content itself with scanty information of what is going on unconsciously in its mind,"[19] the possibilities for autonomous action are quite constrained. The ego does not necessarily express or ensure the possibility of an autonomous or rational will. Analysis may increase one's capacity for self-reflection. Decrease of the powers of rationalization and the influences of unconscious deference to authority will not necessarily follow. In its relations with the id, the ego "too often yields to the temptation to become sycophantic, opportunist and lying, like a politician who sees the truth but wants to keep his place in popular favor."[20]

Analysts may track the complicity between ego and superego forces, including political authority. However, they are often more reluctant to explore the impact of such influences on their own theories and practices. One of the important lessons of both postmodernism and feminism for psychoanalysis is that clinical treatment cannot be politically or socially neutral. The knowledge that informs psychoanalytic practices, like all knowledge, contains traces of the relations of power that circulate through it.

Psychoanalysis has played an important part in generating categories of identity and standards of normalcy and health, especially for practices of sexuality, child rearing, and gender. The normalizing veils of scientific language and claims to the objective discovery of "natural" forces, identities, or drives disguise the operation of these standards. More critical examination reveals the congruence of these identities and standards, especially those of femininity/masculinity, good/bad mother, healthy/deviant, and homosexuality/heterosexuality, with the practices and commitments of other dominant power/knowledge configurations.

In its normalizing and regulatory aspects, psychoanalysis is empowered by and contributes to a modern form of power, "biopower." Biopower signals and reflects shifts in the constitution of modern Western states and their legitimating discourses. The legitimacy of these states now rests and depends upon the politics of life rather than those of death.[21] Older forms of the state exercised juridical power. In these states, the ultimate and definitive expression of state power was its right to kill those who transgressed its law. While these aspects of power have not disappeared, a new one has gradually become pivotal—the power of life, or biopower. The legitimacy of the state is now grounded in and depends upon its ability to maintain and improve the health and welfare of its citizens. Thus it is not surprising that issues such as health care or the treatment of AIDS often dominate contemporary political discourses.

The concrete and precise character of the modern state's knowledge of and interest in human bodies is unusual. The humanistic rubric of the state's interest in and obligation to the creation and protection of the "well-being" of its inhabitants justifies increasingly pervasive surveillance of them. Biopower is based in and effects a "real and effective 'incorporation' of power. It circulates through and roots itself in the concrete lives of individuals and populations through multiple and variegated means."[22] The production of new sorts of truth and particular disciplinary and confessional practices generate and constitute biopower. These practices are supported and exercised both by the state and by newly elaborated discursive formations, especially medicine and the human sciences. The state needs experts to amass the knowledge it requires and to execute the policies said to effect and maximize this well-being and protection. Instances of such knowledge and associated practices include medicine, education, public health, prisons, and schools.

One purpose of biopower is to ensure a more tractable public body. The heterogeneous elements of a population can be made less dissonant through practices of "normalization." Concepts of deviancy, illness, maladjustment, and so forth are products of the same discourses that create the normal. These concepts also name the dangers the normal must be protected against. They justify the need for new and better knowledge to control the problems and for the exercise of power. This knowledge is simultaneously individual and global. It entails the study of specific "traits" possessed by individuals that cause their deviations and the search for methods that can be applied to all such individuals to effect the desired disciplinary results in the populations as a whole. "Prevention" of disease or crime requires the at least potential extension of these knowledges and practices to everyone.

The state's interest is in ensuring regularity of behavior, not only in punishing crimes after the fact. The more peaceful (e.g., controlled) the population, the more the state's power is legitimated and ensured. As the state becomes more powerful, it can dispense disciplinary legitimacy. It supports, regulates, and enforces the monopoly of certain professions over specific domains and practices. Failure of disciplinary practices becomes the basis for "experts" to ask for more resources and power to pursue and exercise their knowledge for the public good.

Along with the processes of normalization and discipline, the individual subject is created through confessional practices. The primary exemplars of these practices are psychoanalysis and psychiatry. Psychoanalysts and others believe in the existence of a particular form of being, the "individual." They teach us we have an individual "self" about which knowledge is possible. This individual has certain "natural," "universal," or "true" traits. These discourses create the idea that there is something "deep inside" us, something hidden but at least partially knowable by consciousness, a source of both pleasure and danger. We experience this self as true and foundational.

However, the constitution of this individual and our belief in its existence is an effect of biopower. Such experience is not "true" in some ontological or essentialist sense. It is an effect of a subjectivity constituted in and through certain discourses, including psychoanalysis. In other discourses such notions and experiences might not exist.

The discourses of biopower produce dangerous forces within us such as sexuality, controllable only by the person exercising surveillance upon her- or himself. This surveillance is said to lead to "self-knowledge" and freedom from the effects of these forces. However, to attain such self-knowledge and self-control, the individual must consult an expert whose knowledge provides privileged access to this dangerous aspect of the person's "self." By transforming pleasure into "sexuality," these confessional discourse/practices generate further practices/knowledge of self-control and self-knowledge. Simultaneously they ensure their own replication and an expansion of their domain.

While psychoanalysis contributes to and benefits from biopower, it also subverts it. The norms it posits and the categories it produces are notoriously ambiguous.[23] Unlike many other discourses, excess and excluded material are readily accessible and available to disrupt conversation or move it in a different direction. This is a strength of psychoanalytic discourse. Analysts should exploit this ambiguity rather than trying to standardize the meanings of its concepts and occlude their productive instability. Psychoanalysts claim tolerance of ambiguity is a sign of psychological well-being. It should become a norm for the health of psychoanalytic discourse as well.

Clinical practice subverts biopower in other ways. It can offer relationships that escape such modern binary oppositions as subject/object, work/play, instrumental/affective, child/adult, inner/outer, and public/private. Analysis is a form of relational work. It is an open-ended and mutually constituted field of activity in which multiple aspects of activity and experience come into play. Language, visual images, dreams, passion, reason, bodily experience, childlike wishes, and adult responsibility are all components of analytic discourse. Analytic time is not linear. Analysis is not oriented to material production, nor is it governed by a precise definition of output. Cost/benefit analysis cannot capture the utility or qualities of its activities or effects. This complexity is one of the strengths of analysis. Analysts err and even risk destroying analysis when they try to exercise order or control by marking one aspect as the true, foundational, or curative one.

The multiplicity of analysis and its emphasis on relationships help to account for the devaluation, identity crises, and current social dislocations of psychoanalysis. Its relational qualities place it within the female side of gendered circuits of identity and power. The confounding of binary oppositions disrupts its potential place within discursive formations, for example, some empirical sciences, whose knowledge and practices produce and depend upon their existence and stability.

3. Disciplinary Training and Practices

If psychoanalysts try to cling to the medical model and to establish analysis as clinical science, psychoanalysis will not survive in the postmodern West. The knowledge-producing practices of psychoanalysis cannot meet the regulatory standards of other discourses, such as medicine or biochemistry, nor should they. Without discourse-specific standards, questions such as who should be authorized to practice analysis cannot be resolved. Satisfactory answers will require more discursive consensus about which knowledge legitimates analytic practices.

If psychoanalysis is to survive in the postmodern world, it must broaden the topics considered legitimate within its discursive conversations. It should increase the number and kinds of partners with whom it converses and explore the implications of their knowledge for analysis. Analysts can have productive conversations among themselves and with others concerning the discourse-specific qualities of their own knowledge and practices and the implications of these for other discursive formations. Such conversations should address the politics of psychoanalytic knowledge and practices and the complex networks of discipline, confession, and resistance within which psychoanalysis circulates. These networks are components of both the internal practices of psychoanalysis and its relations with other discourses.

The paradoxical existence of increasing fragmentation and concentration of disciplinary practices and powers pervades the postmodern world. Psychoanalysis cannot be immune from the consequences all citizens of such a world must face. We find ourselves sometimes in an inadvertent but unavoidable complicity with powers whose ethical and political practices are ambiguous at best. Simultaneously we experience both vulnerabilities and responsibilities to other discursive communities whose practices are (if we are lucky) only partially compatible with ours. Perhaps more than ever, psychoanalysts need to establish new colleges of psychoanalysis. In itself this will not be sufficient for psychoanalysis to survive, much less to flourish. However, intolerance of difference, disorder, and complexity or a wistful political innocence will doom the discourse of psychoanalysis to increasing marginality and obscurity in the postmodern world.

3

Forgotten Forms of Close Combat
Mothers and Daughters Revisited

Women no doubt reproduce between them the peculiar, forgotten forms of close combat in which they engaged with their mothers. Complicity in the non-said, connivance in the unsayable, the wink of an eye, the tone of voice, the gesture, the color, the smell: we live in such things, escapees from our identity cards and our names, loose in an ocean of detail, a data-bank of the unnameable. . . . In this weird feminine seesaw that swings "me" out of the unnameable community of women into single combat with another woman, it is perturbing to say "I" . . . A piece of music whose so-called oriental civility is suddenly interrupted by acts of violence, murders, bloodbaths: isn't that what "women's discourse" would be?

Julia Kristeva, "*Sabat Mater*", *The Female Body in Western Culture: Contemporary Perspectives*

Feminist writers have provided powerful and persuasive accounts of the psychological, political, and philosophical importance of mother-child relations and of their reverberations throughout our lives. This work has stimulated productive analyses of some of the patriarchal fantasies that underlie and engender the productions of Western culture.[1] The frequent displacement of fantasies from maternal to paternal sites even within psychological theorizing has become more evident.[2] Our understanding of female subjectivity and human development is richer and more complex.

Despite these gains, I find the maternal turn so prevalent within recent feminist theorizing increasingly disturbing and suspicious. I am convinced this turn is neither accidental nor innocent. Deconstruction of the functions within feminist discourses of maternal fantasies is urgently needed.[3] The following questions would be among those posed in such a deconstruction: Why has the story of "woman" become the story of mothers and daughters? Why have the conflicts, sacrifices, and confinements of these relations receded or been obscured in a valorization of women's connectedness? Why have mothers become central agents in the constitution of subjectivity? What purposes are served by this framing of the story? What aspects of female subjectivity are repressed or denied in this retelling? Where are stories of paternal power and relations of domination among women? What else determines gender identity? What are the relationships between gender and female subjectivity?

In 1976, Dinnerstein suggested myriad possible paths to pursue.[4] She brilliantly analyzes some of the work fantasies about mothers do. They help to relieve humans of a sense of responsibility and fallibility, of the limits of our powers, and the lack of coincidence between intent and outcomes. Evidently even Dinnerstein underestimated the power, prevalence, and persistence of these fantasies. They continue to reverberate throughout feminist discourses.

I will trace the operation of some of these fantasies through an interaction between a patient and myself. Then I will pursue their circulation through feminist theorizing more generally. I intend this analysis to provoke further conversation about the recurrent valorization of maternity and female relatedness within contemporary feminist discourses.

PASSIONATE ATTACHMENTS

Recently one of my patients arrived at her session in an agitated state. M is a white, professional woman in her late twenties from a relatively wealthy and socially prominent family. She told me the following story. M had dinner the previous week with a man from out of town whom she met on a business trip. After dinner (their first date), as they were walking away from the restaurant, he told her he did not have a place to spend the night. He claimed it was too late to return home. She named several hotels in the immediate neighborhood, but he pressured her to let him stay at her house. M demurred, saying there was nowhere for him to sleep. He said he did not mind sleeping on the floor. They discussed this for about ten minutes, and finally she agreed to let him stay with her.

At her house they talked and watched TV for a while (both sitting on the bed). Early in the morning M said she was exhausted and wanted to go to sleep. She changed into a sweatshirt and pants and went under the bed covers. A short time later she awoke to find the man under the covers with her, his hand on her shoulder, sighing loudly. She took his hand away, but he returned it to her body, moving it down her thigh and continuing to sigh. Again she flung the hand off, but he returned it. Finally she yelled at him, "what are you doing," took a blanket and went to sleep on the floor. He left early the next morning and later called her. She did not return the call.

The patient was very upset. She felt the man took advantage of her. She was also angry at herself for "being nice" and trying to avoid conflict by letting him stay. She called her mother to discuss the incident. Before M finished telling her about the dinner, her mother (as the patient felt it) began to criticize her for not giving the man a chance. The mother claimed her daughter was too particular. There must be something wrong with her; she had dated so many men but had found no one she wanted to marry. When would the daughter settle down? The daughter then continued to tell the mother the rest of her story. The mother began to criticize her daughter again; this time for being incautious. How could she let a man she hardly knew into her house? What was she thinking? How could her judgment be so poor?

The daughter felt furious and rejected by the mother. She could do nothing right; she would be condemned whether she gave the man a chance or not. She felt intruded upon and ashamed. Why couldn't her mother have empathy for her feelings? Why couldn't she help M figure out the regulation of distance, propriety and potential connections with men? What was her mother's agenda, other than wanting the daughter to be married? Why wasn't the daughter's professional success and power enough to please her? What was faulty in her handling of this situation, in her expectations of and response to her mother, and in her relations with men?

The context of the patient's questions included my three-year relationship with her. A major theme in M's therapy has been the lack of attunement between her parents and herself. This lack contributed to M's low sense of self-esteem and her insecurity. M's insecurity was exacerbated by a continual struggle between her sister and herself for first place in the family. She is ambivalent about sexuality, intimacy, and aggression.

In asking her questions she hoped for several contradictory responses. These include empathy for her pain, anger and shame about the situation and her mother's replies. She would like me to be a "good mother." A good mother would provide reassurance and restoration of her sense of self-worth and her capacity to love and be loved. She would encourage M to be a sexual being on her own terms. M also expects me to offer critical but sympathetic analyses of her behavior. She wants me to help her sort out conflicts about the wishes evoked by her mother. I am to assist M in resolving her ambivalence about sexuality and relations with men.

M's questions confronted me with a dilemma. This story, I felt then, and even more on reflection, exemplifies many problematic elements in the constitution of female subjectivity. These include sexuality, power, and relations between and fantasies about mothers and daughters. I bring a feminist sensitivity toward issues of power, gender, and rape to my therapy relations. I wish to avoid the culturally sanctioned tendency toward simplistic mother blaming. However, I also have the psychoanalyst's suspicion of split-off and denied feelings. These include envy, desire, aggression, ambivalence, and ambition. Women develop investments in certain kinds of relationships and images of the self, maternity, and "good" girls. These investments and passions affect mothers and daughters (and therapists) and the relationships between them.

My sometimes conflicting theoretical commitments influence my relations with patients, especially in the choice of interventions and the content of interpretations. In my relationship with M I have expressed my conflicting loyalties. I try to increase M's empathy for her mother's history while also encouraging M to explore her own split-off passions.

However, competing theoretical commitments are certainly not the only determinant of my interventions. I have also been influenced by our culture's fantasies of the good mother. My immediate response to M's questions was to empathize with the pain caused by the lack of attunement in her mother's response. I related it to the ongoing history of their relationship. My response to her question about what she wants from men was to highlight her need for a high level of emotional attunement in present relationships to repair the past. However, by focusing on connection and attunement, I also avoided M's rage. This feeling would have been evoked had I immediately suggested she look at her own behavior and motives more critically.

As I reflect upon this session, I grow more suspicious of my own behavior and motives. I wonder about what is gained and lost by focusing on relational (mother-daughter; therapist-patient) issues first. Does this perpetuate or reinforce certain fantasies and wishes of M and myself concerning being or having a good mother? Did I, like the mother, shut off access to the daughter's knowledge or experience of her sexuality to preserve our dyadic relationship? Shouldn't I also foster autonomous expressions of her sexuality and aggression? Am I encouraging M to shore up her identity as a blameless and attached daughter? By so readily assuming the role of the good mother, am I sustaining unrealistic and harmful fantasies of the perfectly attuned partner? How much frustration is necessary for the development of self-reflection and a realistic sense of agency and the necessary limits of any relationship?

In retrospect, I also wonder if I was doing M a disservice by withholding my questions about her ambivalence about sexuality, ambition, aggression, and power. A feminist sensitivity to date rape and sexual politics is certainly war-ranted. The man had access to contacts extremely useful for M's business. Yet, aren't ambiguities necessarily conveyed in sharing a bed with someone? Don't women sometimes wish to exploit a certain seductiveness or sexual tension for their own purposes, despite or even because of the fact that it can be used against them by men? Although women still suffer under male domination, can't sexual politics be played out by both genders?

From a feminist perspective it is reasonable to invite M to understand (not blame) her mother and the forces operating on her. It is certainly sensible for any mother to be concerned about her daughter's sexual vulnerability. M's mother expressed wishes widely shared in her community when she communicated the hope of having her daughter married. She grew up with very traditional white heterosexual middle-class expectations of women's place and marriage. In this mother's experience, tradition paid off. She enjoyed her marriage to a successful man, motherhood, and a second career when the children were older.

Yet, are my motives or effects so benign? Did I replicate or foreclose exploration of other less admirable behaviors? For example, shouldn't we pay attention to mothers' roles in regulating their daughters' sexuality? What about their envy in our youth-oriented, heterosexist culture of the daughter's potential pleasures and attractiveness to men? Can't mothers feel ambivalent that many career options are more thinkable to their daughters than they were to them?

What about this daughter's ambivalence about her mother's attachments? Why does the daughter still turn to her mother to mediate her relations with men and resolve her quandaries about sexuality, guilt, aggression, and autonomy? M experiences much rage and envy because her father and not she occupies central place in her mother's affections. She envies her mother's powerful and absorbing connection to her husband and her obvious pleasure in it. Why does she continue to hope her mother will change into a more sat-isfying partner for her?

WHOSE BODY IS IT ANYWAY?

M's story epitomizes the complex enmeshment of mothers and daughters in issues of subjectivity, embodiment, and sexuality. Mothers represent the impossible borders, the confounding of the dualities of Western culture.[5] A pregnant woman is simultaneously nature and culture; subject and other. A nursing mother is food (nature) and care (environment); her substance is inner and outer. "I'm in the milk and the milk's in me," sings a child in one of the stories I read to my son. The nursing mother's breast also transgresses the border between sexuality and maternity, between woman as the (man's) object of desire and as the mother of (his) children.

One strand of psychoanalytic thought, spun out of the work of Melanie Klein, stresses the centrality of the mother's body in the infant's fantasy life and development.[6] Her body is literally our first home and often the first source of food as well. As infants, her smell, feel, voice, and touch pervade our senses. They provide a bounded sense of space within which security and continuity become possible.

Yet this being is also our tormentor. She is the source of denial and frustration as well as gratification. Maddeningly separate from us, she has resources we desire within her, to give or not as she chooses. The feeding breast comes and goes, sometimes out of synch with the rhythms of the child's hunger and need. Each of us lives inside our own skin. What is in mother is not necessarily accessible or available to the child. Thus for daughter or son, connection with mother is suffused with desire, aggression, and ambivalence. Prebirth merger can never be restored. With each expression of desire or need we risk frustration, rejection, or damage to the other.

While the question, to whom does the mother's breast belong, is enigmatic, another is equally so. To whom does the nursling's mouth belong? It signals and experiences a need, yet its satisfaction resides in part in the body of an Other. Hence food and love and feeding and control intermingle. This compounding provides rich material for the manifold potentialities of "eating disorders" and the disciplining of the body and its pleasures.[7] One of these pleasures we call "sexuality." Contrary to Freud's beliefs, these pleasures cannot be external to power (or civilization).[8] Power shapes their very "nature" and their naming as such. What can appear as sexuality depends upon complex networks of disciplinary practices, of power circulating between (among others) mothers and children, men and women.

Part of the painful interplay between many mothers and daughters is the initial evoking of desire and then forbidding it. Mothers often participate in turning daughters into objects of desire for men, not for themselves and not for women or their children. As my patient's mother implied (and my patient, too, believes), something is wrong with a grown woman without a husband, a man with property in her person/sexuality.

On the other hand, just as my patient did, many daughters turn to mothers for permission to be sexual and for information about how to do it properly. Frequently they are taught that some (but not too much) sexual display and exchange is necessary to "catch" a man. Daughters, of course, sometimes reject their mother's teachings. What do mothers think when their daughters develop different sexual orientations? How do mothers respond when daughters develop their own erotic interests outside the circuit of reproduction? How do mothers feel when their daughters decide not to become mothers? Of course I do not think mothers or daughters respond in any singular manner to these circumstances. I simply indicate how obscure so much of this terrain remains.

THE VIRGIN MOTHER

What is still missing from my patient's—and my—story? Daughters as well as sons have difficulties with and investments in managing the threatening content and unpredictable boundaries of embodiment, maternity, aggression, and female sexuality. The daughter's conflicts, resentment and ambivalence about the mother's individuality, sexuality, and power are often split off or repressed. The dyad's hostile feelings toward one another are often disavowed. Feelings such as envy, rage, and desire for control and suppression of difference are denied. Alternately these feelings are assigned predominance solely in the constitution and psychodynamics of masculine identities.

Female sexuality outside the circuits of reproduction or relatedness is threatening to many women and men. Many men and women have trouble with the idea that they might simply be an object of women's desire or that sometimes women might experience sex as an end in itself. Sex is not necessarily imposed on women or something we suffer or enter into for its extrinsic rewards (a baby, feeling close to you).

This is part of the emotion stirred by abortion; that sex and motherhood are

not intrinsically connected. "What if your mother aborted you?" a bumper sticker proclaims. This sticker intimates our terror of the maternal power over life
and death. It also suggests our fear of the (potential) power of women to refuse
to be mothers or to be perpetually in relations with others.

Without such denial or displacement the simplistic claims that the gender-
based continuity of identity between mother and daughter has a predominantly
beneficial influence in the constitution of feminine subjectivity would be less
plausible. This continuity is said to provide a motive or ground for women's
allegedly greater propensity for relatedness and connection. Some feminists celebrate the "female" virtues of (a now sanitized) connection and care. Relatedness
and connection are seen as relatively straightforward and positive virtues.

Women are now praised for their greater immunity to "bad" forms of individuality. Bad forms of individuality are ones in which the nonrelational aspects of
the self are given priority over maintaining connections with an Other. One
must repress many aspects of experience to represent mother-daughter relations,
connection, or relatedness in this way. The powerful connections established
through hate or envy are defined away as "not genuine" forms of relatedness.
The dangers, aggression, and potential abuses of or within relationships are
rarely acknowledged. Connection can be represented as a relatively unproblematic good and as a basis for an alternative and implicitly superior subjectivity only
after such repression has occurred.[9]

The construction of femininity within the circuit of mother/daughter provides
a number of secondary gains. These include shielding the privilege of heterosexuality and reinforcing cultural prohibitions on women's aggression and wishes for
separation. Images of maternity are desexualized.[10] The split between sexuality
and maternity prevalent in our culture is replicated and recreated. The costs and
deformations of contemporary femininity, so powerfully named by early radical
feminists such as Rubin, recede from view.[11] Like all disowned material, these
aspects of female subjectivity surface elsewhere.

Desexualized accounts of maternal practices also reinforce beliefs about sexuality and the dangers of the body/passion and mortality that are some of the
most dubious aspects of contemporary white Western culture.[12] How often do
white, middle-class women acknowledge that we actively participate in the constitution and deployment of our sexuality? How often do white heterosexual
women admit that we like sex (sometimes), even or purposely outside a "meaningful" relationship or the gaze of an (masculine or feminine) Other?

Feminist discourses are marked by their own unconscious fantasies about such matters.[13] For example, a curious dynamic has emerged in feminist writing. Female sexualities are increasingly disowned, deconstructed, projected outward, or made an effect of the actions of others as the maternal dimension of femininity is valorized (and homogenized). Sexuality becomes a mark of the victimization of women or is diffused into symbiotic merger.[14] Agency is shifted to maternity—or nowhere.[15] Sexuality may be exploited, distorted, and misshaped by patriarchal power and heterosexuality, but maternity is portrayed as a relatively free space for the constitution and expression of female virtue.

The conflation of woman/mother carries with it a necessary horizon of heterosexuality. Despite efforts by Rich among others, heterosexuality is protected and reinforced.[16] In a heterosexist society, the lack of questioning of how the mother got pregnant permits the almost automatic assumption of the existence somewhere of a man/husband/father to rest undisturbed. In our current discourses, woman/mother often presumes or requires the simultaneous existence of two related dyads: child/mother; father/mother. Consider, for example, the curious term "single" mother. How can a mother be single, since by definition she is a being in some relation to an Other? Obviously she is "single" because she "lacks" a husband; she operates outside the normal rules of the Name of the Father. Maternity without paternity is a deviant form.

Desexualized maternity also implies a lack of desire directed at the child. In psychoanalytic accounts the child has desire for the mother, and much is made of the girl's enforced shift from maternal to paternal love object. Yet what of the mother's desire? How does it shift between child and (adult) lover? In our justified concern with child abuse, are we denying the erotic charge of maternity, the bodily intimacy and the pleasures of that kind of knowledge of an Other? Can the child not bear the idea that it exists as an object for the mother, as much as she exists for it? What images do daughters have of their mothers as sexual beings, of passionate attachments that exclude and may come before and outside them? How does the daughter experience the father as a rival for the mother (not just the mother as a rival for him)?

What if your mother refuses her gaze, turns her attention elsewhere? Does not serve as your mirror, your nurturance, your ground of continuity of being or of the semiotic, fertile source of aesthetic meaning ungoverned by the Father's Law? If she is no longer outside, but inside, power? If she wields power not as care, nurturance, preservative love, but as assertion, need, or desire of her own? Or if she is off playing, with other women or men? Or in her own head? Can daughters stand to be cut off, outside the dyadic circuit? If their mothers don't need them to be women, do they need their mothers? If women don't need babies, do they need men?

MOTHER'S WORK IS NEVER DONE:
THE POLITICS OF MATERNAL FANTASIES

Feminists have barely begun to explore the mutually determining or constituting effects of maternity, sexuality, female subjectivity, and one's racial and class identities.[17]   White feminists have paid too little attention to the ways race and class circulate through and stamp our discourses and choices of tropes, foregrounding certain images of femininity and marginalizing others. The generative effects of relationships of power and domination are rarely explored except in discussions of masculinity.

The constituting effects of racism in white feminist discourses continue to be obscured. The predominance of abstract and nonsituated maternal images serves to perpetuate white women's political innocence. We (white women) become complicit in the intersections of racism/sexism by not challenging the treatment of black mothers and by replicating purified images of white ones (nurturing, caring, empowering, ethical, etc.).[18]

By denying our own pleasures and expressions of aggression, assertion, and control, we represent ourselves as innocent victims outside circuits of power. As mothers, we are somehow universalized and freed from complicity in relations of domination. Our participation in and marking by racism disappears. This desexualized and deracialized "goodness" then becomes the basis of our ethical contribution to the public world. Desexualized white women can be "purely" mothers.

This status was denied black women in captivity. It was then turned against them in the many accusations against the black "matriarch."[19] Isn't it odd that white women are valorized for the very relation (nearly exclusive responsibility for the emotional care of their children) that is now declared to be the cause of innumerable ills in the black community?

Racism serves both white men and women by locating active sexuality as alien to white women, especially higher-class ones. Class operates similarly as in the construction of the pure wife and the loose servant. Traditionally, white women are portrayed as pure/superior, because, unlike black women, our sexuality is modest and constrained.[20] Absence of aggressive, self-generated, non-object-related sexuality is a mark of her race/class. In contrast to the more wild and dangerous sexuality of black men and women, white women's sexuality can be more easily controlled and satisfied. White men can claim to be the protectors of its "purity," and this legitimates their control over other men (potential defilers).

Property in women is an intrinsic aspect of the modern meanings of masculinity. Women's sexuality is inscribed as the possession (or contested terrain) and effect of men. Men's identity is partially defined/expressed by their control over female sexuality. The more women one has access to, the better man/person one is.[21] This ideal of masculinity has a regulatory effect. It influences men throughout the hierarchies of masculinity and even enters into ideas about emancipation and self-respect. As the characters in the recent Spike Lee movie, *Jungle Fever*, discuss, "liberation" for a black man is often taken to include control of "his own" women and sexual access to white ones.[22]

This view of women's sexuality as an effect and perogative of masculine power has been too uncritically adopted by some feminists. Feminists such as MacKinnon treat it as an accurate description of female sexuality. Instead such claims should be deconstructed. They reflect a complex mix of women's and men's struggles, resistance, wishes, and power. Control over female sexuality is exercised and resisted in various ways and for many conscious and unconscious purposes. Access to such control and the possibilities of successful resistance to it vary by race, geographic location, age, sexual identities, and class as well as gender. Sexuality does not spring from a free space outside circuits of power; however, it is not simply a sum of their effects.

GOD IS DEAD, LONG LIVE MOTHER?

> If it is true than an ethics for the modern age is no longer to be confused with morality, and if confronting the problem of ethics means not avoiding the embarrassing and inevitable issue of the law but instead bringing to the law flesh, language, and *jouissance*, then the reformulation of the ethical tradition requires theparticipation of women. Women imbued with the desire to reproduce (and to maintain stability); women ready to help our verbal species, afflicted as we are by the knowledge we are mortal, to bear up under the menace of death; mothers.[23]

Maternal fantasies serve ontological as well as political purposes. Note the slippage here, between women and mothers, reproduction and immortality; the evasion of human finitude. If feminism succeeds in displacing the Name of the Father, or God the Father and his traditional paternal functions, in whose Name will it be done? Will we install a regnant Holy Mother, and thus protect/ preserve the possibility of innocence?

Contemporary Western cultures glorify, denigrate, and isolate maternity. If women might say what they want of the maternal, it could be that we do not want to confront its limits and ambiguities. Mothers and daughters are complicit in evading our full, mutual disillusionment. Motherhood is a heterogeneous and conflictual set of experiences, wishes, fantasies—some of which have nothing to do with the child. Mothers may sometimes have an interest in preserving life, but they cannot save the species or redeem our messy worlds. Maternity is not an essence, nor does it exhaust categories of woman or the feminine.

Perhaps such thinking reveals the recurrence of certain infantile fantasies— only I can satisfy the mother, she needs me (the child) to reach her unique being. Yet, motherhood is not an exclusionary state, separate and clearly differentiated from all others. Being a mother calls upon and evokes a heterogeneous set of capacities and feelings within a multiple subjectivity. While it might conflict with or require the temporary suspension of other capacities (as do many other practices) it does not transport anyone into a unique form of being. We go on hating, thinking, etc., as mothers and otherwise.

Daughterhood also is not the royal road to an understanding of woman, subjectivity, or gender. These are all shaped by heterogeneous forces whose relative power is often undecidable in individual instances. It too is a status overdetermined by many factors including race, class, geography. Daughterhood is not the mirror image of motherhood. We will not exhaust its meanings by analysis of maternity; nor is maternity its necessary end or destination. The daughter's desire does not originate or terminate in her relations with her mother.

Stories about mother-daughter relations reveal the recurrent power of our desire for a benign force or agent out there in the world looking out for us, attending to our needs, and ensuring their satisfaction. These wishes form part of the common ground upon which women and men form a community through sustaining fantasies about (maternal) possibilities. Certain fantasies about mothers ward off profound anxieties and discontents from which contemporary Westerners often suffer. Such stories can only serve their functions by the simultaneous operation of denial, evasion, and pushing other material to the margins, rendering contradictory aspects of maternity almost unspeakable. The existence of our wishes and the return of the repressed, with its undesired yet acted-upon knowledge, situates maternity as an inevitable space of contention.

We long for knowable origins that connect to guaranteed ends (including the goodness of our purposes and agency) and for a loving home.[24] We wish for a meaningful, purposive, orderly, continuous, stable, nurturing, friendly and comprehensible universe, and for secure roots. We would like protection against the multiple contingencies that destabilize but enable us to live finite lives in humanly constituted worlds. We want to be caught and held securely in an idealized mother's gaze. We ask her to assure us that someone is really still there, to protect us and catch us when we fall. Finitude, evil, death: all can be transcended in the rebirth of the holy, innocent child/mother. We promise to be good daughters if mother won't abandon us. Whose voice can we really hear? An echo, a delusion, a fantasy of a childhood always already past and yet disabling us still.

THREE

POLITICS AND PHILOSOPHY

4

IS ENLIGHTENMENT EMANCIPATORY?

That the step to competence is held to be very dangerous by the far greater portion of mankind (and by the entire fair sex)—quite apart from its being arduous—is seen to by guardians who have so kindly assumed superintendence over them.

Immanuel Kant, "What is Enlightenment."

The meanings of modernity and the nature of modernization are intensely contested. Writers can be located along a spectrum from those who believe there is a (yet unrealized) emancipatory potential within the project(s) of modernity to those who claim that it is morally bankrupt or hopelessly contaminated by its disciplinary imperatives.[1]

While this debate appears to be wide-ranging, from a feminist perspective it is deficient. Few writers appear to notice that the dominant stories about modernity and modernization have necessary but repressed or split-off gendered components. The integrity and coherence of these stories are dependent upon what is not explicitly articulated or included. Their normative appeal rests in part upon the unacknowledged and unexcavated elements remaining undisturbed. Attention to gender will alter our understandings of the meanings of modernity/modernization. These perspectives must be included within our stories about them. Closer examination of the gendered (and gendering) processes of modernity should be an intrinsic component of any appraisal of its emancipatory character and potential.

Nowhere are gendered relations more necessary and constitutive than in one of the foundational articulations of modernity: Kant's essay, "What is Enlightenment?". Read with a feminist eye this essay reveals much about the gendered qualities of modernity/modernization and the modern constitution of gender. Kant develops a gendered geography and defense of modernity that recur in and are further developed by later, equally emminent theorists such as Sigmund Freud and Max Weber. Analysis of his text will illuminate different aspects of modernity and contribute to a fuller evaluation of its emancipatory potential.

WHAT IS ENLIGHTENMENT?

From its opening paragraph, Kant's essay is structured through and pervaded by gendered dichotomies. He begins with the contrast between tutelage and enlightenment. "Tutelage is man's inability to make use of his understanding without direction from another."[2] Not all forms of tutelage are antithetical to enlightenment. Kant acknowledges that all humans must pass through a period—childhood—in which we are unable to use our understanding without direction from another. The first dichotomies are introduced here: child/adult and family/autonomy. Although Kant does not state it directly, both childhood and the family are women's worlds. In premodern and modern sexual divisions of labor, mothers or female caretakers are responsible for protecting us until we can safely walk on our own.

Tutelage itself is not necessarily the enemy of enlightenment, but "self-incurred" tutelage is. The laziness and cowardice of humans render them vulnerable to others who set themselves up as our guardians. Humans who could use their own understanding without the direction of another fail to do so out of a lack of resolution and courage. Guardians play on fear to sustain their own power. They make their charges further dependent on them and even more frightened by autonomy. "After the guardians have first made their domestic cattle dumb and have made sure that these placid creatures will not take a single step without the harness of the cart to which they are tethered, the guardians then show them the danger that threatens if they try to go alone."[3]

Three more dichotomies are put into operation: tutelage/autonomy, guardian/independence, domestic/public. One of the dominant strands of the modernization story emerges here. It will become more overt in Freud's theories and stronger still in those of Lacan.[4] Love and autonomy (or enculturation) are necessarily in conflict. The move from tutelage to autonomy requires an external force strong enough to break those initial ties that bind. "For any single individual to work himself out of the life under tutelage that has become almost his nature is very difficult. He has come to be fond of this state, and he is for the present really incapable of making use of his reason, for no one has ever let him try it out."[5]

Bad guardians (mothers/the fair sex) play on the ordinary person's (child's) fear, even though the "danger is not so great, for by falling a few times they would finally learn to walk alone."[6] They (e.g., the entire fair sex) lack an appreciation of thinking for oneself in themselves and others. The power of domestication (women) is so great that its overcoming requires the counterforce of an entirely different sphere: the public world. These guardians can retain their power only as long as their subjects remain (immature) children outside the public realm. "There are few who have succeeded by their own exercise of mind both in freeing themselves from incompetence and in achieving a steady pace. But that the public should enlighten itself is more possible; indeed, if only freedom is granted, enlightenment is almost sure to follow."[7]

The development of autonomy, true adulthood, and rationality requires first the (boy's) identification with a (male) tutor who will encourage autonomy. "For there will always be some independent thinkers, even among the established guardians of the great masses, who after throwing off the yoke of tutelage from their own shoulders, will disseminate the spirit of the rational appreciation of both their own worth and every man's vocation for thinking for himself."[8] Such development must occur slowly, because old prejudices are difficult to overcome. The father/tutor must be incorporated, not overthrown. Rebellion or revolution cannot bring true maturity. "Perhaps a fall of personal despotism or of avaricious or tyrannical oppression may be accomplished by revolution, but never a true reform in ways of thinking. Rather, new prejudices will serve as well as old ones to harness the great unthinking masses."[9]

Note that in this account autonomy is understood as the opposite of connection: walking alone, not holding someone's hand. Good guardians enable us to grow up and leave home/childhood, but to do so they must have access to the public world. Without such access they cannot give the child (boy) what he needs to enter this world and be emancipated from the family (the domestic harness). "For this enlightenment, however, nothing is required but freedom, and indeed the most harmless among all the things to which this term can properly be applied. It is the freedom to make public use of one's reason at every point."[10]

Kant introduces what will become a key theme of modernization: the necessary separation and differentiation of the private (family) and the public, the world of dependence and the world of freedom. He does not overtly acknowledge here that this differentiation is gendered and in turn reinforces gender differentiation. While some theorists such as Habermas repeat this omission, others including Rousseau and Freud do not. Freud writes, "women soon come into opposition to civilization and display their retarding and restraining influence—those very women who, in the beginning, laid the foundations of civilization by the claims of their love. Women represent the interests of the family and of sexual life. The work of civilization has become increasingly the business of men, it confronts them with ever more difficult tasks. . . . His constant associations with men, and his dependence on his relations with them, even estrange him from his duties as a husband and father. Thus the woman finds herself forced into the background by the claims of civilization and she adopts a hostile attitude towards it."[11]

Freud attributes this differentiation to the "natural differences" between men's and women's natures. Feminist theorists suggest that it is not a consequence of nature but of culture and more specifically of force.[12] Women must be "domesticated" and kept in their familial place (wife/mother) by not-so-kindly guardians and legal arrangements.[13] Labors of love must continue to be performed by *someone*. Participation in nonfamilial worlds "estranges," perhaps disables persons (men) from carrying out such tasks. Women may be "hostile" toward civilization, but both our exclusions from parts of it and our labors within its necessary "outside" continue to be ironic necessities.

One of the marks of modernization, then, is the emergence of a distinctive ideology of the family as the world of love/family/dependence/women and children. Men are differentiated; as fathers they bridge the gap between family and the public world. Fathers represent the family in the state. They represent the demands of the public as they tutor their children (sons) into a proper (masculine) maturity. Women are not differentiated. We remain in the background, as dangerous but necessary guardians of those who are not yet able to think for them (or our) selves.

Kant's text also marks another important form of differentiation within men: between "public" and "private" reason. These distinctions map onto another significant set of dichotomies: knowledge/freedom as opposed to work/duty/obedience. "By the public use of one's reason I understand the use that a person makes of it as a scholar before the reading public. Private use I call that which one may make of it in a particular civil post or office which is entrusted to him."[14] Public (emancipatory) and private (instrumental) reason are born simultaneously. They are two different uses of the capacity to think. They are deployed in distinct contexts. Their differences reflect the demands of these contexts and the varied qualities required for man's differentiated roles—this time as scholar and worker/official.

Contrary to the claims of some[15] these two aspects of reason are interdepen-

dent and mutually constituting and constraining. While used for different purposes neither can exist without the other. Man must exert an internal form of
surveillance and discipline to recognize which capacity a context requires.[16]
Modern society, as Kant understands, cannot function if "public" reason is
deployed outside its appropriate context. "Many affairs which are conducted in
the interest of the community require a certain mechanism through which some
members of the community must passively conduct themselves with an artificial
unanimity, so that the government may direct them to public ends, or at least
prevent them from destroying those ends. Here argument is not allowed—one
must obey."[17]

The constraint on public reason is not justified by reference to the unique *content* of the knowledge required within the realm of duty. Indeed, Kant argues
that, "so far as a part of the mechanism regards himself at the same time as a
member of the whole community or of a society of world citizens, and thus in
the role of a scholar who addresses the public (in the proper sense of the word)
through his writings, he certainly can argue without hurting the affairs for which
he is in part responsible as a passive member."[18]

The overriding consideration is one of utility. Kant, like Weber later, is aware
of the corrosive or "disenchanting" effect of "public" reason. The obedient civil
servant must preserve some order while the scholar/scientist or politician is
engaged in the process of creative destruction.[19] Any society, however enlightened it may become, will still require institutions such as religion and the family
in which obedience rather than criticism is required. Even in the most emancipated society, the state will also command a certain amount of uncritical obedience.

The "unlimited freedom" of the scholar "to use his own reason and to speak in
his own person,"[20] depends on the existence of these countervailing spheres.
Another modern dichotomy is put into play: individual/community. The individual is defined as one who is self-determining, who does not have to represent or
obey the will of another. Working within an organization is antithetical to freedom. Whenever one has duties, "he is not free, nor can he be free, because he
carries out the orders of another."[21] Although scholars may be autonomous,
independent individuals, they must still live within communities to survive.
Certain public ends (and private arrangements) are necessary to preserve communities. These ends could not withstand the rational evaluation of the members
of the mechanism who must implement them. Hence the subject must remain

split between he who obeys the guardians and he who uses his own reason and says what he thinks.

However, precisely because the realms of emancipatory (public) reason and private duty are split, such restriction is not an obstacle to enlightenment. Public reason has its own sphere, a world of freedom, of writing and speech. "The public use of reason must always be free, and it alone can bring about enlightenment among men."[22] This reason is the primary source of better knowledge and progress. It answers only to itself and must conform solely to its own dictates. Any law that seeks to restrict the free use of public reason must be invalid. "That would be a crime against human nature, the proper destination of which lies precisely in this progress."[23]

What is the purpose of allowing the free development and expression of reason? Partly, it is an end in itself. Development and exercise of this reason are the distinctive features and highest capacities of the (adult) human. Kant urges rulers to see that "there is no danger to his lawgiving in allowing his subjects to make public use of their reason and to publish their thoughts on a better formulation of his legislation and even their open-minded criticisms of the laws already made."[24]

Reason will also eventually generate laws to which that other public—the state—must conform. Kant claims, "that in freedom there is not the least cause for concern about public peace and the stability of the community."[25]

However, Kant must confront the problem of disenchantment. He recognizes the corrosive effects of public reason. He concedes that, "only one who is himself enlightened, is not afraid of shadows, and has a numerous and well-disciplined army to assure public peace, can say: 'Argue as much as you will, and about what you will, only obey!'"[26]

This quote both reveals and conceals a central paradox of the modernization of the self. Kant acknowledges that "the propensity and vocation to free thinking"[27] develop within relatively authoritarian structures (family and state). These guard the subject until he can become his own guardian. The "character of the people" must be changed. One of the effects of this change is that they "gradually become capable of managing freedom."[28] Only then will this progressive development of the capacity for public reason affect the principles of a government, "which finds it to its advantage to treat men, who are now more than machines, in accordance with their dignity."[29]

Modernization in Kant's story depends upon and reinforces a series of splits and renunciations. The world is split into two private spheres: the world of work and the family and two public spheres: the world of scholarship/knowledge and the state. The world of work requires a constrained form of private reason disciplined by a strong sense of duty. Here one exists as a selfless official, as a member of a mechanism of which one is merely a cog. The ends of the organization dictate how and to what extent each member is to deploy his reason. *Qua* official, one cannot question the intrinsic rightness of these ends.

The family guards children until they are able to develop the capacities of reason and autonomy. It is primarily a world of duty and obedience marked by the absence of reason. Here one is cowlike, attending to bodily and developmental needs until sufficiently mature to leave, or in the case of the (male) adult, until vocations call.

The world of scholarship/knowledge is a world of freedom, populated by individual minds bound only by laws generated by reason itself. This is the world of speech and writing, in which minds speak to themselves and others. In this world all ends can be submitted to critical evaluation as long as the rules of argument, evidence, and consensus-seeking are obeyed.

The world of the state is a heterogeneous one in which both public reason and duty play a part. Insofar as public reason cannot attain consensus on which ends the community should pursue or which laws should bind it, force (armies) and duty (conformity to laws I myself would not legislate) must continue to play a part.

The individual must learn how to manage differentiation and freedom. He must know when to be a citizen and when to be a subject. He must understand when to demand the right to subject all laws and practices to criticism and when to obey in silence; when to guard or demand obedience; and when to let go or let others alone. Public reason will not be emancipatory without a background of such practices and assumptions. Without such practices social order will be undermined by the corrosive force of public reason.

CRITIQUE OF ENLIGHTENMENT

Is Enlightenment emancipatory? We can first consider the promise of enlightenment. What is to be gained as it progresses? The answer to this question appears to be well known: rationalization. Society is to be ordered so that reason can be fully developed. Public reason will be given its autonomous sphere, guarded and anchored as long as necessary by countervailing institutions such as the family and the state. In turn, as reason develops it will produce knowledge that is useful and beneficial. This knowledge will be used in the public sphere of the state, in the private sphere of work, and within the subject himself.

Eventually as the subject becomes more rational, he will become adept at managing freedom.[30] Like a child who becomes an adult, his need for counter-vailing (constraining) institutions will diminish. General enlightenment will progress, and the great mass of humans will become rational. Then the mass will be able to order subjectivity and practices according to the ever-expanding knowledge that an unconstrained reason can produce.

In the public world of the state, humans will be self-determining. They will live by the dictates of reason and without irrational constraint. Hence the public world of the state will approximate the public world of reason. Both will become spheres in which autonomous, equal individuals can engage in argument, rule by a rationally attained consensus, and enjoy freedom.

However, these rational individuals will also recognize when reason cannot rule. In such cases, we must renounce our demands for freedom and self-determination. The family is one such case. It is a relationship among dependent unequals whose purpose is to guard those (women and children) unable to employ their own reason. Institutions such as bureaucracies and the army are other instances. They cannot serve the ends for which they are intended if their mechanical parts engage in a rational critique of these purposes or their authority.

The plausibility and appeal of this promise require at least two tacit assumptions. One is that reason *can* operate autonomously (differentiation will be successful). The second is that ordering our selves and our practices according to reason's dictates *is* emancipatory. Why should we accept the validity of either of these claims? These assumptions rest upon a prior set of beliefs. These include ones about the constitution of the subject and the structure of the external world. There are many reasons to doubt these assumptions and beliefs. Many contemporary writers dispute the claim that reason can operate autonomously. They also question whether even if reason could do so, the resulting knowledges and practices would be necessarily or universally emancipatory.

I. The Constitution of Subjectivity

The plausibility and coherence of Kant's story depend upon the assumption that an innate, homogeneous form of reason exists within all (male?) humans. As contingent beings we are all different, but as bearers of reason we are all the same. We must also assume that this reason is not determined or affected by heterogeneous factors such as desire, patterns of child rearing, or other historical experience and social relations. All such experiences must be merely contingent and in principle separable from pure reason.

The subject must be irrevocably split internally. Without such a split the rational kernel cannot unfold unaffected by its bodily and social experiences. Humans must have privileged access to the operation of their own reason. To insure the purity of reason and the separation of the contingent from the universal, we must be able to analyze reason's intrinsic limits and a priori categories. Otherwise, the reason that is our lawgiver might itself be contaminated by particularity and contingency and we would never know it. Reason might be heterogeneous and affected by forces outside its control. A reason that is not transparent to ourselves could not be a reliable source of knowledge about the self. It also could not be a trustworthy discoverer of objective truth or a neutral authority that a noumenal being ought to obey.

Many psychoanalysts deny that a pure transparent reason is possible. While the capacity to reason may or may not be innate, it develops in interactions with the other parts of the child's inner world and social relations.[31] The child's relations with its guardians are internalized and become part of an internal guardian (the conscience or superego). The boundary between conscience and reason is not fixed or impermeable and the effects of one on the other cannot always be accessible to consciousness. Aspects of reason can be unconsciously repressed by either desire or conscience. What is experienced as rational may be partially determined or pervaded by other aspects of the psyche. Because the internal world is heterogeneous and conflicted, its constitution is never finished, fixed, or constant. Aspects of outer worlds can be brought in to effect inner change; inner conflict can be managed by projection outward. Identity is never permanent, impermeable, or determined "simply" from the inside or outside.

The ego is initially a bodily *I*. Reason may be pervaded by desire—or the desire not to desire. The boundaries between psyche and soma or between desire, embodiment, and thought are not impermeable or fixed. Our contingent experiences, for example, how each person is held, nurtured, attended to, or stimulated, may deeply affect how and what we think. Unconscious processes operate outside and by different rules from those of rational thought. Their effects on rational ones can never be transparent or fully controlled.

Rationalization acquires a double meaning. It not only means to become more

rational but to be more able to rationalize. We become more adept at constructing a postiori reasons for fantasy, impulse, or conscience-driven behavior.

If we can offer good reasons to believe that reason cannot have the character
that the Enlightenment story both posits and depends upon, why do people
remain committed to this belief? Feminist theorists, with their emphasis on gender, can pursue this question in ways that psychoanalysts alone cannot.

While it is partially a consequence of modernization, feminism nevertheless
represents a profound challenge to it.[32] Feminists have begun to question whose
differentiations, whose renunciations, and whose emancipation modernization
both effects and requires. Is the modern subject/subjectivity emancipated, and
at what (and whose) cost? Is justice possible within the gendered spheres and
practices of modernization? What happens if feminist commitments are inserted
into these practices?

Feminists point out that the split between reason and heterogeneous contingency is gendered. The very *appearance* of neutrality or universality of reason
depends upon an interdependent and simultaneous set of moves. These include
naming women as different, that is, unlike the true measure of humanity: men;
devaluing difference; and suppressing men's dependence on and complicity
in this difference. Our understanding of reason depends on what it is not. It
is defined by its difference from and superiority to other faculties such as
the passions.[33]

In the modern West the split between reason and its others also reflects a particular division of labor. Some people (generally privileged men) only or primarily engage in abstract thought. Others (generally women and less privileged men)
take care of the necessities that arise out of embodied existence. These necessities include the reproduction of daily life, childbearing and rearing.[34]

As Kant and Freud acknowledge, modernization alters but reincorporates previously existing divisions between household/private and public/rational/politi-
cal worlds. The household remains the realm of unfreedom. It is the sole
domain of only some of its inhabitants, primarily women and children. The
household is the locus of passion, tutelage, feeling, the concrete and particular,
the subjective, the mortal, the familial and kinship. It represents the childhood of
every adult and of the species. These qualities are posited as existing in opposition and inferior to reason, the abstract, autonomy, maturity, the universal,
objective, immortal (reason and knowledge) and the productive (value produc-
ing) employment of labor or thought.

Philosophers have traditionally argued as Kant does that engagement in such activities disqualifies one from the life of reason. No true knowledge can arise out of such activities and indeed involvement in them impedes or clouds "true" thought. They produce biases that must be "controlled for." Hence only those who can separate themselves from embodiment and reproduction can be rational producers of true knowledge. We must (and can) leave the private/domestic world to engage in public/reason. Identifying women with the body and the particular are two of the necessary conditions for the possibility of conceptualizing a disembodied and universal faculty (e.g., the Cartesian ego or Kant's pure reason). Woman = the body; therefore men are not possessed/determined by it. The effects of male embodiment and social experiences on reason and its products are defined out of existence. With the contaminating effects of difference suppressed or denied, reason can take on its unitary and universal appearance.

2. The Metaphysics of Enlightenment

Kant's story rests on untenable assumptions about the nature of subjectivity and reason. It also depends upon problematic beliefs about the nature of the external world and the possible fit between reason, knowledge, and practice. Part of the appeal of Kant's political philosophy is its promise to solve a problem that has plagued modern politics: how to reconcile knowledge, power, and freedom.

Many philosophers and political theorists have wished to solve this problem in a way that could maintain the innocence of knowledge, power, and themselves. The position of the intellectual is part of what is at stake in arguments about enlightenment. Foucault criticizes this "universal" position while others such as Habermas wish to uphold its possibility.[35]

Innocence would be possible if Kant's arguments were true. He claims that there is a particular kind of truth "out there" that reason can grasp, although only through its own innate categories. This truth is simultaneously universal and benign. Governing according to its principles will result in the best for all and the domination of none.

If knowledge is grounded in and warranted by a universal reason, not particular "interests," it can be simultaneously "neutral," positive, and socially beneficial (powerful). The accumulation of more knowledge (the getting of more truth) results simultaneously in an increase in objectivity (neutrality) and in progress. Insofar as power/authority is grounded in this expanding knowledge, it too is progressive. It becomes more rational and expands the freedom and self-actualization of its subjects. Rational power can be other than and not productive of new forms of domination. Such power is neutral. It does not favor or hurt anyone and is transparent in its exercise and effects.

The philosopher/intellectual has a unique ability to investigate and establish the conditions of knowledge and to adjudicate truth claims. This epistemological skill/privilege grounds and warrants their position as guardian and benign representative of humanity's emancipatory interests.

This set of beliefs rests on a number of wishes. These are subject neither to rational proof nor disproof.[36] We must assume that the social as well as the physical universe is governed by uniform, benign, and ultimately harmonious and homogeneous laws. Conforming our behavior to contradictory or malevolent laws would generate conflicts and differences that could not themselves be lawfully resolved. If the universe is pervaded by random and chaotic forces, neutral "decision procedures" could not exist. It would be difficult to resolve conflict without privileging one position rather than another. Order will have to be (at least to some extent) imposed rather than discovered.

A chaotic or random universe would thwart our wish for the kind of rational, stable, and universal knowledge necessary to ground enlightenment politics. Knowledge would be partial, and at best it could temporarily capture aspects of unstable processes. Which aspects we highlight would depend partially upon our interests and will. Actions generated by knowledge unmoored by the real will have unpredictable and differential effects. What counts as knowledge would vary according to different purposes. Different kinds of knowledge would be useful for some (persons and effects) and oppressive to others. Lacking grounding in a rational, benignly lawful universe both knowledge and power lose their purity.

3. Is Enlightenment Emancipatory?

Feminists answer this question in at least two contradictory ways. Some argue there is nothing intrinsically gender biased about the process of modernization. The process has generated sexual divisions of labor in the family and in the economy. Women have been excluded from the public worlds of work and knowledge production. These outcomes are merely contingent and reversible. Women can be integrated into the differentiated spheres of the public and private/economic. Men must assume more responsibilities in the private/domestic one. The Enlightenment promises of equality, justice, and rationality will then be redeemed.[37]

Others argue that the locations and representations of women within modernity are not contingent. The splits and differentiation that mark modern Western societies reflect and sustain intrinsic relations of domination, including gendered ones. It would be a mistake to adopt the modern ("universal") practices of reason and citizenship as regulative ideals. Feminists will comply with and reinforce a regime of domination in which differences of many kinds become the basis for asymmetrical relations of power. Integration is a delusory and self-destructive strategy. Women can integrate into these cultures only at the expense of our femininity. We must be willing to reject or annihilate everything that is "different" about us. The male/universal is not challenged as the norm in this strategy. Difference remains the "other" of its superior "same."[38]

The second position is more compelling. Advocates of the first position are not nearly critical enough of the Enlightenment story of modernization and its idea of emancipation. None of the spheres of modern life are or can be clearly differentiated. The possibility of justice or emancipatory political practices requires more than self-government, the neutral rule of law or discursive consensus. There are rational aspects of domination, and emancipatory promise can be found within the nonrational.

Tracking the organization and effects of gender relations makes it evident that the claim of differentiation reflects the experiences of and benefits (at best) a few privileged (white) men. It is often asserted to preserve relations of power and privilege. For example, the private/family extends into the private/work sphere in many ways. Sexual harassment, predominantly of women by men, is prevalent at work. It is in part motivated by a wish to resituate women within familial relations even in a work context. Differentiation is invoked when women attempt to reconcile the contradictory demands of private/family and private/work by questioning the contemporary standard of a good worker. The good worker is usually available to the employer and is willing to place organization demands above all others. This model assumes either that the worker is childless or that someone outside the paid labor force is available to care for others.

No clear line of demarcation between public/state and private/family exists.

The modern state regulates aspects of family life such as marriage, child custody and support, and divorce. However, "separate spheres" is invoked when male privilege is threatened in case of wife battering or marital rape. Children become private obligations/possessions of their parents when alternative arrangements for child care or the redistribution of resources to the poor are proposed.

4. The Poverty of the Public Sphere

I am skeptical that feminist visions of gender justice or political life can be accommodated within any liberal or democratic-socialist state. A full defense of this skepticism is beyond the scope of this paper, but I can indicate several reasons here. The concepts of justice available within or congruent with such states, at least as articulated by theorists such as Rawls or Habermas, are inadequate for feminist purposes.[39]

These theorists argue that our practices and theories of justice must be deontological, that is, disconnected from claims about the good life. Since people's views about the good life differ irreconcilably, it is not possible to obtain rational consensus about its nature. Justice is a process by which we articulate rules of argument and policy formation. Problems that cannot be formulated according to the rules must be ruled out of order. Questions about the good life must be excluded from considerations of justice.

Neither of these theorists adequately acknowledge that their view of justice is itself driven by and congruent with some visions of the good life and not others.[40] Models of democracy based on the characteristics of the ideal speech situation or on the distribution of primary goods reflect deficient visions of public life. Political life remains impoverished in its absence of ritual, sensuality, spectacle, community, moral education, and aesthetics.

Habermas claims that a fully realized and autonomous public sphere is necessary to fulfill Enlightenment promises of emancipation. Fraser extends his argument by including multiple and competing public discourses and more space for the articulation of material interests within public life.[41] Neither of these writers confronts the extent to which problematic and repressive acts of exclusion typical of Enlightenment thinking are left undisturbed and unexamined within their vision of the public sphere. Neither author adequately addresses the structural limitations of Enlightenment concepts of the public and the domination of a certain form of reason within them.

The privileging of speech and rational argument over other qualities such as nurturance and caretaking (traditionally female activities) or a commitment to beauty or pleasure remains unquestioned within these theories. All individuals are to value a certain kind of rationality as the superordinate public virtue. One may not speak out or make public demands out of desire or aesthetic commitments. Consensus is privileged over conflict; the productive uses of conflict in developing and maintaining civic virtue are never explored. The importance of spectacle, drama, rhetoric, painting, sculpture, or music in constructing a rich public life (as, for example, in the classic Greek polis or the French revolution) is nowhere acknowledged or incorporated.[42] Many social aspects of public life, for example, the contributions of personal/political associations in building and sustaining political interest and loyalty, are also ignored.

These theorists do not question the biases that are built into their view of the modal person who is to engage in argument. The family/public split is replicated. As in classical liberal theory, adults simply spring up in the public sphere like mushrooms.[43] Inquiry into how we become persons capable of demanding and sustaining a rich public is absent. Apparently all relevant parties in the processes of justice are equal, autonomous, rational, individual adults who can speak for themselves. This assumption is problematic because in some policy debates the interests of the speechless (children, animals, the environment) may be very much at stake.[44] Even discourse might be very different if we imagined ourselves in the variety of positions most people do find themselves in eventually. These positions include ones in which we are helpless like infants, dependent on the care of others, or are physically or mentally incapacitated. Public discourse will remain impoverished as long as we assume someone else (mostly women in private/families) will tend to these Others.

The conflating of discourse and reason is also quite problematic. It excludes many other qualities that are often necessary for a full public life or speech about it. These qualities include loyalty, empathy, fantasy, courage, and a sense of righteous rage, for example. Subjectivity is partially constituted in and though public life. If public life does not demand them, qualities necessary to the full development of public actors will be absent.

We cannot have a rich public life if questions of the visions of the good to which we are committed are excluded. Politics is inextricably connected to such visions. It always involves assumptions and questions about what kinds of people we want to be, what kinds of practices and obligations people believe are right or necessary, and what resources (family, economic, political, knowledge, emotional, etc.) are required to make such practices and people exist. These questions have public and private dimensions and cannot be neatly mapped onto one or the other domain.[45]

My dissatisfactions with these visions of the public sphere do not arise out of a longing for an organic (premodern) totality that, in any case, as feminists are quite aware, never existed. They speak to and from a preference for further differentiation—for the play of differences *within* a single domain rather than a distribution across them. Whether acknowledged or not, our modern institutions rarely are governed by a single set of purposes, interests, or mode of reason or affect. As any academic knows, for example, rational arguments are often motivated by and deployed for quite other purposes than the discovery of truth. Our institutions are already interdependent and mutually constituting. Modern, instrumental rationality could not survive without its interconnected "opposites." These include the worlds of nurturance (family) and "free" subjectivity/expressivity (including "high art"). All three of these qualities are expressions of the multiple subjectivities of modern individuals. The partially illusory construction of any of them as isolated "pure types" renders them increasingly impoverished. This delusory singularity makes it difficult for people to understand and articulate what they dislike or would want to be different.

It has become increasingly clear that no institution can thrive if we pretend it is the unique locus of or has the sole responsibility for any of these capacities. For example, Kant and others are correct to argue that families cannot withstand the corrosive effect of public reason. Freud is correct to claim that the demands of work estrange people from the capacities necessary to be good parents and lovers. It need not follow that the private/family should be exempt from rational criticism or that efforts should be made to constitute it as a true "haven" from a "heartless" world. Rather, we need to find modes of justice appropriate to family life and modes of nurturance appropriate to work.

Modern Westerners would probably be better off if our worlds were less heartless and if both genders in many forms of relations could move more easily between and within domains. This does not entail collapsing completely the public and private. Both spheres require transformation. In more emancipated societies, the variety of needs and motives already at play will no longer be distributed by and through the differentiated disciplining of men and women. Emancipation would undermine the replication of gender-based relations of domination.

One insight we can derive from looking at modernization from a feminist perspective is: differences can be simultaneously colonized and repressed. Cores and peripheries are mutually constituting, impoverishing, and interdependent. Our emancipatory impulses have the best chances to deconstruct the iron cages they invariably construct out of and for themselves if we set differences to play across boundaries.

5

MULTIPLES

ON THE CONTEMPORARY POLITICS OF SUBJECTIVITY

AN ELUSIVE SUBJECT

Subjectivity is a central concept in post-seventeenth-century Western thought. Stories about subjectivity concern a crucial figure in the modern West—the subject. This subject must do an enormous amount of work. It plays essential roles in philosophy and politics. In philosophy the subject grounds, represents, or generates knowledge and our accounts of it. In politics it grounds the possibility of freedom—freedom from determination and domination, freedom to be self-determining and sovereign.

Considering the weight the modern subject bears, it is not surprising that a central debate in contemporary Western political discourse concerns the nature of subjectivity and its possible relations to emancipatory action. Contemporary critics have undermined the plausibility and desirability of many modern Western theories of subjectivity. These include rational, empirical, instrumental, and transcendental ones. Each grew out of and reflects particular historical projects, practices, and pressures that have either been exhausted or are no longer useful to us. Crises of representation, interpretation, knowledge, power, and legitimacy intensify as old ways of understanding subjectivity are thrown into doubt. It is increasingly evident that their credibility has required repression or denial of many other, interrelated aspects of subjectivity.

Many theorists argue that the decentered/postmodernist forms of subjectivity some critics advocate as replacements for older ones cannot exercise the agency required for liberatory political activity.[1] Are the claims of Enlightenment philosophers from Kant to Habermas correct? Does emancipatory action—and the very idea and hope of emancipation—depend upon the development of a unitary self capable of autonomy and undetermined self-reflection?[2] Can there be forms of subjectivity that are simultaneously fluid, multicentered, and effective

92

in the "outer" worlds of political life and social relations? Could multicentered and overdetermined subjects recognize relations of domination and struggle to overcome them?

I believe a unitary self is unnecessary, impossible, and a dangerous illusion. Only multiple subjects can invent ways to struggle against domination that will not merely recreate it. In the process of therapy, in relations with others, and in political life we encounter many difficulties when subjectivity becomes subject to one normative standard, solidifies into rigid structures, or lacks the capacity to flow readily between different aspects of itself. While we might want to foreground a mode of subjectivity for certain purposes, problems arise when we decide in advance that what we should be or find is *one* definitive quality. No singular form can be sufficient as a regulative ideal or as a prescription for human maturity or the essential human capacity.[3]

I will argue below that it is possible to imagine subjectivities whose desires for multiplicity can impel them toward emancipatory action. These subjectivities would be fluid rather than solid, contextual rather than universal, and process oriented rather than topographical.[4] Emancipatory theories and practices require mechanics of fluids in which subjectivity is conceived as processes rather than as a fixed atemporal entity locatable in a homogeneous, abstract time and space. In discourses about subjectivity the term "the self" will be superseded by discussions of "subjects." The term "subject(s)" more adequately expresses the simultaneously determined, multiple, and agentic qualities of subjectivity.

To clear spaces for such discussions, I will deconstruct some of the prominent misconceptions about subjectivity. We can at least be clearer about what subjectivity is not. Some approaches to it are likely to prove particularly unproductive. Our imaginations too often are imprisoned by an inability to think about subjectivity as multiplicities that are neither fixed nor fragmented. Often theorists posit an apparently dichotomous choice between two ideas of subjectivity. Subjectivity is depicted either as a coherent entity or as formerly solid ones that have (or should) now splinter into fragments. These ideas are actually mirror images of and dependent on each other. We can develop more adequate accounts of subjectivity if it is conceived as heterogeneous and incomplete processes.

Psychic "structures" are constituted by the interweaving of many heterogeneous experiences and capacities. These include complex clusters of capabilities, modes of processing, altering and retaining experience, and foci of affect, somatic effects, and transformation of process into various kinds of language, fantasy, delusion, defenses, thought, and modes of relating to self and others. Subjectivity also has its own forms of and relations to time. Subjective time is highly variable in its range and intensity. Subjectivity can dwell in many moments of time simultaneously or move relatively freely through past, present, and (projected) future experiences (its own experience, and to some extent, that of others).

The processes of subjectivity are overdetermined and contextual. They interact with, partially determine, and are partially determined by many other equally complicated processes include somatic, political, familial, and gendered ones. Temporary coherence into seemingly solid characteristics or structures is only one of subjectivity's many possible expressions. When enough threads are webbed together, a solid entity may appear to form. Yet the fluidity of the threads and the web itself remains. What felt solid and real may subsequently separate and reform.

THE MODERN SUBJECT IN CONTEXT

The development of modern physics in the seventeenth century had a doubly disruptive effect on people's understanding of subjectivity and the universe. Science contributed to the dislodging of the religious world view in which God was seen as the cause and guarantor of order and revelation and faith as privileged sources of knowledge. Modern physics also confronted people with the problem of determinism. A new order was posited in which the physical universe is determined by objective and impersonal laws of nature. While expanding the possibilities of human power, this view also generated profound problems for people's understandings of themselves. Is there anything human that is not determined? How can belief in freedom and free will be sustained? Descartes provides one response to this quandary: split mind and body and define mind as incorporeal and hence not subject to physical determinism. The mind operates according to its own principles, which are accessible through self-study and the unique methods appropriate to it (thought).[5]

Kant provides a further move in rescuing a (relatively) free subjectivity. In his account, objective knowledge of the world or thought about it is dependent upon reason. Philosophy is the master discourse, the queen of the sciences. Through its study of reason, philosophy can tell us what makes knowledge possible, what kinds of knowledge exist, and how to adjudicate between rival truth claims.

Even if the mind's intrinsic categories limit our ability to acquire knowledge of the world, critical reason can understand its categories, taxonomy, and capabilities.[6] Epistemology becomes the cardinal field within philosophy. Through its rigors, the mind can be analyzed and disciplined and the validity of its truth claims assessed. Proper procedures ensure that eventually error will be identified and corrected, and objective truth will emerge.

The possibility that truthful knowledge can be generated through an objective mind is essential for the success of Enlightenment political projects. Kant and other Enlightenment philosophers hoped to solve the problem of authority by grounding it in reason. They believed there is no natural form of authority. Thus, its exercise must be justified and its legitimacy established. Since subjects are naturally free and independent, they must be sovereign. Subjects can be sovereign only if they are self-governing; the laws they obey must be ones they give to themselves. Rational authority requires a subject who is fully able to exercise a reason that can recognize the existence and compelling nature of such laws. Rational subjects will agree to be bound by rules that accord with their reason.

Since the universe is predictable and ordered by natural law, it must be possible to find such rational rules. There must be a set of truthful propositions, discoverable by reason, that can govern our behavior. Such rules will be objective—neutral and equally binding on all. Only under these conditions can authority be other than domination.

This set of propositions constitutes part of a metanarrative of Enlightenment.[7] This metanarrative requires a certain form of subject—an undetermined one, who can be the discoverer of truth. It requires a particular view of reality—rational, orderly, and accessible to and through our thought. It also requires a particular view of freedom and law. The subject can be simultaneously sovereign and subject through obedience to its own rational laws. Rule by rational law necessarily excludes domination.

TROUBLED SUBJECTS

In the modern West, being a self and subjectivity are inseparable. Subjectivity in other cultures might be constituted through kinship or one's relationship to God or the natural world. Modern understandings of subjectivity are rooted in the idea of self we adopt. Two views of the self have been dominant in post-seventeenth-century Western cultures. One is the Cartesian idea of the self as an ahistoric, solid, indwelling entity that grounds the possibility of rational thought. In turn the self is accessible and transparent to such thought. The defining characteristic of this self is its ability to engage in abstract rational thought, including thought about its own thought. Such thought is said to be undetermined by the empirical, social, or bodily experiences of the thinker.[8] The second idea is the Humean-empirical one. This self and its knowledge are derived from sense experience. Any adequate account of subjectivity and thought must therefore be rendered in terms that can be expressed in, referred to, or tested by intersubjectively transmissible empirical experience.[9]

Neither view of the self is very compelling. Twentieth-century theories of language and the constitution of sense experience have rendered the classic rationalist and empiricist philosophies obsolete.[10] Contemporary discourses such as psychoanalysis, feminism, and postmodernism propose and require alternate ideas of subjectivity.

The psychoanalytic tenet of the existence of unconscious processes calls into question the possibility of the clear boundaries between mind and body that both rationalism and empiricism require. According to psychoanalysts such as Freud and Lacan, the subject is always internally divided. Her actions are unavoidably affected by forces outside conscious awareness and control.[11] The idea that the self can have transparent access to and be the master of its own processes is no longer tenable.

Postmodernists insist that subjectivity is a discursive effect, not a transcendental, ahistoric, and unchanging objective status, entity, or state. These theorists have begun to delineate the political genealogies of subjectivity and how its "nature" is constituted and transformed over time.[12] They also insist concepts of subjectivity operate as regulative ideals within historically delimited contexts. Such ideals can never be neutral or universally true and binding. They cannot be understood as the result of "value free" scientific or rational/philosophical thought. Rather, such ideals are the product of complex knowledge/power networks. These networks generate interdependent categories of subjective experience such as health/pathology that underwrite and legitimate therapeutic and punitive social interventions.

For example, "normal" acquires meaning only in and through its function as the (apparent) opposite of deviant. Such categories function to create and justify social organization and exclusion. They also serve as the rationale for creating new groups of "experts" whose function is to sort people into the relevant groups. Only these experts can develop appropriate treatments for the deviants or protect the healthy from them. If such categories are successfully established the experts can perpetuate their client groups and their power.

Feminist concepts of gender have many implications for concepts of subjectivity.[13] Feminists tend to argue that our thinking about and practices of gender are historical artifacts. Gender is an effect of complex, historically variable sets of social relations in and through which heterogeneous persons are socially organized as members of one and only one of an exclusionary and (so far) unequal pair—man and woman. Masculine and feminine identities are not determined by a pregiven, unchangeable biological substratum. They are created by and reflect structures of power, language, and social practices and our struggles with and against these structures. While it may seem that there are only two genders, this is not the case. There are many highly variable and particular determinants and experiences of "being a woman" (or man). Gender itself interacts with and is partially constituted by other social relations such as race.

Although gendering is a heterogeneous and often contradictory experience, it profoundly shapes and determines subjectivity. There are no genderless persons in contemporary Western cultures. Attention to gendering reveals the delusory character of self-determining, individualistic, and autonomous ideas of subjectivity. Gender is one of the conditions of possibility of modern subjectivity. It is intrinsic both to (apparently) abstract notions and individual experiences of subjectivity.

Gendering is an integral part of the process of becoming and being an individual subject. One becomes a boy or a girl, not a person.[14] The meanings of gender for and as oneself cannot be completely idiosyncratic. Vocabularies and social practices already exist through which (gendered) subjectivity is constituted and by which one makes sense of it to oneself. Since gendering is such a complex and overdetermined process, it is not possible to be conscious of all its determinants, effects, and consequences. Even if this was possible, one cannot simply choose to opt out of such arrangements. However complicated one's own subjectivity may be, gender is a major category of social organization. We must work and have relationships with other persons. To do so, our gendered selves must be made to fit with and be intelligible to other, equally determined persons. One will be inserted into preexisting, gendered social locations and practices.

IMPEDIMENTS TO THINKING SUBJECTS IN PROCESS

Despite their many contributions to the undermining of unitary or fixed notions of subjectivity, psychoanalysts and postmodernists retain or replicate aspects of these subjectivities within their own discourses.[15] Each discourse impedes as well as contributes to development of more fluid accounts of subjectivity. Each highlights some aspects of subjectivity while obscuring or denying others. Each discourse tries to order the heterogeneous components of subjectivity within one master narrative or category. It would be more fruitful to treat contradictory elements of subjectivity as evidence for its multiplicity. We will need multiple stories in a variety of styles to appreciate its complexity.

In conceptualizing subjectivity, it is difficult to avoid replicating the mind/body split that is so prevalent in modern Western culture. One of its current manifestations is particularly harmful to an understanding of subjectivity. Nature or biology is split and treated as intrinsically other than culture, discourse, or the person.

Perhaps there is something about our bodily experience that predisposes us to assign either a false concreteness or abstraction to subjectivity. Bodies themselves can be understood as intersections of complex processes. How people think about, categorize, and analyze bodies change radically over time and vary even within one culture.[16] From another perspective, however, our bodies seem subject to a pregiven, linear set of events that we ultimately cannot alter: birth, maturity, childbirth (for some women), aging, death. Sometimes this sequence is altered, as when someone dies young or a woman miscarries. Then we tend to feel the "natural order" has been violated. This feeling confirms the "normality" of the "usual" order of things.

However, we never encounter a person without a body or discursive practices without embodied practitioners. Embodiment is simultaneously somatic, psychic, and discursive. Researchers may try to understand "the brain" purely in somatic or chemical-electrical terms. They soon discover to their chagrin that the "ghost in the machine problem" (e.g., the subjective qualities of mind) will not stop haunting them.[17]

Therapists may also replicate the dysfunctional effects of the mind/body splits and individualism still prevalent in white middle-class American culture. It is just as difficult for therapists as anyone else in our culture to resist collusion with its dominant beliefs, even if some of these harm our patients. We may not subject such ideas to the same critical analysis that other aspects of their thinking receive. Like many other members of their cultures, for example, some of my patients believe that dependency is weakness. A strong enough will should be able to triumph over any problem. Diseases that affect mood are treated differently than those that affect "the body." Moods are seen as a (disembodied) mind phenomena. Hence they are subjective and should be subjectively controllable. Somehow the body is not the self, and one is not responsible for its illnesses in the same way. This kind of Cartesian individualism makes it difficult to develop adequate accounts of certain forms of human suffering. There may be no particular reason or meaning for why one person rather than another should have a mental disorder. At the same time, it could happen to anyone, despite their will or intelligence.

It is important to do justice to social, discursive, psychodynamic, or interpersonal aspects of illness, but this should not entail the exclusion of somatic ones. The brain can misfunction like any other part of the body and have profound effects on one's subjectivity. Whatever the mix of biosocial determinants may be, when an affective illness like depression is in full force, it can become the dominant aspect of subjectivity. We may deconstruct the genealogies of categories such as mental illness, alter the meanings we assign to them, or seek through research to improve their treatment. Nonetheless, they may continue to force us to pay attention to them at times and in ways we and our patients would not choose. Such states may at least temporarily have a high degree of independence from our interpretative activities or discursive relations.

Psychoanalysts from Freud on have seemed to feel the need to develop teleological narratives of subjectivity. These narratives begin with the premise that there is a unitary substance (or potential) present from the beginning. Given "good enough" environmental conditions, this substance will unfold in definite, innate stages toward its "natural" end or purpose (adult maturity/health). If deviance from this descriptive-prescriptive narrative erupts, we work backwards from the present to discover where things went wrong. We even create diagnostic categories that define illnesses by the defective stage.[18]

This approach obviously assumes that individual humans all share an essence with a common developmental pattern. This pattern is or should be rational, sequential, purposive, and additive. Naturalizing and universalizing this developmental history obscures its fictive qualities and prescriptive purposes. The posited end becomes a given whose political and ethical components disappear behind the supposed neutrality or scientific nature of the "description."

The construction of such stories and norms also reveals psychoanalysts' dependence on and complicity with the metanarrative of Enlightenment. Order and purpose are privileged over and at the expense of multiplicity, randomness, and contingency. (Unconscious?) complicity in this metanarrative exposes psychotherapists to the risk of participating in the disciplinary and normalizing practices that pervade this society without evaluating the ethical consequences of such participation.

Postmodernists stress the importance of discursive practices in the constitution of subjectivity. They claim these practices can take on objective, thinglike qualities that act as important constraints against as well as enablers of further discourses. Yet the same writers tend to ignore or deny the potentially empowering, limiting, constraining, and partially autonomous effects of our psychic-somatic processes.

Even if we stress the discursive construction of "nature" and human "being," it does not follow that nothing exists except our constructions. We may choose to believe that nothing else exists for us. Therefore either nothing else really exists, or its potential existence is irrelevant. However, this is a rather narcissistic and grandiose view of our powers and importance. Extradiscursive phenomena and experience can both empower and limit our constructs. Postmodernists produce curiously attenuated accounts of human practices when they ignore affects and somatic processes. In these accounts people never seem to be born, have attachments to others, feel, fantasize, or die.

Postmodernists insist on the play of differences, on the irreducible multiplicities constituting past and present existence. This celebration of difference can mask the hegemony in postmodernism of a singular category—discourse (or textuality). No singular category can do justice to the vast and highly differentiated variety of processes in and through which subjectivity can be constituted and expressed. An implicit privileging of language, speech, and writing circulates through this one. Many aspects of subjectivity and its practices are denied, obscured, or marginalized. Discourse is a particularly inapt synonym for practices (for example, ballet or breastfeeding) which are predominantly affective, sensuous, visual, tactile, or kinetic. These qualities are important in the constitution and expression of subjectivities.

SUBJECTIVITY IS NOT LANGUAGE IDLING

Postmodernists and feminists are correct to criticize any unitary approach to subjectivity and to expose the historically constituted character of all ideas about "human nature." They are also correct to insist that all such notions are necessarily prescriptive and to question the purposes of those who would constitute such norms. In contemporary Western society such norms reflect and function within knowledge/power systems. The modern state exercises its power and gains legitimacy partially by defining and then tending to the health/illness of the "body politic."

Similarly, gender systems operate to normalize standards of femininity and masculinity that are necessary for the replication of gender-based relations of domination. All women and most men fail to met these standards, but we fail in different ways and degrees. Many women and men lack class, race, heterosexual, or other privileges necessary to (almost) meet the stipulated standard for their gender. Relations of domination *among* women (and among men) are reinforced by these standards and our varying allegiances to them.

What follows from the claim that subjectivity is not unitary, fixed, homogeneous, or teleological? It does *not* follow that subjectivity is an empty or outmoded category that we can happily discard along with other modern hangups. To make such a claim would be to privilege one view of subjectivity; if it is not that, it is nothing. It also does not follow that we can make no claims about what we believe to be better or worse ways of being a person. We cannot fall back on reassuring, universal standards to justify our beliefs. However, we can, do, and must make judgments about how to be with and treat ourselves and others (since one aspect of subjectivity is intersubjectivity).

As theorists and political actors, we orient ourselves in part by at least implicit notions of what it means to be subjects in our inner and outer worlds. As reflective beings, we seek ways to understand, practice, and improve our particular subjectivity. As persons in relations to others, we attempt to comprehend subjectivities other than our own. Without such comprehension any form of prediction, cooperation, and/or control is extremely difficult to effect. Perhaps in some future reality we would not continue to do these things. However, in the near term, I cannot foresee what could replace such practices. Furthermore, it is not clear to me why we should abolish them; although the need for improvements in the ways we do them is compelling.

Attempts to develop a unitary, linear, prescriptive, or universally true narrative of the development and nature of "the self" will fail. We can, however, develop phenemenologies of different ways of organizing subjectivities. These phenemenologies can help us to assess some of the benefits and limitations of various modes of subjectivity and the practices that are required to generate and sustain them. These benefits and limitations are always context specific. We must also specify and defend these as our norms.

Experiences with my patients are part of the reason I have come to advocate multiple, fluid subjectivities. I will discuss two ways in which people's subjectivity can be ordered—schizoid and borderline—and the processes and dilemmas that pervade such modes of subjectivity. The categories "schizoid" and "borderline" are constructs. They are created and employed to order and make sense out of a heterogeneous set of phenomena. Like all such categories, they serve as a shorthand by which persons engaged in similar practices can communicate with each other. Like all categories also, they have consequences that exceed the intentions of and elude their creators. The existence of the categories, but not necessarily the phenomena, is totally dependent upon these persons, their practices, and the context in which they operate.

The dilemmas of schizoid and borderline persons can contribute to our understanding of subjectivity and its vicissitudes. Many of the debates about subjectivity implicitly assume less extreme forms of one or the other as a danger or a possible norm. The schizoid form is an exaggeration of a kind of subjectivity currently valued in the West. The instrumental, split subject who can adapt behavior to achieve predetermined ends while appearing to be an authentic person who is also genuinely concerned for the welfare of others does well in many segments of the postmodern world. The capacity to split reason and feeling, attachment and destruction is highly useful in certain occupations, for example, managing large corporations, designing "smart bombs," or defending dangerous chemical plants.

Postmodernists' critique of reason sometimes presupposes that rationality's only possible locus or consequence is a schizoid Cartesian subject. They celebrate the fragmentation of subjectivity or an egoless experience of the sublime, pleasure, or the Other as alternatives to this oppressive subject.[19] Postmodernist accounts of decentered subjectivity can obscure the need for moments of ruthless organization and the ability to separate fantasy and consensual reality. Fragmentation may be pleasurable in moments of ecstasy or aesthetic experience. However, while I advocate decentered forms of subjectivity, I do not think fragmentation is the only desirable or plausible alternative to a false sense of unity. Fragmentation also entails many risks. In many contexts it is inappropriate, useless, or harmful. People can achieve coherence or long-term stability without claiming or constructing a (false or true) solid core self. Lacking an ability to sustain coherence, one slides into the endless terror, emptiness, desolate loneliness, and fear of annihilation that pervade borderline subjectivity.

PHENOMENOLOGIES OF TROUBLE

Thinking rationally does not necessitate a schizoid split, any more than having intense emotions requires borderline fragmentation. Neither form of subjectivity can make use of the multiplicity of subjective processes that are available to others. Each is an excessively imperfect attempt to solve problems many humans share— how to manage the multiplicity that different contexts require, how to feel and think (especially simultaneously) without destroying ourselves and others.

Both forms of subjectivity exemplify some of the dangers and costs of the lack of fluidity. Schizoid subjectivity is unnecessarily rigid and compartmentalized. Borderline subjectivity is so fragmented and inconstant that fluidity cannot cohere into usable shapes or meanings. Schizoid and borderline persons suffer a common difficulty. Neither can experience *simultaneously* the *distinctiveness* of different aspects of subjectivity and their *mutuality*. They cannot experience how each aspect interacts and intersects with and is mutually determined by but differentiated from the others.

1. Schizoid Compartments

Schizoid is defined here as Winnicott and other object relations theorists use it.[20]   Schizoid subjectivity tends to be organized so that feeling is divorced from thought and psychic and somatic experiences are isolated. Modes of experience and dimensions of a subject's history are encapsulated and rigidly separated from others. Breaches of internal barriers are often accompanied by intense anxiety. Interactions with schizoid persons often leave one with a sense of hollowness and emptiness. There seems to be a shell lacking a human inhabitant.

People develop such subjectivity for many reasons. Part of the story involves the dynamics of particular family systems. In some families, the boundaries between adult and child are too unclear. Parents may abuse their children emotionally or physically, neglect them, or be too intrusive. Any of these behaviors can impede the development of children's private fantasy worlds. Lacking the security of adult control (and adults in control of themselves and appropriately attentive to others) children find fantasy frightening and impulses dangerous. Inner and outer become too confused and unbounded; each cannot exist in its own appropriate way. Lacking a reliable adult who could set and respect appropriate limits, a child attempts to establish boundaries for herself. To lose control takes on threatening, crazy connotations.

In defense, children may seek to control their own feelings and impulses totally. Especially in girls and women this may take the form of "being good." Being good means attending to other people's needs. One should not expect people to recognize and attend to one's own needs or to appreciate the aspects of subjectivity that require independence from or resistance to others. Soon it can become difficult to tell the difference between dangerous acting on impulse and any feelings. It is safer to suppress or split off many of them. One can no longer feel the difference between a self-regarding selfishness and a reckless and potentially harmful disregard for the needs of others.

The schizoid person's childhood experiences are ruthlessly repressed along with aspects of fantasy, healthy selfishness, anger, aggression, and the pain of abandonment. The isolation of many aspects of one's past means childlike ways of understanding the world cannot be moderated or balanced by adult ones. Their emergence into conscious awareness is often experienced as alien and dangerous. This isolation also cuts off access to certain kinds of playfulness and an erotic pleasure in life. The absence of goals and responsibilities is frightening. Vacations and weekends can be burdens. Without access to inner resources, they are literally empty time. Intimate relations with others are difficult, because trust and dependence expose one to possible abuse or the return of split-off feelings. Schizoid people can attend to others very well, but although they yearn to be cared for, they will not allow others to attend to them.

2. Borderline Disequilibrium

Borderline persons are notable for the intensity and isolation of affect states. Affective experience fluctuates from one absolute state to another (for example, rage to despair). Relations with other persons are also absolute and encapsulated. Other persons and relations with them can be all good or all bad. Similarly, feelings about oneself tend to fluctuate wildly. Experiences with others do not moderate preexisting fantasies about the world. Such experiences are reworked so they become either more of the same or an absolute unassimilatable difference.[21]

Unlike the schizoid person's carefully closed and barricaded compartments, borderline subjectivity is marked by a somewhat unpredictable whirl of fragments. A schizoid person comes to feel imprisoned within an excessively rigid equilibrium. Certain aspects of subjectivity cannot be reached and fluidity between and within subjective processes is blocked off. On the other hand, a borderline person experiences a profound sense of disequilibrium.

Each fragment has its own emotions, fantasies, thoughts, and intra- and inter-subjective modes of relating. Transitions between one fragment and another are difficult. Sometimes one predominates so intensely and absolutely that the others feel in danger of being permanently eclipsed. This constant emotional vertigo means that no fragment can be appreciated or enjoyed. Any stable moment of rest and continuity feels tenuous and insecure. Lacking secure moments of constancy, the particularity of the different aspects of subjectivity and the interconnections between them tend to be lost. Fluidity is frightening. It cannot be distinguished from the beginning of an uncontrollable slide into a complete dissolution or annihilation of subjectivity.

People are frightened by how much energy it takes to contain the centrifugal force of their fragments and "pass for" normal or feel at home anywhere. Borderline people suffer from a profound sense of loneliness and emptiness, a black hole or nothingness inside. This black hole feels powerful enough to suck up all the fragments and annihilate them. It feels quite different from the hopelessness often experienced during a depression. Depression seems more like an almost alien state (analogous to the flu) that takes over and then passes. The void is experienced as highly personal, all-pervasive, and much more destructive to oneself and others.

Borderline people are extremely sensitive to the relationship between themselves and others, including therapists. My patients would like me to understand their inner worlds well enough to help them name the various fragments and differentiate among them. Such differentiation is a necessary precondition for the development of stability in inner and outer worlds and a sense of perspective. If I am that close to them, they worry that I will either be sucked up by the void or be too solid and displace their own modes of subjectivity. Hence, our time together is itself fragmentary. It often shifts between moments of intense attunement followed by frightened flight, clever stories to keep my attention, intense emotional pain and terror, anxious disclosure of valued ways they are different from me and others in which they long to have bits of me in their own ways. I receive frequent requests to sort out something in their inner and outer worlds or offer parental advice. Borderline patients want me to flow enough to stay in contact with them. A too-solid subjectivity would feel impossibly alien and unreachable. While I must be multiple, I cannot fragment. Then I could no longer help them stave off the subjective dissolution and annihilation that continually threaten their precarious balance.

FLUID SUBJECTIVITIES: SOME IMPLICATIONS FOR THEORIZING

The concept of fluid, multiple subjectivities has many implications for theorizing. First, theorists will try to keep in mind the multiple components of subjectivity. These include: temperament and orientations to the world; biological vulnerabilities and needs; capacities for abstract thought, work, and language; aggression; creativity; fantasy; meaning creation; and objectivity. The intrasubjective and intersubjective relations among subjectivities are important as well. The qualities and importance of these components within any subjectivity will vary over time. Vast variations across subjectivities will occur as well. These multiple determinants mean that we cannot construct a unitary theory of subjectivity.

We also cannot assume there are always reasons or explanations for what happens to us. Such an assumption is only plausible as an act of faith grounded in contestable beliefs about the nature of being, history, reality, or God.[22]   It is equally likely that there is much random, inexplicable nastiness in the world that affects individuals impersonally and unpredictably. While it may seem paradoxical, these are often comforting and empowering ideas. They encourage a less grandiose view of the extent of one's own powers and a more workable sense of responsibility. Attention to the limits of our powers is often desirable. It encourages us to attain a degree of detachment from the immediacy of affective experience or fantasy. Without such distance, it is difficult to enter empathically into the experiences of others or to respect their differences.

Subjectivity is so complex that we can never be certain what causes a person to be the way they are or to change. Hence, we will also need to be more circumspect in asserting the efficacy of any mode of treatment. We will not discover one correct technique that is the treatment of choice, the best form of psychotherapeutic relationship, or the "real work," even for one sort of illness. Therapy can accomplish a variety of tasks. Their value should be determined by the patient's need, not the therapist's commitments. Since humans are embodied social beings, both somatic and intersubjective interventions are often equally important aspects of treatment.

This need for flexibility and multiplicity in both patient and therapist can be seen quite clearly in the treatment of mood disorders such as depression. In a mood disorder such as depression, medication can alter the affective and somatic facets of experience. However, depression also has cognitive and intra- and intersubjective dimensions. While these may not change without attention to its affective and somatic aspects, they can develop into semiautonomous features of subjectivity. People begin to think and relate to themselves and others in distinct, depressed ways. These will not necessarily disappear when the affective dimension changes. Therapy can be quite helpful in making people aware of their ways of organizing subjectivity and of possibilities for changing them.

However, such work cannot occur when the person is overwhelmed by the affective and somatic effects of a mood disorder such as depression. Attempting to do such work at this point may make the patient worse, exacerbating her already pervasive feelings of failure and incompetence. Seeking reasons for the depression may result in the intensification of the patient's already overwhelming sense of guilt and inappropriate responsibility.

Therapy can make more dimensions of subjectivity available to people. It can encourage the development of the aspects of subjectivity that evoke and enjoy multiplicity. People can develop more tolerance for and appreciation of differences, ambiguity, and ambivalence. Therapy can also increase our ability to engage in appropriate self-protective behavior and to sustain an internal equilibrium within and against the constraints of the inner and outer worlds. These aspects of subjectivity are not the superordinate I/ego of the ego psychologists. They are instead a set of capacities that are so well practiced as to become almost automatic. However, other aspects of subjectivity sometimes must rebel against or interrogate these capacities. Automatic vigilance can be transformed into punitive compliance with unnecessary forms of authority.

The task of therapy cannot be the discovery (or construction) of a solid, unitary, pristine, and undistorted self lying somewhere deep down inside. The person could then be true to this self and use it to orient all actions, choices, and relations in an uncontradictory way. If this is our definition, patients are bound to be disappointed and feel inadequate and defeated. Subjectivity is not an illusion, but the subject *is* a shifting and always changing intersection of complex, contradictory, and unfinished processes. Total access to or control over these processes *is* an illusion, for (among other reasons) the outer world will not provide the resources for us to discover all of them or the space to express them.

Theorists will also have to abandon the idea that we can develop one story that will make sense of all subjective experience. Even constructing multiple narratives and interpreting people's experience are only parts of any therapy. Their importance will vary with the person and over the course of treatment.[23] We will not find one root cause of all illness and health and hence have one grand theory that accounts for them all. Different aspects of subjectivity may require different modes of storytelling. In some kinds of stories intention and will may be relevant, in others they may not be.

Ideas like taking responsibility may vary in meaning and importance depending on which aspects of subjectivity and time we are discussing. For example, as a child someone might have been a helpless victim of abusive parents. As adults we may have to take responsibility for tending to the present consequences of such experiences. One can be simultaneously victimized and responsible; neither negates the other.

Similarly, we cannot assume that the developmental stories we create to make sense of childhood processes also explain adult experiences. There is no singular past waiting in a pristine state for our (re-)discovery. Experience is constantly reworked in conscious and unconscious ways as our cognitive and linguistic skills and intra- and intersubjective worlds and purposes change. Meanings of our experience are affected by and shift within different intra- or intersubjective contexts. The (temporary) content and endings of stories about our experience are partially determined by the questions we and others pose. They are also shaped by the interventions and effects of outer social structures and bodily changes that occur while we are (re-)constructing our narratives.

Dilemmas originally encountered in childhood (like separation-individuation) may persist within our subjective experience. However, as adults we generate and must confront new challenges for ourselves. These cannot be understood solely as a replication or higher level of or reparation for past problems or experiences. Indeed, we get into trouble when we do this. For example, in parenting we may reexperience aspects of our own childhood dilemmas. For our children's sake, we have to find ways to be an adult for them that respond to their particular needs for a parent. Such responses require capacities for empathy, detachment, and appreciation of difference and a desire to foster the unique subjectivities of an Other. These are not notable features of childhood.

POLITICS OF SUBJECTIVITY

We also cannot use parent-child relations as a direct model for citizenship or political action. Citizenship and politics occur within radically different contexts. These contextual differences transform problems of power, authority, and responsibility.[24] Many aspects of political contexts existed before the persons who find themselves within them. We will also have to take into account the effects of these contexts and ongoing action in the world on the continuing constitution of our subjectivities. People are not enclosed, finite systems. Subjective development continues throughout the life cycle. Active political participation, for example, may stimulate the development of aspects of subjectivity that cannot exist outside it.

An analysis of different forms of subjectivity can, however, contribute to an understanding of some of their political consequences. Our notions of subjectivity and our choices among them do reflect and reinforce political and social forces. In this disrupted moment, the ability to tolerate and the will to encourage fluid and multiple forms of subjectivity are imperative and fully ethical positions. The unitary self is an effect of many kinds of relations of domination. It can only sustain its unity by splitting off or repressing other parts of its own and others' subjectivity.

Too much isolation of one dimension from others will have serious intra- and intersubjective effects. Such isolation can be achieved only by turning other aspects of subjectivity into dangerous and alien others requiring punitive control. Since these others are integrally related to the favored part, a hierarchical relation of domination must be established and maintained. Ambiguity and boundary-crossing are increasingly intolerable. Even if the initial motive for such isolation was emancipatory, eventually its repressive consequences will be evident. The long-term costs of such a strategy will outweigh its immediate gains. To retain control, the dominating part must establish perpetually uneasy and insecure relations of mastery over its lesser "others." The creation of presents and futures more congruent with feminist, psychoanalytic, or postmodernist ethics will require the sustained efforts of multiple subjectivities. Only multiple and fluid subjects can develop a strong enough aversion to domination to struggle against its always present and endlessly seductive temptations.

6

THE PLAY OF JUSTICE

DIFFERENCES AND THE NEED FOR JUSTICE

The conflict, resolution, or recognition of differences is among the most urgent contemporary political problems. Modern politics are increasingly pervaded by explosions of differences that cannot be integrated into a unitary whole. Political theorists are constrained in their treatment of this problem, because the canon provides often unsatisfactory solutions to it. However, one of the central concepts in the discourses of political theory—justice—does offer particularly rich resources for more adequate treatments of differences.

In this essay I will outline an approach to justice that is congruent with my feminist commitments to overcoming relations of domination and my postmodernist interests in fostering the play of differences. Ideas about subjectivity are intrinsic to this approach. Since discussions about justice implicitly or explicitly assume and generate assumptions about who "we" are and why we are living together, discourse about justice cannot do without concepts of subjectivity. Better theories of justice will require different accounts of what subjectivity might be. It is both possible and necessary to develop nonrationalist concepts of subjectivity and justice.

I intend to show by example that the arguments that postmodernism is necessarily depoliticizing and cannot be reconciled with feminist or other ethical commitments are wrong. All differences are not equal nor do they deserve the same political consideration. However, positing abstract principles or essentialist claims about human nature will not help us sort out which differences ought to be respected within particular political arrangements. Such principles or claims cannot determine which arrangements are best for specific purposes. They are not particularly useful in struggles against those who have the power to impose radically different ones.

Essentialist claims may be useful in building solidarity among members of a particular group. However, if a group is victorious it tends to use such principles as a warrant for oppressing others. In the twentieth century the costs of deploying such claims have far outweighed their benefits.[1] Our best hopes for more just practices lie in abandoning such illusions about the sources of justice. Postmodernism encourages us to recognize these ideas as illusions and to analyze more carefully our continuing attachments to them.

Justice is not a finite state or a permanent set of rules or principles (contrary to the arguments of writers as diverse as Plato or Rawls). It is an ongoing process in and through which our goals and purposes will change. Justice can be better understood and approximated if we think of it as interrelated practices. These practices have the best possibility of developing and being sustained and effective within transitional spaces.[2] Such spaces are generated by, depend upon, and reflect more than the operation of any form of reason. The domination of certain forms of reason may actually inhibit or block their development.

JUSTICE AND THE PLAY OF DIFFERENCES

Theorists since the classic Greeks have recognized that the need for justice arises in part out of the play of differences. Political life is partially constituted through and necessitated by the tensions generated between two recurring human characteristics: our differences and interdependence. People have different skills, resources, qualities, claims on each other and the community, and opinions about the good. Since none of us is self-sufficient, we must find ways of living together and maintaining relationships. Differences must somehow be confronted, accommodated, or harmonized within a whole that strives to achieve the good(s) for all and in which relations of domination are minimized.

Traditional approaches to justice have often incorporated or resulted in a hierarchical treatment of difference in which only a few qualities are truly respected or valorized.[3] Alternatively, a universal sameness is posited that marginalizes differences and disguises ongoing forms of domination, for example, gender relations.[4] Neither of these approaches is adequate today. Our postmodern worlds require new processes of justice. These will address issues of difference, relatedness, and domination in new ways.[5]

In the contemporary West, the recognition of differences seems inseparable from the creation or reproduction of asymmetric dualisms. Within contemporary Western cultures, differences appear to generate and are certainly used to justify hierarchies and relations of domination including gender-based (or ascribed) ones.[6] Gender relations and the inability to recognize and allow the free play of differences are integrally interconnected and mutually sustaining. Contemporary theories and practices of justice apparently presuppose or require asymmetric gender relations and the suppression or misnaming of differences for their realization.[7]

In the modern (post-seventeenth-century) West, gender has been constituted through a vicious circular logic. Gender connotes and reflects the persistence of asymmetric power relations rather than "natural" (biological/anatomical) differences. A range of "differences" (e.g., mind/body, reason/emotion, public/private) is identified as differences and as salient to and constituent of gender. These differences are also conceived as oppositional, asymmetric dualisms on a hierarchical, binary and absolute scale rather than as pluralisms in an indefinite and open-ended universe. "Woman" is defined as and by the cohering of certain elements, always the lesser side of the dualistic pairs. Man, her superior opposite, "naturally" incorporates and is constituted by the greater.

Modern liberal theorists recommend equality as the remedy for relations of domination. However, it is increasingly uncertain whether equality, however defined, is adequate to or even appropriate for overcoming gender-based relations of domination. It is not clear that equality can mean anything other than assimilation to a preexisting male norm.[8] Western liberal thought itself is partially constituted by "homosexual" tendencies. Differences are reduced to either confirmation of the superiority of the (masculine) same or deviations from it.[9]

Equality appears to require the positing of some characteristic shared by all humans. Our possession of this quality serves as the warrant for the claim of equality. However, the universal sameness posited within liberalism has a distinctly masculine character.[10] The stories philosophers or psychologists tell about the subjects who possess the necessary quality tend primarily to reflect the experiences, problems, and acts of repression of stereotypical white Western masculine ones.[11] Integrating more "feminine" qualities into these stories will not provide satisfactory solutions to the problem of domination. Any universal quality has to be constructed at such a level of abstraction that it will necessarily exclude and do violence to many differences. Among these differences will be many of the ones that make political life meaningful and interesting and just practices possible. It is also likely that the plausibility of any universal claim depends upon its congruence with existing relations of power. The appearance of universality may require that the qualities central to the least powerful are rendered invisible. Some practices of justice may replicate and justify their exclusion.

Feminist movements are not exempt from the exclusionary and constituting effects of the denial or suppression of differences. Contemporary white feminist movements were inspired by the ideas that there is a universally shared female experience and that it is possible to represent the claims of woman. However, more recently it appears that the plausibility of such claims requires excluding effects of other relations of domination including race. Racism in white feminist movements has confronted white feminists with the necessity of devising better theories and practices of difference.

White feminists create our own binary oppositions. We have trouble imagining freely floating differences in which there is no (at least tacit) homogeneous identity or standard for the category "woman." Struggles with our own forms of injustice have impelled white feminists to rethink issues of identity, justice, and equality.[12] In pursuing our interests in overcoming relations of domination feminist theorists (however reluctantly) find ourselves occupying and mapping terrain that overlaps with that of many postmodernist philosophers.[13]

Postmodernists do not treat equality, whether defined either as equal treatment for equals or due process for all, as necessarily essential to justice.[14] However, it does not follow that postmodernists lack a compelling interest in justice. The postmodernist engagement in and preference for play, fragmentation, and differentiation has a quite serious, even normative purpose.[15]

The skeptical and disrespectful rhetorical, antifoundational, and antiessentialist moves of postmodernist writers are partially strategic devices. They are meant to disrupt and erode the power of the grand normalizing discourses, including rationalistic theories of subjectivity and justice. Normalizing discourses put into action and legitimate patterns of dominance characteristic of post-Enlightenment states. One purpose of these deconstructive projects is to contribute to the clearing of existing public spaces. In these altered spaces many disorderly or local forms of life could flourish. The play of differences cannot be very wide-ranging when relations of domination are pervasive.

One aspect of these deconstructive projects is to loosen the hold of transcendental or rationalistic theories of subjectivity and justice. There are good reasons to undermine our belief in such ideas. We believe that objective truth and justice are interdependent, but this is not necessarily the case. It is unnecessary and even dangerous to assume that the existence and practice of justice requires any transcendental grounding.[16] Even if we abandon all notions of transcendental truth and a reason capable of grasping it, we can still formulate and articulate theories and practices of justice. Our choice is not necessarily between grounding justice in objective truth claims (judged by reason) or domination.

We need not assume that only a transcendental reason or the recognition of universally shared human qualities can impel or recognize claims to justice. The belief that humans can recognize or construct an objective set of rules, principles, or neutral laws that will protect us from each other is a seductive but dangerous illusion. It reflects a fantasy of a powerful, Godlike, socially isolated, pure mind detached from embodied, interrelated persons. Human control over or independence from subjectivity, others, and the environment is necessarily limited and imperfect, not omnipotent or objective. To sustain such a fantasy, lesser others must be created whose domination becomes essential to the self. The failures of the products of this pure mind can be attributed to the influences of the inferior "others" (women, other races, the body) over whom perfect control has yet to be fully established. Hence far from making us free, such approaches to justice generate and require relations of domination.

THE SUBJECT OF JUSTICE

Politics cannot be understood as the psyche writ large.[17] There are forces in public life for which there are no accurate analogues in individual psychic existence. Examples of these forces include the levels of violence potentially and currently wielded in politics or the kinds of impersonal yet concerned relations between people that citizenship can entail. It would be a mistake to generalize directly from familial relations, for example, those of mother and child, to political ones.[18] Issues of responsibility and power arise at the political level that radically differ from those in intimate, immediate relations.

There are no simple determining relations between individual psyches and politics. Public life and subjectivity mutually affect each other. Persons are not fixed or closed systems, and psychological development continues throughout the life cycle. Certain forms of ethical maturity and judgment as well as a broadened sense of history, responsibility, and relatedness to others may only develop through active participation in political life.

Even if we experience and express ourselves in transformed ways, humans do not become completely different beings when we enter public worlds. One of the purposes for constructing theories of human subjectivity is to explore our capacities' possibilities and limits. If these capacities are simply a product of past practices and discourses, this does not render them meaningless or utterly suspect.[19] If people are the tissue of our practices, we can still evaluate what resources might be available for use. This evaluation need not conflict with genealogical investigations of the constituting effects of human practices and discourses on our ideas about subjectivity. We can also continue to imagine alternate constituting practices that might make possible different forms of subjectivity.

The problems with concepts of justice such as those of Plato, Locke, Kant, and Rawls do not arise simply because these theorists depend upon or assume ideas about subjectivity. However, problems do occur when these theorists rely upon ideas about subjectivity that are inadequate for generating or supporting just practices. These theorists inappropriately privilege the rational aspects of human subjectivity and posit abstract, impersonal, and disembodied concepts of reason. Justice is made to depend upon the operation of this kind of reason.

An abstracted reason, for example, is the necessary grounding for either a Lockean natural rights or a Kantian theory of justice. Rights for Locke are grounded in a universal, rational natural law, which reason can recognize and is obligated to obey. For Kant, justice depends upon the capacity of reason to recognize the binding effects of universal, rational principles such as the categorical imperative. In Rawls' theory, reason can transcend (or draw a "veil of ignorance" over) interests, including those of empirical experience and personal ties and obligations. This capacity grounds and guarantees the legitimacy of the decision procedures through which the principles governing the basic social structure are ratified. The justice of the principles is guaranteed by the rationality of the procedure.

It is questionable whether there are any necessary or intrinsic relations between reason, however defined, and justice. Why should we believe that reason is privileged or primary for the self or justice? There are many factors upon which the development of subjectivity, self-understanding, and justice depends. These factors include political practices; child rearing and education; the absence of economic, race, or gender-based relations of domination; empathy; fantasy; feelings; imagination; and embodiment. Why should we believe that reason is, can, or should be independent of the contingencies of intersubjectivity, embodiment, language, social relations, or the unconscious?[20]

Rationalistic approaches to justice are doomed to fail and are counterproductive. They block the development of other capacities, such as empathy and appreciation for otherness, which are required for the effective exercise of justice. They encourage and depend upon pathological forms of subjectivity similar to what Winnicott calls the "mind-psyche."[21] Thinking is radically split off and experienced as operating independently of the rest of subjectivity, including our relatedness to and dependence on others. The development and maintenance of such forms of abstract rationality require intrapsychic and interpersonal relations of domination. The effects of such domination cannot be contained by rational principles or law or social structures devised by philosopher-kings.

CHANGING THE SUBJECT OF JUSTICE: FEMINIST AND POSTMODERNIST CONTRIBUTIONS

Psychoanalysts' views of subjectivity as embodied and desiring as well as reasoning and their suspicions of any "pure" concept of reason generate a new subject of and for justice.[22] However, these approaches require tempering by postmodernist skepticism about essences and unitary or homogeneous substances and a feminist attention to gender.[23]

Feminists point to the pervasive effects of gender relations and to a division of labor in which relationships, nurturance, and caretaking necessarily conflict with autonomy, reason, and history making. Relational work and capacities are assigned to women, defined as irrational or arising purely out of bodily necessity, and devalued. The isolated agent and (his) pure reason become the social/political hero.[24]

Postmodernists point to the logocentrism at the heart of Western culture— with its equating of the rational and the human and its collapsing of the rational and the real. They expose and trace our denial of the many intersections between reason, the allegedly autonomous subject, and power. They also encourage us to be skeptical about any essentialist definitions of human nature. Genealogies of such definitions uncover their generation in human practices and relations of power. Conceptions of subjectivity should be read as narratives whose construction and motives are provisional and subject to doubt.

Like D. W. Winnicott and other object relations psychoanalysts, many feminist theorists stress the central importance of sustained, intimate relations with other persons or the repression of such relations in the constitution, structure, and ongoing experiences of a self. Unlike many psychoanalysts, however, feminists conceptualize the families in which we first experience relations with others as constituted by more than the dyads (or triads) of many psychoanalytic accounts. Families and individuals are located within wider contexts of social relations. Some of these relations, for example, race and gender, are structured by and through domination. Questions of power are essential aspects of the constitution and analysis of subjectivity.

Furthermore, feminists analyze the consequences of a fact that is treated as "natural," unremarkable, or unproblematic by many psychoanalysts. In many cultures, the first person(s) we are in an intimate, social relationship with is a woman, a mother or her substitutes or relations. Feminist theorists argue that the repression, especially by men, of these primary relations and the relational aspects of our subjectivity is necessary for the replication of male dominant cultures.[25]

The possibility and plausibility of many theoretical claims and social practices rest in part on the evasion, denial, or repression of how important human attachment is in the constitution of the subject and cultures more generally. Claims dependent on such moves include the positing of a pure mind detached from its social context and subjectivity and rationalistic theories of justice. The first experience of such attachments and their power occurs in early childhood, especially in mother-child relations. In male-dominant cultures the importance of such relations is simultaneously romanticized, devalued, denied, repressed, and placed firmly outside the public realm.[26]

PLAYING AND REALITY: D. W. WINNICOTT AND THE LOCATION OF JUSTICE

Any adequate account of subjectivity would have to do justice to a being who is simultaneously embodied, fantasizing, rational, language-using, related to others, endowed with a distinctive temperament and inner world, socially constituted, and desiring. This being is able to express a range of emotions and capacities including envy, aggression and greed, love and altruism, child rearing, aesthetic appreciation and creation, work of other sorts, and participation in the public world.

Subjectivity is not a closed system in which clearly delimited and identifiable or isolated and independent influences are at play. The very complexity, historicity, and heterogencity of subjectivity render it impossible to make definitive statements about an invariant or foundational human nature. The categories we use to conceptualize ourselves are themselves our constructions. To an unknowable extent these categories bear the traces of all that we are trying to isolate or explain. I would not claim that any theory of subjectivity reveals the truth about our "nature." However, some are more adequate than others in recognizing or leaving space for subjects' complexity.

One particularly promising resource for the development of better accounts of subjectivity is the work of D. W. Winnicott. Winnicott argues that humans live simultaneously in three realities: inner (the subjective), external (the objective), and transitional. At birth the infant is embodied, that is, she or he is a "psyche-soma." Mental and physical experiences are interrelated, permeable and not clearly bounded. For example, the mother's holding and physical caretaking, if in tune with the baby's needs, translates into a feeling of well being and existential continuity for the baby. If the mother's caretaking is radically out of tune with the baby's needs, we "find *mental functioning becoming a thing in itself,* practically replacing the good mother and making her unnecessary. . . . This is a most uncomfortable state of affairs, especially because the psyche of the individual gets 'seduced' away into this mind from the intimate relationship which the psyche originally had with the soma. The result is a mind-psyche, which is pathological."[27]

Winnicott believes each child is born with a unique temperament and the capacity for a variety of cognitive skills and emotions. He places special emphasis, however, on the ways these and embodiment unfold or are impeded within the matrix of the mother-child dyad. Subjectivity in his account includes more than asocial isolated qualities or drives. Subjectivity has a social dimension. It develops partially in and through powerful, affective relationships with other persons. These relations are not simply lived out in the external world; the term "socialization" does not begin to capture their complexity. The subject also has its own inner world with dynamic systems of internal relations. This inner world is partially constituted in and through networks of relations, fantasies, and expectations among and about internal objects (persons with whom we have relations, fantasies, and wishes). Relations with others and our feelings and fantasies about them, along with experiences of embodiment also mediated by such relations, contribute to the constitution of subjectivity. This subjectivity is simultaneously embodied, gendered, social, unique, bounded, determined, open, and unfinished. It is capable of telling stories about and of conceiving and experiencing itself these ways.

Initially the child has no bounded concept or experience of subjectivity. She or he is merged with the mother. The child is not an individual but is rather the "total set-up" of the "environment-individual." The infant begins to move out of this merger after the first six months of life. With good enough care, a distinct person with its own sense and (eventually) concepts of an inside and an outside begins to emerge:

> By good-enough childcare technique, holding and general management the shell becomes gradually taken over and the kernel (which has looked all the time like a human baby to us) can begin to be an individual. . . with good enough technique the centre of gravity of being in the environment-individual set-up can afford to lodge in the centre, in the kernel rather than the shell. The human being now developing an entity from the centre can become localized in the baby's body and so can begin to create an external world at the same time as acquiring a limiting membrane and an inside.[28]

Aggression and frustration can play crucial, constructive roles in this process. Both enable the infant to put experience outside, to begin to distinguish me and not me. After the first six months, babies benefit from their mothers' appropriate failures in caretaking. These failures provide a space in which the infant's own growing capacities can be employed to provide for itself. The infant can also begin to create an idea of the mother (an internal object with whom it has ongoing relations). This idea eventually becomes quite elaborated and a persistent part of the baby's own inner world. The infant's growing sense of a not-me world paradoxically enables it to develop an extensive capacity for fantasy. Fantasy "is only tolerable at full blast when objective reality is appreciated well. The subjective has tremendous value but is so alarming and magical that it cannot be enjoyed except as a parallel to the objective."[29]

Paradoxically also, only if the mother can be put outside the baby can aggression against her be risked. The infant can then test the limits of its powers and control by destroying the mother in fantasy while and only if she survives in the external world. Gradually it suffers a process of disillusionment, as it realizes neither it or the mother is omnipotent.

The concept of transitional phenomena is one of Winnicott's most important contributions to social theorizing. Transitional spaces are, among other things, ways of handling "the immense shock of loss of omnipotence"[30] of the mother and the subject. The transitional space is an "intermediate area" between the infant's illusion of omnipotence and "objective perception based on reality testing."[31] Winnicott describes it as a "third world" that is neither subjective nor objective, neither purely inner nor outer. This world has its own processes, tasks, and ways of making sense out of experience. Transitional spaces are a permanent facet of our mental life. They are not products of a stage of development that is necessarily incorporated into some subsequent or higher state. However, these spaces continue to grow in complexity and richness.

This space is transitional only in the sense that it is both made possible by and bridges the gaps between self and other and inner and outer reality. Transitional spaces can emerge only if there is neither too much nor too little impingement from either the inner or outer world. If the gaps are too great or too small, transitional spaces cannot emerge. Under such conditions the child's ability to create or use transitional objects will be impaired. Often, for example, disturbed children find it difficult to engage in imaginative play or make creative use of toys.

Originally this is the space of play and of attachment to special "not me" possessions (a blanket or toy, etc.) that must always be accessible to the baby. The child's ability to choose and use a transitional object also signals that it has begun to engage in the process of symbolization. The capacity to play and the process of symbolization associated with it eventually "expands into creative living and into the whole cultural life of man."[32] Culture, like play, exists in this third area, the potential space between the inner life of the individual and objective reality. Without something to make use of (tradition out there), no creativity or culture is possible. The creative transformation by the individual of what exists independently in shared reality distinguishes art from dreams or individual delusion. Without pregiven structures and systems of signification, no creativity would be possible. On the other hand, the individual can creatively transform what is given, including language, texts, and games of various sorts, in part by bringing something of inner reality into the process.

Unlike Freud or Lacan, Winnicott does not conceptualize symbolization and culture itself as something alien to the individual, imposed over and against the inner subject. The primary material of culture is not the repression and sublimation of instinctual impulses. It does not operate with a logic purely external to those subjected to it. Culture arises out of that third world, giving us pleasure and a sense of vitality and continuity. However, it does not follow that humans could ever be conflict free. In Winnicott's view, conflicts are endemic to human subjectivity. Each of us must engage in lifelong processes of reconciling subject and other and inner and outer realities:

> It is assumed here that the task of reality acceptance is never completed, that no human being is free from the strain of relating inner and outer reality, and that relief from this strain is provided by an intermediate area of experience. . . which is not challenged (arts, religion, . . .). This intermediate area is in direct continuity with the play area of the small child who is "lost" in play.[33]

THE PLAY OF JUSTICE

Both our capacities to seek justice and our needs for it arise in part out of transitional spaces and the lifelong process Winnicott describes. However, justice must be held and nurtured within public, political-economic contexts rather than the dyadic ones of early childhood. Processes of justice can be intermediate areas of experience in which relief is found from the strain of the isolation of our inner worlds and the press of necessity and regulation from the outer world. Designing or engaging in just practices offers the possibility of modes of relatedness with others. In these processes other persons and their creations are objects neither of fantasy nor desire. They are also not fellow objects of law or necessity. Processes of justice can turn a necessity (bridging various gaps) into a potential source of pleasure and creativity. Such practices also both are and generate spaces in which bits of fantasy can be turned into creative use of outside resources. Something can be created that has meaning or use for others as well as ourselves. They also contain us and add to our sense of security that proper boundaries between inner and outer worlds will be maintained.

Justice can also reconcile us to or even increase our appreciation for the existence of perpetual gaps between our selves and others. If truly different others and the structures of external reality did not exist, we would become isolated prisoners of our inner worlds. Aggression could not be channeled into creativity and the capacity to play. Symbolization would be stunted or impoverished.

Justice is best understood as an ongoing process rather than a fixed set of procedures or a pregiven standard to which we must conform. Transitional spaces serve as defenses against the fear of multiplicity, ambivalence, and uncertainty. This fear often tempts us to try to collapse all our worlds into one.

Justice teaches us how to reconcile or tolerate differences between subjects and others without domination. It generates processes in which we can differ with the other without feeling a need to annihilate her. It shows us how to challenge or play with the limits or restrictions required by the outer world. Justice requires us to confine the playing out of hurtful fantasies to the inner world.

Like transitional objects, justice cannot bridge inner and external reality if it is conceptualized in purely objective (transcendental) or subjective (values or arbitrary wants or power) terms. In play, there is no subject or object; play transforms subject and object into and through process:

> The transitional object and the transitionalphenomena start each human being off with what will always be important for them, i.e., a neutral area of experience which will not be challenged. Of the transitional object it can be said that it is a matter of agreement between us and the baby that we will never ask the question "Did you conceive of this or was it presented to you from without?" The important point is that no decision on this point is expected. The question is not to be formulated.[34]

Understood as a process, justice is one of the ways individuals manage the strain of being simultaneously public and private, alone and related to others, desiring and interdependent. On a collective level, justice is one way groups manage the strain of mediating between the individual subjectivities of which they are composed and the objectivities that those individuals did not create but to which they must respond. These objectivities include limited resources, past traditions, and the consequences of past decisions and practices.

The management of such tensions necessarily involves the exercise of various forms of power. Power can be productive and generative. Relations of domination are not the only result of the exercise of power or of the conflicts and strains endemic to individuals singly and collectively. Power has many forms other than restraint or the direct imposition of external standards upon individual subjects. The consequences of exercises of power depend in part on the relative absence or presence of processes of justice. Depending upon how tensions are managed, empowerment and relief may result. Political spaces may become more open, heterogeneous, and hospitable to new forms of difference.

As a process, justice incorporates at least four aspects:

1. *Reconciliation:* This involves reconciling diversities into a restored but new multiple unity. Justice requires a unity of differences; mutuality

and incorporation rather than annihilation of opposites and distinctions. Claims to justice may be motivated by a desire to extend or preserve the play of difference rather than a sense of obligation to a uniform standard or sameness Transitional spaces enable humans to live simultaneously in three worlds. Such spaces enable us to do this without psychotic fragmentation. We can resist denial of any of our worlds or destruction of the differences among them.

2. *Reciprocity:* Reconciliation is not passive. Justice requires the active complement of reciprocity. Reciprocity connotes a continuous though imprecisely defined sharing of authority and mutuality of decision. It does not require equality of power but does preclude domination. Domination may be present whenever the third space is transformed into a mirror of one set of "objective" standards or "normative" practices. Transitional phenomena or practices help us to manage the frustration and aggression engendered by the inevitable gaps between our wishes and ways of resolving conflict and those of others. They enable us to make creative use of the difference of others and of different sorts of relations. However, they also press us to resist false accommodation to ill-fitting demands.

3. *Recognition:* Recognition includes acknowledging the legitimacy of the others. This requires taking others into account or giving them due honor and consideration. It is often difficult to manage the tensions generated by the demands of accepting the separateness and difference of others while also identifying with them.

Transitional phenomena enable people to engage in the continuous struggle to accept first the mother and later others as existing separate from yet related to us. Mother and child once were one; each became a part of the other's inner world. Mother and child also share a common project—the development of the child into its own person. Yet, ideally, each also comes to accept and appreciate the distance between their fantasies of the perfect mother or child and the realities of the qualities of the other and their relationship.

We cannot make others into exactly what we want, but if we could they would not exist apart from our wishes. The possibility of being alone, together, and apart arises in this gap between fantasy and otherness.[35] Absolute power would entail a terrifying solitude. Differences enable us to experience separation as other than abandonment or domination. A sense of related separation, of identity and differences must exist before we can recognize the obligation to respect the privacy and needs of others and the integrity of each person's inner world. Without distance we cannot experience mutuality and cooperation.

4. *Judgment:* Judgment involves a process of balancing and proportion, of evidence and reflection, of looking forward and backward. This requires the capacity to see things from the point of view of another. It calls upon qualities like empathy and imagination as well as logic and objectivity. Judgment is also connected to action. We must evaluate the consequences of past decisions and place current, potential choices within the context of the needs of both individuals and collectivities. Thus justice is dependent upon a quality of care that arises out of a sense of attachment, connection, and obligation to others. We must be able to imagine vividly the (potential) experiences of concrete others. Sometimes a still-related distance is required to think about the needs of the collectivity as a whole.

Transitional phenomena help us to play with, tolerate, appreciate, or imagine ways to remake the variety of relations, authority, and rules we find present in the external world. Within them we can suspend the demands of both internal and outer realities, to see things anew. They also enable us to move back and forth within multiple realities, including those of others as well as ourselves. Processes of justice encourage us to tolerate ambiguity and ambivalence without losing a sense of individual location and responsibility.

While needs for and capacities to engage in justice depend in part on "private" aspects of human experience, justice can only be exercised in public, intersubjective spaces. Justice is necessarily connected to an active notion of citizenship. Active citizenship is essential for creating public spaces in which justice can be nurtured and held. Without it, politics will remain a restricted, private space in which the transformational processes of justice cannot occur. Citizenship is also another transitional practice that helps manage the strain between the subjective and objective worlds. By diffusing access to power, it serves as a positive defense against the possibility that the outside world will be one that can inappropriately impinge upon transitional spaces.

Citizenship has at least two major aspects: the transformation of private need into public action and the transformation of necessity into freedom. Inner realities and external ones are modified in this transitional process. The transformation of private need into public action requires at least three processes. A need must be seen as publicly actionable, not just as one's private misery. This is part of the feminist claim that the "personal is political." The two are not identical nor should they be merged. Rather, what was formerly borne as one's private misery is now understood, at least to some extent, as caused and transformable by a pattern of human decisions and practices.

In bringing a private need to the public, the spirit in which this is done must itself be transformed. The "I want" must be transformed into the "I and others in my situation are entitled to." This necessarily situates oneself as a member within a public that is shared by others. In some ways these others are like the subject and yet each person, even those we may share a claim with, are not exactly like us. For example, the category "women" obscures many differences and conflicts.[36] Women may suffer from certain pervasive cultural practices (e.g., rape) but the ways we articulate claims to remedy such experience may differ. African-American women may be more mindful of the past racist uses of rape law than white women and hence may frame remedies in different ways.[37] In recognizing differences as well as mutuality, one is forced to negotiate with others. We are required to see the limits of our claims as well as one's mutual responsibility for and dependence upon the character of the "we."

In this process of recognizing and negotiating with the we, one begins to see the subject as not completely driven by necessity. One is part of a community that can collectively act to change its joint practices. Communities can take responsibility for the forces in which we are individually and collectively embedded. To take responsibility collectively requires at least three conditions: (1) an open, accessible community of discourse that cares for its transitional spaces; (2) individuals capable of desiring justice; (3) visible connections between speech, deliberation, empathy, and outcomes.

To have a community of discourse there must be rules, norms, and practices that govern and nurture collective discourse and action. These themselves are open to renegotiation and must be understood as generated by the community itself, as dependent on nothing outside it. The power of rules or laws lies in the collective human agreement to be bound by them. We must agree to include other persons within their protective spaces. Lacking such agreement, and rejecting the practices such agreements codify, some of us will not be secure against the aggression of others. People are quite capable of defining some groups as less than fully human and hence as beyond the relations of justice or the protection of law.

A complex network of practices, beliefs, and feelings inhibits this aggression and keeps it at bay. Our obedience to law and the meaningful inclusion of persons within its protection are symptoms that such a network is in place. Law alone—whether grounded in the attribution of natural rights, a neo-Kantian theory of transcendental justice, natural law, reason, or communicative competence—can never create such a network nor compensate for its absence.

In such circumstances we must recognize that we are in a different domain. When the outer world will not allow us to play justly we too must act differently. This differentiation does not negate the importance of developing theories and practices of justice. On the contrary, since practices of justice are contextual we must acknowledge that in some contexts they will not be useful. Ideas about justice can operate as anticipatory motivation, as, for example, potential excellence at a skill can motivate one to practice it. However, we cannot expect such ideas alone to generate a desire to acquire a skill or a mode of relating to others.

Theories of justice will require complementary theories and practices of injustice. In such theories the uses of aggression and relations to others will take different forms. In some ways the problems will remain the same—how to employ aggression creatively without annihilating the others or one's own capacities for other practices. Developing responses to injustice are critical aspects of any theorizing about justice, but I have not begun to think through such problems. This lack is a crucial absence in my theorizing. Addressing it may significantly change what I have written here.

Discourse is not meaningful outside contexts of action and power. To be aware of the consequences of acts, either individually or collectively, one must be able to take responsibility in a meaningful way. Responsibility is not meaningful without power to act and without having more than an illusion that one is the author of one's acts. To be able to see the consequences of one's acts also requires the elimination of relations of domination. Such relations are in part made possible by rendering some of a community's members and the consequences of individual or collective actions invisible.

To have and sustain these processes of justice, there must be people who desire reciprocity. These people will accept the responsibility of struggling to acknowledge without terror our interconnectedness and mutual dependence. They will also strive to honor and do justice to our separateness and to the distinctiveness and integrity of each other person. To have subjects capable of desiring justice requires persons who need connections with others. These persons will try to see how their own acts affect others. They will work to tolerate the prospect of engaging in an open process without a guaranteed end, result, or privileged position within it. Such subjects will worry when discourse becomes too monovocal, stable, or unitary.

They will recognize that there is nothing outside our tissue of practices, our mutually created transitional spaces, that can help us make decisions and relate to each other justly within them. Yet they would also be aware of their location within external realities, such as past practices and the physical environment, that impose their own limits and boundaries. People would resist allowing their inner worlds (or those of others) to dominate or be collapsed into transitional or external worlds.

Ultimately, justice as well as truth is of this world. Its existence is dependent solely upon our fragile, unstable, embodied, and heterogeneous selves. Any one interested in justice has much to gain and little to lose in encouraging ongoing processes and discourses of disillusionment without which (and partially through which) transitional spaces emerge.

FOUR

IN-CONCLUSION

7

THE END OF INNOCENCE

And although I sensed that everything going on inside me remained blurred, inadequate
in every sense of the word, I was once more forced to admire the way in which
everything fits together with a sleepwalker's precision: the desire of most people
for a comfortable life, their tendency to believe the speakers on raised platforms and the
men in white coats; the addiction to harmony, and the fear of contradiction of the many
seem to correspond to the arrogance and hunger for power, the dedication to profit,
unscrupulous inquisitiveness, and self-infatuation of the few. So what was it that didn't
add up in this equation?

Christa Wolf, *Accident: A Day's News*

PART OF A STORY

In the Spring of 1990 I was invited to discuss an earlier version of this paper with
a group of women who teach in a well-known and successful women's studies
program. I had just spent two days as the only woman at another conference at
the same university, and I was looking forward to a more friendly and productive
exchange. Instead, I was quite surprised by the atmosphere of tension and hostility that erupted as soon as I entered the room. The last time I recall experiencing
such hostility from a group of expected allies was in 1967 when conflicts about
Black Power and the role of whites erupted in the Civil Rights movement. The
intensity of feelings and the sense that one's integrity, history, identity, and place
were at stake reminded me of those earlier and equally painful encounters.
Other participants in this meeting commented on the tension, but no one could
explain or alter it.

The participants repeated many of the claims that some feminists make about
postmodernism. "You cannot be a feminist and a postmodernist," I was told.
Postmodernists are apolitical or even antipolitical. They are relativists; if we
take them seriously, any political stance will be impossible to maintain or justify.
Feminists must generate and sustain a notion of truth so that we can adjudicate
conflicts among competing ideas and legitimate the claims of (some) feminist

theorists and activists. Since postmodernists believe there is no truth, conflict can only be resolved through the raw exercise of power (domination).
Postmodernists' deconstructions of subjectivity deny or destroy the possibility
of active agency in the world. Without a unitary subject with a secure identity
and an empirical sense of history and gender, no feminist consciousness and
hence no feminist politics is possible. Since postmodernists believe meanings
are multiple and indeterminant, if you write clearly and comprehensibly you cannot be a postmodernist. Postmodernists write obscurely on purpose so that
no one outside their cult can understand them. One must choose between
total acceptance and rejection of their position. Acceptance entails abandoning
Feminism or annihilating its autonomy and force, subordinating it to a destructive and inhospitable male-dominated philosophy.

Neither these claims nor the evident emotional investments were illuminated
in this particular encounter. The experience did highlight some of the most contested issues in feminist debates about postmodernism: what are the relations
between knowledge, power, and action? What kind(s) of subjectivities can
demand and support feminist politics? What are the relationships, actual and
potential, between feminist theorizing and the practices of feminist politics?
Does the actualization of feminist visions of the future depend upon the production of better feminist knowledge or epistemologies (and in what sense is this
so)? What are the positions of feminist intellectuals, especially those who teach
in universities, to each other, to other women and to power of various kinds?
What forms the self-consciousness of feminist intellectuals? What motives and
desires (including unconscious ones) drive us to make claims about our subjectivity and the nature and status of our theorizing? Can feminist theorizing (and
women's studies programs) develop best in isolation from nonfeminist modes of
thought? Should feminist theorists try to produce new grand theories as inclusive and self-sufficient as Marxism claimed to be?

DREAMS OF INNOCENCE

Postmodernism is threatening to some feminists because it radically changes
the background assumptions and contexts within which debates about such questions are usually conducted. It is often recognized that white feminist politics in
the West since the 1960s have been deeply rooted in and dependent upon
Enlightenment discourses of rights, individualism, and equality. However the

epistemological legacy that feminists have inherited from these discourses has only recently been called into question.[1] Postmodernism, especially when compounded by certain aspects of psychoanalysis, necessarily destabilizes the (literal and figurative) grounds of feminist theorizing. It has this effect on many forms of Western philosophy. If one takes some of its central ideas seriously, even while resisting or rejecting others, postmodernism is bound to induce a profound uneasiness, or threatened identity, especially among white Western intellectuals. Our consciousness and positions are among its primary subjects of critical analysis.

One way to read postmodernism is as an articulation of the identity crisis among certain white Western intellectuals. As much as we might like to imagine ourselves as outside or immune to the conditions that produced this crisis, white feminists are deeply affected by them. We cannot simply dismiss reflections on this crisis as irrelevant to our own positions and self-understandings. Our race and geographic location and (generally) our relative economic and social status implicates us in it.

While there are many aspects of the threat that postmodernism poses to the self-understanding of white Western intellectuals, there is one I will emphasize here. Postmodernism calls into question the belief (or hope) that there is some form of innocent knowledge available. This hope recurs throughout the history of Western philosophy (including much of feminist theory). While many feminists have been critical of the content of such dreams, many have also been unable to abandon them.[2]

By innocent knowledge I mean the discovery of some sort of truth that can tell us how to act in the world in ways that benefit or are for the (at least ultimate) good of all. Those whose actions are grounded in or informed by such truth will also have *their* innocence guaranteed. They can do only good, not harm, to others. They act as the servant of something higher and outside (or more than) themselves, their own desires, and the effects of their particular histories or social locations.[3]

One of the great promises of Enlightenment is that truth will set us free. Those whose actions are grounded in truth and whose work gives them a privileged relation to it will be the agents of progress and freedom for all. This story deeply affects white Western intellectuals' sense of identity and guarantees us a special place in modern political life.

Conflicts between truth and power can be overcome by grounding claims to and the exercise of authority in reason.[4] Reason both represents and embodies truth. It partakes of universality in two additional ways: it operates identically in each subject and it can grasp laws that are objectively true, that is, are equally knowable and binding on every person. Power grounded in such truth will never generate domination, only freedom.

Three of the discourses feminists have attempted to adapt to our own pur- poses—liberal political theory, Marxism, and empirical social science—express some form of this Enlightenment dream. The coherence and moral force of each theory are dependent upon its grounding in some of these Enlightenment beliefs. Liberal political theorists from John Locke to John Rawls attempt to distinguish legitimate authority from domination by listening for and recording reason's voice. They claim they are articulating a set of rules or beliefs in Reason's own language. To hear Reason's language a rite of purification must be undergone (imagining a "state of nature" or drawing the "veil of ignorance" around oneself)[5] to strip away the merely contingent or historical. The rights or rules that are truly Reason's own and hence binding on all will then re-present themselves. Conformity to these (neutral) laws by the state and its subjects guarantees the rationality, justice, and freedom of both.

Marxists have their own variant of this dream. Their "objective" ground tends to be History rather than Reason. However, in their account, History itself is ultimately rational, purposive, unitary, law governed, and progressive. In the Marxist view, events in history do not occur randomly; they are connected by and through an underlying, meaningful, and rational structure comprehensible by reason/science. The pregiven purpose of history is the perfection of humans (especially through labor) and the complete realization of their capacities and projects. Marxist theory and its articulator (the Party, the working class, the engaged intellectual) have a privileged relation to History.[6] They speak but do not construct its "laws" and legitimate their actions by invoking its name. Since History, like Reason, has an essentially teleological and homogeneous content, we can look forward to its "end." Then all sources of irresolvable conflicts or contradictions will disappear. Authority will take the form of the administration of things rather than the domination of persons. Power will be innocent and human actions in conformity with our highest and most emancipatory potentials.[7]

Empirical social science also inherits, reflects, and is the beneficiary of Enlightenment dreams. Here the relationship between knowledge and power is mediated by science, or at least by a particular understanding of science. Science is the paradigm of knowledge for Enlightenment thinkers. Modern philosophy, as exemplified by Kant, began with the task of explaining *how* scientific knowledge is possible. Kant's particular problem was how physics could develop such accurate and reliable knowledge of the physical world.[8] Until recently, most influential modern philosophers did not interrogate the belief that science does generate such knowledge.

Social scientists also rarely questioned science's relationship to the Real. Their concern was whether such knowledge *could* be obtained about the *social* world and if so what methods were most likely to produce such results.[9] They adopted the Enlightenment belief that science is the ideal form of knowledge, the model for the right use of reason, and the methodological paradigm for all truth claims. They accepted a story about science created by pre-Kuhnian philosophers. Science progresses according to this story because its practitioners are governed by a universal and neutral "logic of discovery."[10] Use of the proper scientific method guarantees that investigators will not distort the data they gather. This method and the scrutiny of the scientific community ensure that investigator bias will be controlled and errors corrected. If social scientists adhere to the rules intrinsic to this logic they too can generate reliable cumulative truth about the Real.

A grounding in science preserves the innocence of the social scientist. Knowledge acquired by the proper methods must reflect the Real (which is also the rational, the benevolent, and the true). Hence knowledge produced by social science can be simultaneously (and without contradiction) neutral, useful, and emancipatory. It can be on the side of good and has no unjustifiable costs. Social scientists' knowledge and power can be innocent of bias, prejudice, or ill effects for anyone. Its innocence is warranted by the (universal) truth/laws in which it is grounded.

The plausibility, coherence, or even intelligibility of these claims depends upon a set of unstated background assumptions. These assumptions include a belief that truth and prejudice are clearly distinguishable and dichotomous categories. There is a neutral language available to report our discoveries. The "logic of discovery" operates independent of and without distorting either its subject (user) or object of investigation. The "scientific" process is self-correcting and governing. It will gradually but necessarily eliminate any biases or false knowledge. The social world is stable, homogeneous, and lawfully structured. Its laws are good and not contradictory; they work to the equal benefit of all.

We can then assume that there is no fundamental disjunction between the discovery and the administration of social laws. The real of science has an unchanging and unchangeable existence independent of the knower. It is not merely created or transformed by humans in the process of doing science. The scientist speaks with and represents the voice of the Real. Therefore "primary" and "applied" social science are merely two facets of the same process—displacing ignorance and prejudice and replacing it with the neutral rule of reason. Action grounded in scientific/expert knowledge is an innocent form of power. Its operation and effects are as transparent and universally accessible as the scientific enterprise. Expert rule generates neither privilege nor domination in its exercise. Instead it results in the good of all.[11]

TWENTIETH CENTURY NIGHTMARES: THE CENTERS WILL NOT HOLD

The modern Western sense of self-certainty has been undermined by political and intellectual events. The meanings—or even existence—of concepts essential to all forms of Enlightenment metanarrative (reason, history, science, self, knowledge, power, gender, and the inherent superiority of Western culture) have been subjected to increasingly corrosive attacks. The challenges to Western political-economic hegemony and to political and cultural colonialism, the rise of nationalist movements in the Third World, women's movements everywhere, and antiracist struggles have disrupted the order of things.

Western intellectuals' sense of epistemological security has also been disrupted by internal dissent. The "essential contestibility" (and the "all too human" contingency) of the constituting notions of Enlightenment metanarratives have been exposed. This creates a crisis of innocence, since these notions then become mere artifacts that humans have created and for whose effects and consequences we alone are responsible. It is difficult for humans to live without secure grounds below and ontological or transcendental guarantees from above.

Psychoanalysts, postmodernists, and feminists have contributed to the undermining of the foundations of Western thought. They are also ambivalent about and partially complicit with it. Psychoanalysts call into question the autonomy of reason, the equation of consciousness and mind, and the unity and stability of the self. They emphasize the existence and partial autonomy of an inner world pervaded by desire and fantasy. This inner world has unconscious and uncontrollable effects on other aspects of human subjectivity such as thought. Postmodernists compose more complex and less hopeful stories about the relationships between knowledge, power, history and subjectivity.[12] Feminist theo-

rists argue that ideas about knowledge are dependent upon and made plausible by
the existence of specific sets of social relations, including gender.[13]

Postmodernists believe philosophy occupies a constituting and legitimating
position within metanarratives of Enlightenment that continue to structure
Western culture. Hence, the deconstruction of philosophy is a political responsibility (and at least *qua* philosophers) their most salient and subversive contribution to contemporary Western culture. Western philosophy remains under the
spell of the "metaphysics of presence."[14] Most Western philosophers took as their
task the construction of a philosophic system in which something Real would and
could be re-presented in thought. This Real is an external or universal subject or
substance, existing "out there" independent of the knower. The philosopher's
desire is to "mirror," register, mimic, or make present the Real. Truth is understood as correspondence to it.

For postmodernists this quest for the real conceals most Western philosophers' desire, which is to master the world conclusively by enclosing it within an
illusory but absolute system. They assert such systems re-present or correspond
to a unitary Being beyond history, particularity, and change. To mask his idealiz-
ing desire, the philosopher must claim his knowledge is not the product, artifact,
or effect of a particular set of historical or discursive practices. It can only be the
Real expressing itself directly in our thought.

The philosopher also obscures another aspect of his desire: to claim a special
relation and access to the True or Real. The presence of the Real for us depends
on him—the clarity of his consciousness, the purity of his intention. Only the
philosopher has the capacity for Reason, the love of wisdom (philo-sophia), the
grasp of method, or the capacity to construct a logic adequate to the Real. The
Real is the source of Truth. So the philosopher as the privileged representative
of the Real and interrogator of truth claims must play a "foundational" role in all
"positive knowledge." Epistemology acquires an essential place within modern
philosophy. It serves as the means to purge, clarify, or demarcate the philosopher's consciousness, for himself, for the benefit of other philosophers, and ultimately for humanity as a whole.

Postmodernists attack the "metaphysics of presence" and the Western philosopher's self-understanding in a number of ways. They question the philosophies of
mind, truth, language, and the Real that underlie and ground any such transcendental or foundational claims. Postmodernists claim that there is (and can be) no
transcendental mind. On the contrary, what we call mind or reason is only an
effect of discourse. There are no immediate or indubitable features of mental

life. Sense data, ideas, intentions, or perceptions are already constituted. Such experiences only occur in and reflect a variety of discursively and socially determined practices. The problem of the relation between the "mind" and "things in themselves" becomes infinitely more complex. One cannot even assume that the mind has some universal, transcendental, a priori categories or concepts that always shape experience in the same, even if unknowable, ways. Instead the categories or concepts by and through which we structure experience are themselves historically and culturally variable. "Mind" is no more homogeneous, lawful, and internally consistent in or over time than is History.

Truth for postmodernists is an effect of discourse. Each discourse has its own distinctive set of rules or procedures that govern the production of what is to count as a meaningful or truthful statement. Each discourse or "discursive formation" is simultaneously enabling and limiting. The rules of a discourse enable us to make certain sorts of statements and to make truth claims. The same rules force us to remain within the system and to make only those statements that conform to these rules. A discourse as a whole cannot be true or false because truth is always contextual and rule dependent. Discourses are local, heterogeneous, and often incommensurate. No discourse-independent or transcendental rules exist that could govern all discourses or a choice between them. Truth claims are in principle "undecidable" outside of or between discourses. This does not mean that there is no truth but rather that truth is discourse dependent. Truth claims can be made by those who accept the rules of a discourse or who are willing to bridge across several. However, there is no trump available that we can rely on to solve all disputes. Prior agreement on rules, not the compelling power of objective truth, makes conflict resolution possible.

Since truth is discourse dependent, genealogy replaces older concepts of epistemology. Postmodernist investigations do not focus on identifying the general rules or conditions that produce truthful statements. They are not particularly interested in the relationships between our knowledge and the real. Instead they encourage us to pay more attention to the varying conditions under which conflicting truth claims can be put forward or resolved. We cannot understand knowledge without tracing the effects of the power relations that simultaneously enable and limit the possibilities of discourse. Sometimes disagreements can be settled through discourse but often only political actions, including the use of force, are sufficient. While force or domination is not required to settle all disputes, discourse alone cannot resolve irreconcilable differences. Even consensus is not completely innocent, since traces of force may be found in the history of any set of rules that attain and maintain binding effect.

Truth is discourse dependent also because there is no stable, unchanging, and unitary Real against which our thoughts can be tested. Western philosophers create an illusory appearance of unity and stability by reducing the flux and heterogeneity of the human and physical worlds into binary and supposedly natural oppositions. Order is imposed and maintained by displacing chaos into the lesser of each binary pair, for example culture/nature or male/female. The construction of such categories as and through opposition expresses and reveals the philosopher's desire for control and domination. Once these oppositions are seen as fictive, asymmetric, and conditions of possibility for the philosopher's story, then a premise that underlies all variants of the metaphysics of presence can be revealed. This premise is: to be other, to be different from the defining one, is to be inferior and to have no independent character or worth of one's own.

For example, "woman" is defined as a deficient man in discourses from Aristotle through Freud. The superior member of the pair maintains his innocence. Unlike the inferior, *he* is secure in his independence and natural superiority; he is within but not of the dyad. Like Aristotle's master or husband, his is the active matter, determining and generative within, but never affected *by* his coupling. There is no disorder within him and hence none within Being as such, but there may be disorderly objects requiring the exercise of his mastery. In the Enlightenment self-understanding, this view is an "optimistic," humane, and "progressive" one; eventually all difference/disorder will be brought within the beneficent sovereignty of the One.

Postmodernists regard all knowledge construction as fictive and nonrepresentational. Since it is a product of the human mind, knowledge has no necessary relation to Truth or the Real. Philosophers create stories about these concepts and about their own activities. Their stories are no more true, foundational, or truth-adjudicating than any others. There is no way to test whether one story is closer to the truth than another because there is no transcendental standpoint or mind unencumbered by its own language and stories.

Philosophers and other knowledge constructors should seek instead to generate an infinite "dissemination" of meanings. They should abjure any attempt to construct a closed system in which the "other" or the "excess" are "pushed to the margins" and made to disappear in the interest of coherence and unity. Their task is to disrupt and subvert rather than (re-)construct totalities or grand theories. Postmodernists must firmly situate themselves as constructs within their own discourses. The imperial, impersonal Cartesian ego is to be deconstructed and its desires set free to play within and as language. The "view from nowhere" is replaced by admittedly partial and fragmentary multiples of one.[15]

Feminist theorists also pose profound and still inadequately confronted challenges to many understandings of our social life and knowledge. One of the most important contributions has been to reveal and problematize gender relations. Gender has been reconceived as a highly variable and historically contingent set of human practices. Gender is not a stable thing; it is not a simple consequence of anatomy or biological processes. We do not know what consequences female (or male) embodiment would have in societies without gender-based domination, although feminists think about this question in increasingly interesting ways. We cannot even claim that gender is a universal or unitary relation present in all cultures. It is a category that feminist theorists have constructed to analyze certain relations in our cultures and experiences. The concept must therefore reflect our questions, desires, and needs.

Gender relations have many often-disguised or denied effects on the structuring of individual experience, social relations, and knowledge itself. Feminists have successfully carried out genealogical investigations of the constituting effects of male dominance in knowledge production. We have also begun to explore the suppression and devaluation of knowledge arising from certain dimensions of women's and men's experiences. The necessary connections between the suppression of certain experiences and forms of knowledge and the persuasiveness and power of the claims Western culture makes about the nature of its knowledge have become more evident.[16]

Feminists insist that masculinity and femininity are effects of gender systems. Feminists understand masculine and feminine in terms of power and domination, not as positions in language that any subject can assume. Gender relations are interwoven with and reinforce other preexisting and constituting social relations such as race. Both men and women are marked by gender relations, although in different and unequal ways.

Feminists' conceptualizations of these categories provide a necessary counterpoint to and basis for criticism of the weaknesses (or absence) of postmodernist positions on gender.[17] From a feminist viewpoint it appears (at best) quite odd that many postmodernists are unaware of the problems in their approach to gender. They are emphatic in their claims that the subject is a thoroughly constituted but not a constituting being. However, writers such as Derrida appear to adopt a voluntaristic (indeed almost free-will) approach to gender identity. If subjectivity is constituted by pregiven categories like masculine or feminine, no individual subject can escape the effects of these categories any more than she or he could speak a private language. Unless the entire discursive field (and each subject's unconscious) is changed, these categories will continue to generate particular forms of subjectivity beyond the control of individuals, no matter how freely the subject believes she or he is playing with them.

THE END OF INNOCENCE AND THE CRISIS OF REPRESENTATION

Postmodernist deconstructions of representation and the "innocence" of truth and psychoanalytic displacings of reason are profoundly unsettling for feminist intellectuals. Of these three modes of theorizing, feminist theories are the most overtly and self-consciously political. The action most psychoanalysts seek to effect is an individual therapeutic cure. Postmodernists, especially in the United States, have been primarily concerned with disruptions of discourses whose location in and effects on relations of domination are (at best) highly mediated. Feminist theorists take as their primary objects of investigation and intervention the gender systems that continue to generate and reproduce relations of domination. No other movement or mode of thinking has taken as its central commitments the analysis and elimination of their oppressive effects.

However, postmodernist discourses disrupt master narratives of the West and the language games in which terms like freedom, emancipation, or domination take on meaning. Lacking "privileged" insight into the "laws" of history or reason's operations, firmly situated within discrete, contingent, but constituting gender, class, race, and geographical locations, no longer serving as the neutral instrument of truth or the articulator of a homogeneous "humanity's" best hopes, what authorizes the intellectual's speech? We become hesitant to speak for or prescribe our good(s) for others. Contemplating Auschwitz or the environmental disasters produced by modern technologies we can no longer sustain the illusion or the hope that "true" knowledge is sought only by the virtuous or is a priori generated by the good. When knowledge is put into practice the probabilities it will have only the beneficial results we intend is small. It is more difficult to separate normative discourse from potential exercises of power or to conceptualize power entirely innocent of domination.

Despite postmodernist challenges and their own deconstructions of the gender-based relations of power that generate the content and legitimacy of many forms of knowledge, many feminist theorists sustain the Enlightenment hope that it is possible to obtain "better" knowledge and epistemologies. By better, they mean (at minimum) knowledge and epistemologies less contaminated by false beliefs and dominating relations of power. They believe feminist theories are progressive; that is, they are freer from these effects of error and domination than previous thinking. Therefore they represent a higher and more adequate stage of knowledge. Many feminists also continue to argue for the necessary relationships between better knowledge and better practices.[18] Without the secure ability to make truth claims, the feminist project of ending gender-based domination is doomed.[19]

One of the most persuasive advocates of such positions, Sandra Harding, argues that epistemologies are partially justificatory schemes. Like moral codes, they challenge the idea of "might makes right" in the domain of knowledge claims. Access to such schemes is especially necessary when unequal power relations exist. It is in the interest of the weak to contest on the ground of truth rather than with force. Feminists also need defenses against and alternatives to traditional discourses about women and means of obtaining truth. Both of these may be gender biased. We also need decision procedures that can be articulated to other feminists. These procedures can guide choices in theory, research, and politics. Although traditional grounds for knowledge claims are not adequate we still need to justify our claims to ourselves and to others.

This theorizing should be accountable to many different women. Difference should be taken into account, both as cultural variations and as domination. We also need decision procedures to guide practice; knowledge can be a resource to help organize strategies against domination. Ultimately, Harding seems to think, as do Nancy Hartsock and others, that the success of the feminist projects of creating effective analyses of gender and of ending gender-based domination depend on our ability to make truth claims about the "objective" status of our knowledge and our demands.

I believe these arguments are profoundly mistaken, and to the extent to which they are (unconsciously) intended to maintain the innocence of feminist theories and politics, dangerous. Operating within the Enlightenment metanarrative, these feminist theorists merge three different claims. These claims are: that certain kinds of knowledge are generated by gender-based power relations, that correcting for these biases will necessarily produce "better" knowledge, and that this knowledge will be purely emancipatory (e.g., not generated by nor generative of its own relations of uninnocent power).

These feminists are not content with constructing discourses that privilege some of those who have previously lacked power (at the necessary expense of others). They wish to claim dis-covery of ways to increase the general sum of human emancipation. These theorists assume that domination and emancipation is a binary pair and that to displace one necessarily creates new space for the other. They conceive disruption of the given as entailing an obligation to create something new. The legitimacy or justification of disruption depends in part on the nature of what is offered in place of the old. They fear what will emerge in disrupted spaces if they are not in feminist control. In order for the new to be secure and effective, it must be located and grounded within a new epistemological scheme.

Like other Enlightenment thinkers, they believe innocent, clean knowledge is available somewhere for our discovery and use. Although the discovery of new knowledge may be dependent upon disruptions of previously existing power relations, the effects of its social origins are somehow transformed by epistemological means. Epistemology also gives a force to new knowledge (independent of politics) that it would otherwise lack.

These claims reflect the difficulties of abandoning the Enlightenment metanarrative that cannot, despite its promises, deliver us from domination or enable us to construct or exercise knowledge innocently. Harding and others assume (rather than demonstrate) there are necessary connections between truth, knowledge, emancipation and justice. They also presuppose that truth and force or domination are necessarily antimonies.

On the contrary, I believe we need to rethink all these concepts, let them float freely, and explore their differences. All epistemological talk is not useless or meaningless, but a radical shift of terrain is necessary. I would like to move the terms of the discussion away from the relations between knowledge and truth to those between knowledge, desire, fantasy, and power of various kinds. Epistemology should be reconceived as genealogy and the study of the social and unconscious relations of the production of knowledge. Philosophers would abandon wishes to adjudicate truth claims and instead would engage in linguistic, historical, political, and psychological inquiries into forms of knowledge construction and conflict within particular discursive formations. Such inquiries would include investigations into the philosopher's own desire and place within particular social locations and discourses. We can also analyze some of the effects of different discursive practices and articulate why one set of practices appears to be preferable for certain pragmatic purposes.

RESPONSIBILITY WITHOUT GROUNDS

A belief in the connections between truth and knowledge at this point in Western history seems far more likely to encourage a dangerously blind innocence rather than to prepare the ways for freedom or justice. We should take responsibility for our desire in such cases: what we really want is power in the world, not an innocent truth. The idea that truth is on one's side is a recurrent element in justificatory schemes of all sorts. It is used to justify the actions of terrorists, antifeminists, and producers of dangerous technologies as well as those whose politics are more congruent with feminist ones.

Part of the purpose of claiming truth seems to be to compel agreement with our claim (if it is true, then you as a "rational person" must agree with me and change your beliefs and behavior accordingly). We are often seeking a change in behavior or a win for our side. If so, there may be more effective ways to attain agreement or produce change than to argue about truth. Political action and change require and call upon many human capacities including empathy, anger, and disgust. There is no evidence that appeals to reason, knowledge, or truth are uniquely effective or ought to occupy privileged positions in strategies for change. Epistemologies do not necessarily reassure people that taking risks are worthwhile or convince them that political claims are justified. It is simply not necessarily the case (especially in politics) that appeals to truth move people to action, much less to justice.

Thus Harding confuses the need for justification with the need for power. Arguments can lack force (in the political sense) no matter how well they may be grounded in some epistemological scheme. Furthermore, arguments about knowledge are motivated in part by a wish to maintain an innocence and an innocent form of hope that are quite dangerous. False knowledge can be used to justify or support domination. However, it does not follow that true knowledge will

diminish it or that the possessor of "less false" knowledge will be free from complicity in the domination of others.

A concern for epistemology can mask the desire to claim a position of innocence in which one person's clarity does not rest on the exclusion of an Other's
experience. It can also be motivated by an illusory wish to discover neutral rules
that could provide certain guarantees. Adherence to these rules will not result in
the distortion or erasure of someone's "truth." Speaking in knowledge's voice or
on its behalf, we can avoid taking responsibility for locating our contingent selves
as the producers of knowledge and truth claims. Talk of adjudication and justification assumes that neutrality or at least consensus is possible. This in turn
presupposes there are no irresolvable differences, that harmony and unity are
desirable, and that effective knowledge and political action must rest on a secure,
conflict-free common ground. Consensus is privileged over conflict, rule-follow-
ing over anarchy.

Aspects of contemporary white feminist theorizing exemplify negative consequences of these beliefs. As some feminists have argued recently, an intensified
concern about epistemological issues emerged at the same time as women of
color began to critique the writings of white feminists. The unity of categories
like "woman" or "gender" was found to require the exclusion of many experiences of women of color (as well as women outside the overdeveloped world,
poor women, and lesbians).[20]

As much as, if not more than, postmodernism, the writings of women of
color have compelled white feminists to confront problems of difference and the
relations of domination that are the conditions of possibility for the coherence of
our own theorizing and category formation. Our guilt and anxieties about
racism (and our anger at the "others" for disturbing the initial pleasure and comfort of "sisterhood") also partially account for the discomfort and difficulties we
white women have in rethinking differences and the nature of our own theorizing
and social locations.

Postmodernism is not above criticism or without flaws.[21] I would not claim
that anxieties about race and other differences are the only sources of its rejection. I am trying to make sense of part of the emotional vehemence with which
some feminists reject these writings, sometimes with only minimal knowledge
of them. The intensity of the emotional response is puzzling, especially among
people who generally respond to ideas in a much more complex and nuanced
manner.

Since the projects of postmodernism and of women of color do overlap, I wonder whether there is a racial subtext at work that requires more attention. Directly attacking women of color or voicing our resentment of them (in public) would be politically unthinkable. Is it easier and more acceptable for white women to express our discomfort with difference discourses and the politics of knowledge claims by categorically rejecting postmodernism and branding it politically incorrect? Such constituting acts of exclusion or repression can become evident only when the power relations that enable the construction of knowledge claims are explicitly addressed.

Establishing or adjudicating truth claims will not help us achieve a central feminist objective: to destroy gender-based relations of domination. Claims about domination are claims about *injustice* and cannot be given extra force or justification by reference to Truth. Claims about injustice belong on the terrain of politics and in the realm of persuasive speech, action, and (sometimes) violence. As Machiavelli argues, politics requires a morality and knowledge appropriate to its unique domain. Claims about injustice can operate independently of "truth," or indeed of any corresponding counterclaim about a transcendental good or an ideal form of justice.[22]

Once we begin to make claims about gender injustice, we have irrevocably entered the realm of politics. We need to learn ways of making claims about and acting upon injustice without transcendental guarantees or illusions of innocence. One of the dangerous consequences of transcendental notions of justice or knowledge is that they release us as discrete persons from full responsibility for our acts. We remain children, waiting, if our own powers fail, for the higher authorities to save us from the consequences of our actions. Such wishes depend on and express our complicity with what Nietzsche calls the "longest lie," the belief that "outside the haphazard and perilous experiments we perform there lies something (God, Science, Knowledge, Rationality, or Truth) which will, if only we perform the correct rituals, step in to save us."[23]

To take responsibility is to situate ourselves firmly within contingent and imperfect contexts, to acknowledge differential privileges of race, gender, geographic location and sexual identities. Responsibility entails resisting the delusory and dangerous recurrent hope of redemption to a world not of our own making. We need to learn to make claims on our own and others' behalf and to listen to those that differ from ours. Ultimately there is nothing that justifies these claims beyond each person's desire and need and the discursive practices in which these are developed, embedded, and legitimated. Each person's well-being is dependent on the development of discursive communities that foster (among other attributes) an appreciation of and desire for difference, empathy, even indifference in the others. Lacking such feelings, as the Jews in Europe or people of color in the United States (among many others) have discovered, all the laws and culture civilization can offer will not save us. It is far from clear what contributions knowledge or truth can make to the development of such feelings and communities.

At its best, postmodernism invites us to engage in continual disillusionment of the grandiose fantasies that have brought us to the brink of annihilation. For this is part of what is missing from Crista Wolf's equation: in different situations, people in the West are on both sides, the few and the many. It is extremely difficult for us to accept and live such unstable and painful ambivalence. However, these junctures are exactly where responsibility beyond innocence looms as a promise and a frightening necessity.

ENDNOTES

Minerva's Owl

1. Marge Piercy, "To Be of Use," in her *To Be of Use* (Garden City: Doubleday, 1973), 49. I developed this sense of theorizing early in my work. See Jane Flax, "Women do Theory," *Quest* 5, 1(Summer 1979), 19–26; and my "Mother-Daughter Relationships: Politics, Psychology, Philosophy," in *The Future of Difference*, edited by Hester Eisenstein and Alice Jardine (Boston: G. K. Hall, 1980).

2. Elsa Barkley Brown's article, "'What Has Happened Here': The Politics of Difference in Women's History and Feminist Politics," *Feminist Studies* 18, 2 (Summer 1992), especially pp. 300–307, helped me to think more clearly about this. See also Christina Crosby, "Dealing with Differences," in *Feminists Theorize the Political*, edited by Judith Butler and Joan W. Scott (New York: Routledge, 1992).

3. I do not mean to slight the wonderful work of this sort that exists. See, for example, Evelyn Nakano Glenn, "From Servitude to Service Work: Historical Continuities in the Racial Division of Reproductive Labor," *Signs* 18, 1(Autumn 1992):1–43; Hazel V. Carby,"On the Threshold of Women's Era': Lynching, Empire, and Sexuality in Black Feminist Theory" in *"Race," Writing and Difference*, edited by Henry Louis Gates (Chicago: University of Chicago Press, 1985); Biddy Martin and Chandra Talpade Mohanty, "Feminist Politics: What's Home Got to Do with it?" in *Feminist Studies/Critical Studies*, edited by Teresa de Lauretis (Bloomington: Indiana University Press, 1986); and the essays in *Third World Women and the Politics of Feminism*, edited by Chandra Talpade Mohanty, Ann Russo, and Lourdes Torres (Bloomington: Indiana University Press, 1991).

4. My first article,"Do Feminists Need Marxism?" was published in *Quest* 3, 1 (Summer 1976): 46–58.

5. My temperament disposed me to find Michel Foucault a kindred spirit before I ever read his work. I particularly appreciate the explicitly provisional quality of Foucault's thought and his attempts to demystify intellectual work. See Michel Foucault, "Questions of Method," in *The Foucault Effect*, edited by Graham Burchell, Colin Gordon, and Peter Miller (Chicago: University of Chicago Press, 1991); and his "The Masked Philosopher" in *Politics, Philosophy, and Culture*, edited by Lawrence D. Kritzman (New York: Routledge, 1988).

6.   I have written more about this process in "Mother-Daughter Relationships," in Hester Eisenstein and Alice Jardine (Boston: G.K. Hall, 1980).

7.   See Jane Flax, "Critical Theory as a Vocation," *Politics & Society* 8, 2 (1978): 201–223.

8.   Max Horkheimer and Theodor Adorno, *The Dialectic of Enlightenment* (New York: Herder and Herder, 1972).

9.   See particularly the introduction to *Dialectic of Enlightenment*. Herbert Marcuse's *An Essay on Liberation* (Boston: Beacon, 1969) is moving in its anxiety about whether hope is really possible or wise. The *Dialectic of Enlightenment* can be read as a profound and painful meditation on cultural identity (especially of German Jews). The authors peer over the cliff of total disillusionment that they refuse (or from which they are rescued) by reasserting a faith in the possibility of a (yet to be realized) emancipatory reason.

10.   See for example, Max Horkheimer, *Critical Theory* (New York: Herder and Herder, 1972); and Herbert Marcuse, *Negations* (Boston: Beacon, 1968). I adopt this approach for my own purposes in "Why Epistemology Matters," *Journal of Politics* 43, 4 (November 1981): 1006–1024; and "Object Relations, Political Theory and the Patriarchal Unconscious," in *Discovering Reality*, edited by Sandra Harding and Merrill Hintikka (Boston: D. Reidel 1983).

11.   In Karl Marx, *Capital*, v. 1 (New York: International Publishers, 1967), 71–93.

12.   Especially Georg Lukacs, "Reification and the Consciousness of the Proletariat," in his *History and Class Consciousness* (Cambridge: MIT Press, 1968); and Antonio Gramsci, *The Modern Prince and Other Writings* (New York: International Publishers, 1968), particularly part 2.

13.   Particularly influental was Thomas Kuhn, *The Structure of Scientific Revolutions*, 2nd ed. (Chicago: University of Chicago, 1970) and the debates it generated. Concerning the social sciences, the work of Charles Taylor, especially the essays collected in his *Philosophy and the Human Sciences* (Cambridge: Cambridge University Press, 1985), affected me as did Jurgen Habermas, *Knowledge and Human Interests* (Boston: Beacon, 1971); Sheldon Wolin, *Politics and Vision* (Boston: Little, Brown, 1960); and Hanna Pitkin, *Wittgenstein and Justice* (Berkeley: University of California Press, 1972).

14.   Albert Hirschman, *The Passions and the Interests* (Princeton: Princeton University Press, 1977); C. B. Macpherson, *The Political Theory of Possessive Individualism* (New York: Oxford University Press, 1962); J. G. A. Pocock, *The Machiavellian Moment* (Princeton: Princeton University Press, 1975); and J. Peter Euben, *The Tragedy of Political Theory* (Princeton: Princeton University Press, 1990) have made me particularly aware of the historical oirgins of political vocabularies and of their potential incommensurability.

15. See my "Do Feminists Need Marxism?" *Quest* 3, 1(Summer 1976): 46–58.

16. Christine Di Stephano, *Configurations of Masculinity* (Ithaca: Cornell University Press, 1991); and Isaac D. Balbus, *Marxism and Domination* (Princeton: Princeton University Press, 1982) provide evaluations of Marxist theories that are far more adequate than my own. Some feminist writers initially more enamored of Marxist theories have come to similar conclusions. See, for example, Michele Barrett, *Women's Oppression Today*, rev. ed. (New York: Verso, 1988).

17. Herbert Marcuse, *Eros and Civilization* (New York: Vintage, 1955).

18. Horkheimer, *Critical Theory*, p. 248. Jurgen Habermas' work represents an attempt to fill out exactly such a "materialist concept." He also cannot do without some Kantian rationality, however reformulated (communicative competence, universal pragmatics), to guarantee and ground the entire project. See Jurgen Habermas, *Communication and the Evolution of Society* (Boston: Beacon, 1979); and his *The Theory of Communicative Action*, v. 2 (Boston: Beacon, 1987). These more recent developments exacerbate my sense of distance from this approach. Later, I began a more complex deconstruction of Kantian reason and some of Habermas' arguments. See Jane Flax, "'What is Enlightenment?': A Feminist Rereading," in this volume. Although I am more critical than she is, I have found Nancy Fraser's work particularly helpful in thinking about this material. See Nancy Fraser, *Unruly Practices* (Minneapolis: University of Minnesota Press, 1989).

19. Especially Sigmund Freud, *The Ego and The Id* (New York: W. W. Norton, 1960); and his *An Outline of Psychoanalysis* (New York: W. W. Norton, 1969). I discuss some of the philosophic implications of these theories in Chapter 3 of my *Thinking Fragments: Psychoanalysis, Feminism, and Postmodernism in the Contemporary West* (Berkeley: University of California Press, 1990).

20. See The Frankfurt Institute for Social Research, "The Family," in their *Aspects of Sociology* (Boston: Beacon, 1972). These claims still circulate widely in discourses on the family. Christopher Lasch, *Haven in a Heartless World* (New York: Harper 1977) quite directly appropriates them. I try to develop alternative analyses of "the family" and its relations to other social arrangements the following essays: "A Look at the Cuban Family Code," *Quest* 4, 2 (Winter 1978): 87–93; "A Materialist Theory of Women's Status," *Psychology of Women Quarterly* 6, 1 (Fall 1981): 121–136; "Contemporary Families: Decline or Transformation?" in *Families, Politics and Public Policy*, edited by Irene Diamond (New York: Longman, 1983); and "The Family in Feminist Theory: A Critical Review," in *The Family in Political Thought: Past and Present*, edited by Jean Bethke Elshtain (Amherst: University of Massachusetts Press, 1982). Early exposure to such arguments has prepared me to be skeptical about feminist attempts such as in the work of Sara Ruddick to transvalue maternity. See her "Maternal Thinking," and "Preservative Love and Military

Destruction," both reprinted in *Mothering: Essays in Feminist Thinking*, edited by
Joyce Trebilcot (Totowa: Rowman & Allanheld, 1984).

21. This is less true in *The Dialectic of Enlightenment*. In this earlier work Horkheimer
     and Adorno more fully acknowledge the effects for women men, reason, and soci-
     ety of male dominance. They also seem more concerned about the negative conse-
     quences of such arrangements.

22. Especially my "Object Relations, Political Theory and the Patriarchal Unconscious",
     in *Discovering Reality*, edited by Sandra Harding and Merrill Hintkka (Boston: D.
     Reidel, 1983); *Thinking Fragments* (Berkeley: University of California Press, 1990);
     "The Play of Justice," and "Multiples," in this volume.

23. See Evelyn Fox Keller and Jane Flax, "Missing Relations in Psychoanalyis," in
     *Hermeneutics and Psychological Theory: Interpretative Perspectives on Personality,
     Psychotherapy and Psychopathology*, edited by Stanley B. Messer, Louis A. Sass, and
     Robert L. Wollfolk (New Brunswick: Rutgers University Press, 1988); and my
     "Can Psychoanalysis Be a Science?" in *Journal of Philosophy* LXXVIII, 10 (October
     1981: 561–569; "Psychoanalysis as Deconstruction and Myth," in *The Crisis of
     Modernity: Recent Critical Theories of Culture and Society in the United States and West
     Germany*, edited by Gunter H. Lenz and Kurt L. Shell (Frankfurt: University of
     Frankfurt Press; Boulder, CO: Westview Press, 1986); "Final Analysis?
     Psychoanalysis in the Postmodern West," in this volume; and my *Thinking
     Fragments*.

24. Especially D. W. Winnicott, *Through Paediatrics to Psychoanalysis* (New York: Basic
     Books, 1975); and his *Playing and Reality* (New York: Basic Books, 1971). I draw
     on Winnicott's idea on the transitional space to reformulate approaches to just
     practices in my "Play of Justice"; and my "Beyond Equality and Difference: Justice
     in Feminist Postmodernism," in *Equality and Difference: Gender Dimensions in Political
     Thought, Justice and Morality*, edited by Gisela Bock and Susan James (London and
     New York: Routledge, 1992).

25. D. W. Winnicott, "Mind and its Relation to the Psyche-Soma," in *Through
     Paediatrics*; and Melanie Klein, "Early Stages of the Oedipus Conflict," and "The
     Importance of Symbol-Formation in the Development of the Ego," both in her
     Love, Guilt, and Reparation (New York: Delta, 1975); my "Philosophy," in
     Psychoanalysis and Feminism: A Critical Dictionary, edited by Elizabeth Wright
     (London and New York: Basil Blackwell, 1992); and my "The Subject,"in *The
     Oxford Companion to Women's Writing in the United States*, edited by Cathy N.
     Davidson and Linda Wagner-Martin (New York: Oxford, 1993).

26. I certainly do not think Winnicott's ideas are flawless. In Chapter 4 of *Thinking
     Fragments* (Berkeley: University of California Press, 1990), I discuss some of the
     problematic aspects of his work. Certain absences are especially significant: of the
     mother as a person in her own right and not simply the baby's object, of sexuality

in object relations and subjectivity more generally, and of the social contexts and relations in which the mother-child dyad is embedded and through which it is partially constituted.

27. See Jane Flax "Multiples: On the Contemporary Politics of Subjectivity," in this volume; and my "Remembering the Selves: Is the Repressed Gendered?" *Michigan Quarterly* XXVI, 1 (Winter 1988): 92–110.

28. Gayle Rubin, "The Traffic in Women: Notes on a 'Political Economy' of Sex," in *Toward an Anthropology of Women*, edited by Rayna Rapp (Reiter) (New York: Monthly Review Press, 1975); Nancy Chodorow, *The Reproduction of Mothering* (Berkeley: University of California Press, 1978); Dorothy Dinnerstein, *The Mermaid and the Minotaur* (New York: Harper & Row, 1976). Juliet Mitchell's, *Psychoanalysis and Feminism* (New York: Pantheon, 1974) was important to me for her insistence that we could read Freud as a description rather than prescription of femininity under patriarchy. However, I did not find persuasive her adoption of Althuser's economic determinism in the "last instance" and her dual systems approach (Freud and Lacan for the ideological superstructure; Marx for the material base). See Jane Flax, "Juliet Mitchell," in *The Routledge Dictionary of Twentieth Century Political Thinkers*, edited by Robert Benewick and Philip Green (London: Routledge, 1992).

29. In addition to Chodorow, Rubin, and Dinnerstein, the following works have been particularly helpful to me: Jessica Benjamin, *The Bonds of Love* (New York: Pantheon, 1988); Hazel Carby, *Reconstructing Woman: The Emergence of the Afro-American Woman Novelist* (New York: Oxford, 1987); Madelon Sprengnether, *The Spectral Mother: Freud, Feminism, and Psychoanalysis* (Ithaca: Cornell University Press, 1990); Patricia J. Williams, *The Alchemy of Race and Rights* (Cambridge: Harvard University Press, 1991); Micheline R. Malson et al., eds., *Black Women in America* (Chicago: Chicago University Press, 1988); Michelle Zimbalist Rosaldo and Louise Lamphere, eds., *Women, Culture & Society* (Stanford: Stanford University Press, 1974); and Barbara Smith, ed., *Home Girls: A Back Feminist Anthology* (New York: Kitchen Table Press, 1983). I'll turn to the raced context of this language later.

30. Jane Flax, "The Conflict between Nuturance and Autonomy and its Consequences for Feminism and Anti-Feminism," *Feminist Studies* 4, 2(June 1978): 171–189; and later, my *Thinking Fragments*, ch. 5; and "Mothers and Daughters Revisited," in this volume.

31. See my "Mothers and Daughters Revisited," and "The End of Innocence," both in this volume.

32. See especially D. W. Winnicott, "Hate in the Countertransference," in *Through Paediatrics*. I am thinking in particular of the work of Carol Gilligan, *In a Different Voice* (Cambridge: Harvard University Press, 1982); Jean Baker Miller, *Toward a New Psychology of Women* (Boston: Beacon, 1976); and the Stone Center.

33.   I do not mean to denigrate other equally important points of inquiry. These
       include the construction of sexuality and heterosexuality, ethnicity, and the impor-
       tance of economic positions and access to material resources.

34.   I would have to rewrite "Object Relations, Political Theory and the Patriarchal
       Unconscious" today. The emphasis on gender as a determinant of thought is still
       productive, but I would apply this to feminist thought as well. While I believe
       there are realities out there that exceed and are never exactly captured by our
       thought about them, I would argue that the truth tests for our knowledge are prag-
       matic, not ocular ones. I would look at their consequences (which we can know
       only incompletely) and their utility for specific purposes at specific times for spe-
       cific groups. Since we cannot directly apprehend the real apart from a particular
       description of it, it is useless to try to rank or evaluate knowledges according to
       how accurately they "mirror" the real. I am particularly grateful to Nancy Hartsock
       and Sandra Harding for our ongoing productive disagreements on standpoint theo-
       ries, knowledge, and politics. See Nancy Hartsock, *Money, Sex and Power* (Boston:
       Northeastern University Press, 1985); Sandra Harding, *The Science Question in
       Feminism* (Ithaca: Cornell University Press, 1986); and her *Whose Science? Whose
       Knowledge?* (Ithaca: Cornell University Press, 1991).

35.   I develop these arguments in "Postmodernism and Gender Relations in Feminist
       Theory," *Signs* 12, 4 (Summer 1987): 621–643; "Reply to Tress," *Signs* 14,
       1(Autumn 1988): 201–203; "The End of Innocence"; "The Play of Justice"; and
       "What is Enlightenment."

36.   Simone de Beauvoir, *The Second Sex* (New York: Knopf, 1953); Monique Wittig,
       "One is Not Born a Woman," *Feminist Issues* 1, 2(1981): 47–68. Recent essays by
       Linda Zerilli have stimulated me to clarify my thinking about gender. See Linda
       Zerilli, "Rememoration or War? French Feminist Narrative and the Politics of Self-
       Representation," *differences* 3, 1(1991): 1–19; and her "I am a Woman: Female Voice
       and Ambiguity in *The Second Sex,*" *Women and Politics* 11, 1(1991): 93–107.

37.   Thomas Laqueur, *Making Sex: Body and Gender from the Greeks to Freud* (Cambridge:
       Harvard Univeristy Press, 1990); and Donna Haraway, *Primate Visions: Gender,
       Race, and Nature in the World of Modern Science* (New York: Routledge, 1989) make
       it clear that sex, nature, biology, and gender are mutually constituting categories
       that express and enter into the regulation of social life. Whatever "nature" might
       be in itself, we can know it only as we construct it through vocabularies laden with
       social relations, political purposes, and moral commitments.

38.   Evelyn Brooks Higginbotham, "African-American Women's History and the Meta-
       language of Race," *Signs* 17, 2 (Winter 1–92): 251–276 recently made this point
       with particular force.

39.   Four collections of essays have recently been particularly helpful to me in thinking
       about these complex relationships: those in Henry Louis Gates, Jr.; in Chandra T.
       Mohanty, Ann Russo, and Lourdes Torres; Judith Butler and Joan W. Scott; and

Abdul R. JanMohamed and David Lloyd, eds. *The Nature and Context of Minority Discourses* (New York: Oxford University Press, 1990).

40. Christine Overall traces the construction of this binary pair in "What's Wrong with Prostitution? Evaluating Sex Work," *Signs* 17, 4 (Summer 1992): 705–724.

41. The recent debates over the proper subject of feminist discourse are productively discussed in Kathy F. Ferguson, "Interpretation and Genealogy in Feminism," *Signs* 16, 2 (Winter 1991): 322–339; Brown, "What has Happened Here?"; Nancy A. Hewitt, "Compounding Differences," *Feminist Studies* 18, 2(Summer 1992): 313–326; Rosi Braidotti, *Patterns of Dissonance* (New York: Routledge, 1991); and the essays in Butler and Scott.

42. In Immanuel Kant, *Foundations of the Metaphysics of Morals* (Indianapolis: Bobbs Merrill, 1959) this takes the form of the categorical imperative; in Jean Jacques Rousseau, *The Social Contract* (New York: Penguin, 1968), the general will; in John Rawls, *A Theory of Justice* (Cambridge: Harvard University Press, 1971), the two principles of justice; and in Habermas, the ideal speech situation.

43. My disagreement here does not rest on an assumption that all ways of life ought to be given equal weight or can be incorporated into a particular society. Rather, I object to the claim of neutrality or universality and to the lack of recognition of and taking responsibility for the necessary suppression or exclusion of certain ways of life.

44. See Catharine A. MacKinnon, *Feminism Unmodified* (Cambridge: Harvard University Press, 1987), especially the introduction. I discuss these claims in more detail in "Mothers and Daughters Revisited."

45. Michel Foucault, *The History of Sexuality*, v. 1 (New York: Vintage, 1980).

46. The number of important exceptions to this claim is growing rapidly. Among the ones that have been most helpful to me are: Di Stephano; Laqueur; Wendy Brown, *Manhood and Politics* (Totowa, NJ: Roman & Littlefield, 1988); Hanna Fenichel Pitkin, *Fortune is a Woman: Gender and Politics in the Thought of Niccolo Machiavelli* (Berkeley: University of California Press, 1984); Luce Irigaray, *Speculum of the Other Woman* (Ithaca: Cornell University Press, 1985); Catherine Clement, *The Lives and Legends of Jacques Lacan* (New York: Columbia University Press, 1983) Carole Pateman, *The Sexual Contract* (Stanford: Stanford University Press, 1988); Joan Landes, *Women and the Public Sphere in the Age of the French Revolution* (Ithaca: Cornell University Press, 1988); Evelyn Fox Keller, *Reflections on Gender and Science* (New Haven: Yale University Press, 1985); Janet Adelman, *Suffocating Mothers: Fantasies of Maternal Origin in Shakespeare's Plays, Hamlet to the Tempest* (New York: Routledge, 1992); and Linda Zerilli,*Woman in Political Theory Discourse: Agent of Culture and Chaos* (Madison: University of Wisconsin Press, 1992).

47. Judith Butler, *Gender Trouble: Feminism and the Subversion of Identity* (New York: Routledge, 1990).

48. Walter Benjamin,"Theses on the Philosophy of History" in his *Illuminations* (New York: Schocken, 1969), 225. Later in this same essay, Benjamin writes (p. 257–258): "This is how one pictures the angel of history. His face is turned toward the past. Where we perceive a chain of events, he sees one single catastrophe which keeps piling wreckage upon wreckage and hurls it in front of his feet. . . . The storm irresistibly propels him into the future to which his back is turned, while the pile of debris before him grows skyward. This storm is what we call progress."

49. Jurgen Habermas, *The Philosophical Discourse of Modernity* (Cambridge: MIT Press, 1987); Peter Sloterdik, *Critique of Cynical Reason* (Minneapolis: University of Minnesota Press, 1987).

50. Richard Rorty, *Philosophy and the Mirror of Nature* (Princeton: Princeton University Press, 1979); Jean-Francois Lyotard, *The Postmodern Condition: A Report on Knowledge* (Minneapolis: University of Minnesota Press, 1984). Recently I have been struggling to do justice to the radical difference of Foucault's ideas about power and the state. See especially the essays in Graham Burchell, Colin Gordon, and Peter Miller.

51. I discuss these claims in my "The End of Innocence," in this volume, and "Reply to Tress," *Signs* 14, 1 (Autumn 1988).

52. For a more detailed discussion of my views of better political practices, see "'What is Enlightenment'"; and "The Play of Justice," in this volume.

53. Contrary to the claims of Habermas or John Rawls. Foucault and Stuart Hampshire, *Innocence and Experience* (Cambridge: Harvard University Press, 1989) have been major influences on my recent thinking about politics.

54. Theodor Adorno, *Negative Dialectics* (New York: Seabury, 1979), 364: "The guilt of a life which purely as a fact will strangle other life according to statistics that eke out an overwhelming number of killed with a minimal number of rescued, as if this were provided in the theory of probabilities—this guilt is irreconcilable with living. And the guilt does not cease to reproduce itself, because not for an instant can it be made fully presently conscious. This, nothing else, is what compels us to philosophize."

Final Analysis

1. The definition of psychoanalysis is highly contested and ambiguous. Consider, for example, the range of opinion among the following analysts: Charles Brenner, *An Elementary Textbook of Psychoanalysis* (Garden City, NY: Anchor, 1955); Nancy J. Chodorow, *Feminism and Psychoanalytic Theory* (New Haven: Yale University Press, 1989); W. Ronald D. Fairbairn, *Psychoanalytic Studies of the Personality* (London:

Routledge & Kegan Paul, 1952); Anna Freud, *The Ego and the Mechanisms of Defense* (New York: International Universities Press, 1966); Arnold Goldberg, *The Prisonhouse of Psychoanalysis* (Hillsdale, NJ: Analytic Press, 1990); Otto Kernberg, *Borderline Conditions and Pathological Narcissism* (New York; Jason Aronson, 1975); Melanie Klein, *Love, Guilt and Reparation* (New York: Delta, 1975); Heinz Kohut, *How Does Analysis Cure?* (Chicago: University of Chicago Press, 1984); Jacques Lacan, *The Four Fundamental Concepts of Psychoanalysis* (New York: W. W. Norton, 1973); Ronald Langs/Leo Stone, *The Therapeutic Experience and Its Setting* (New York: Jason Aronson, 1980); Rudolph M. Lowenstein et al., *Psychoanalysis—A General Psychology* (New York: International Universities Press, 1966); Roy Schafer, *The Analytic Attitude* (New York: Basic Books, 1983); Donald P. Spence, *Narrative Truth and Historical Truth* (New York: W. W. Norton, 1982); Harry Stack Sullivan, *The Interpersonal Theory of Psychiatry* (New York: W. W. Norton, 1953); and D. W. Winnicott, *Psychoanalytic Explorations* (Cambridge: Harvard University Press, 1989). Most of these authors address the question of the scientific status of psychoanalysis. On this question, see also Adolf Grunbaum, "Epistemological Liabilities of the Clinical Appraisal of Psychoanalytic Theory," *Nous* XIV, 3 (September 1980); 307–386; Marshall Edelson, *Hypothesis and Evidence in Psychoanalysis* (Chicago: University of Chicago Press, 1984); and Jane Flax, "Psychoanalysis and the Philosophy of Science: Critique or Resistance?," *Journal of Philosophy*, LXXVIII, 10(October 1981): 561-569.

2.   Michel Foucault, "Truth and Power," in Michel Foucault, *Power/Knowledge* (New York: Pantheon, 1980), 119.

3.   Michel Foucault, "Revolutionary Action: 'Until Now,'" in Michel Foucault, *Language, Countermemory, Practice* (Ithaca: Cornell University Press, 1977), 221–222.

4.   Max Weber also stresses the importance of legitimation schemes. His work is an important complement to Foucault's. See especially Max Weber, "Politics as a Vocation;" and "Science as a Vocation," both in *From Max Weber*, edited by H. H. Gerth and C. Wright Mills (New York: Oxford University Press, 1958).

5.   I discuss this in more detail in Jane Flax, *Thinking Fragments* (Berkeley: University of California Press, 1990), ch. 3.

6.   Thomas Kuhn, in *The Structure of Scientific Revolutions* (Chicago: University of Chicago Press, l962), is one of the first writers to question this set of assumptions. His work suggests that the "success" of science is a consequence of certain practices adopted by historically specific scientific communities.

7.   Kenneth R. Hoover, *The Elements of Social Science Thinking*, 4th ed. (New York: St. Martins, 1988), 3–4.

8.   This pattern recurs throughout the history of psychoanalysis. Instances include Freud's battles with former disciples such as Adler or Jung, "the controversial dis-

cussions" in England from 1942 to 1944, and the recent struggles in France and in the International Psychoanalytic Association over Lacan and subsequently among Lacanians themselves. See Peter Gay, *Freud: A Life For Our Time* (New York: W. W. Norton, 1988); Phyllis Grosskurth, *Melaine Klein: Her World and Her Work* (New York: Knopf, 1986); Sherry Turkle, *Psychoanalytic Politics: Freud's French Revolution* (Cambridge: MIT Press, 1981); and Catherine Clement, *The Lives and Legends of Jacques Lacan* (New York: Columbia University Press, 1983).

9. The term *postmodernist* is controversial and ill-defined. I have discussed it extensively in my *Thinking Fragments* (Berkeley: University of California Press, 1990). My account here includes a probably misleading condensation of some of the ideas of Michel Foucault, Jacques Derrida, Jean-Francois Lyotard and Richard Rorty.

10. When philosophers such as Adolf Grunbaum evaluate the epistemological liabilities or scientific status of psychoanalysis without paying attention to or giving a justification of the warrant for their own practices, they operate within this discourse.

11. On this point, see Jacques Derrida, "Violence and Metaphysics," in his *Writing and Difference* (Chicago: University of Chicago Press, 1978); and Richard Rorty, *Philosophy and the Mirror of Nature* (Princeton: Princeton University Press, 1979).

12. Spence and Schafer are among the most important advocates of hermeneutic approaches in psychoanalysis. For an example from philosophy see Hans-Georg Gadamer, *Truth and Method* (New York: Crossroad Publishing, 1984).

13. On what a postmodernist philosopher might do, see the essays in *The Institution of Philosophy*, edited by Avner Cohen and Marcelo Dascal (La Salle, Ill: Open Court, 1989); *After Philosophy: End or Transformation*, edited by Kenneth Baynes, James Bohman, and Thomas McCarthy (Cambridge: MIT Press, 1987); Rorty, ch. 8; Richard Rorty, *Consequences of Pragmatism* (Minneapolis: University of Minnesota Press, 1982); Jacques Derrida, *Positions* (Chicago: University of Chicago Press, 1981); Michel Foucault, *Politics, Philosophy, Culture* (New York: Routledge, 1988); and Nancy Fraser, *Unruly Practices: Power, Discourse and Gender in Contemporary Social Theory* (Minneapolis: University of Minnesota Press, 1989).

14. See the essays in *Gender/Body/Knowledge*, edited by Alison M. Jaggar and Susan R. Bordo (New Brunswick: Rutgers University Press, 1989); *Feminist Challenges: Social and Political Theory*, edited by Carole Pateman and Elizabeth Gross (Boston: Northeastern Press, 1986); *Third World Women and the Politics of Feminism*, edited by Chandra Talpade Mohanty, Ann Russo, and Lourdes Torres (Bloomington: Indiana University Press, 1991); and *Feminists Theorize the Political*, edited by Judith Butler and Joan Scott (New York: Routledge, 1992).

15. Especially the work of Nancy Chodorow, *The Reproduction of Mothering* (Berkeley: University of California Press, 1978); Dorothy Dinnerstein, *The Mermaid and the Minotaur* (New York: Harper and Row, 1976); and Irene Fast, *Gender Identity: A Differentiation Model* (Hillsdale: Analytic Press, 1984). Many psychoanalysts contin-

ue to ignore this work, or it is marginalized as having relevance solely to an understanding of the psychology of women. For example, despite the title of his recent book, Stephen A. Mitchell, *Relational Concepts in Psychoanalysis* (Cambridge: Harvard University Press, 1988) mentions none of these authors. He (as is common with many analysts) does not discuss gender as a crucial social relation in the constitution of modern subjectivity. Object relations theory has many other gender biases. On this point see Flax, pp. 120–126.

16. I discuss some of the difficulties in mother-daughter relations and their consequences for women's subjectivities in "The Conflict between Nurturance and Autonomy," *"Feminist Studies* 4,2 (June 1978): 171–189; and "Mothers and Daughters Revisited," in this volume.

17. Sigmund Freud, *The Ego and the Id* (New York: W. W. Norton, 1960); Melanie Klein, "Early Stages of the Oedipus Conflict," in *Love, Guilt and Reparation*; D. W. Winnicott, *Playing and Reality* (New York: Basic Books, 1971); and D. W. Winnicott, "Mind and its Relation to Psyche-Soma," in his *Through Paediatrics to Psycho-Analysis* (New York: Basic Books, 1975).

18. Cf. the discussion of the bodily ego in Sigmund Freud, "The Unconscious," in *Collected Papers*, v. 4, edited by James Strachey (New York: Basic Books, 1959).

19. Sigmund Freud, "Analysis Terminable and Interminable," *Collected Papers*, v. 5 (New York: Basic Books, 1959), 353.

20. Freud, *The Ego and the Id*, p. 46.

21. Michel Foucault, *The History of Sexuality*, *Volume I, An Introduction* (New York: Vintage, 1980), especially part 5.

22. Michel Foucault, "Truth and Power," in his *Power/Knowledge*; and Michel Foucault, *History of Sexuality*.

23. For example, Sigmund Freud, *Three Essays on the Theory of Sexuality* (New York: Basic Books, 1975) is an exemplar of ambiguity. It would be quite revealing to track the eruptions of tensions and multiple definitions of crucial terms throughout this text.

Forgotten Forms of Close Combat

1. See, for example, Wendy Brown, *Manhood and Politics: A Feminist Reading in Political Theory* (Totowa: Rowman & Littlefield, 1988); Sandra Harding and Merrill Hintikka, eds., *Discovering Reality: Feminist Perspectives on Epistemology, Metaphysics, Methodology, and the Philosophy of Science* (Boston: D. Reidel, 1983); Hanna Fenichel Pitkin, *Fortune is a Woman: Gender & Politics in the Thought of Niccolo Machiavelli* (Berkeley: University of California Press, 1984); and Gayatri Chakravorty Spivak,

"Feminism and Deconstruction Again: Negotiating with Unacknowledged Masculinism," in *Between Feminism & Psychoanalysis*, edited by Teresa Brennan (New York: Routledge, 1989).

2.   Jane Flax, *Thinking Fragments: Psychoanalysis, Feminism and Postmodernism in the Contemporary West* (Berkeley: University of California Press, 1990), 73–88; Coppelia Kahn, "The Hand that Rocks the Cradle: Recent Gender Theories and Their Implications," in *The Mother Tongue: Essays in Feminist Psychoanalytic Interpretation*, edited by Shirley Nelson Garner, Claire Kahane, and Madelon Sprengnether (Ithaca: Cornell University Press, 1985); and Madelon Sprengnether, *The Spectral Mother: Freud, Feminism and Psychoanalysis* (Ithaca: Cornell University Press, 1990).

3.   See, however, Elizabeth Abel, "Race, Class and Psychoanalysis? Opening Questions," in *Conflicts in Feminism*, edited by Marianne Hirsch and Evelyn Fox Keller (New York: Routledge, 1990); Patricia Boling, "The Democratic Potential of Mothering," *Political Theory* 19, 4 (November 1991): 606–625; Nancy Chodorow with Susan Contratto, "The Fantasy of the Perfect Mother," in Nancy Chodorow, *Feminism and Psychoanalytic Theory* (New Haven: Yale University Press, 1989); Hilary Manette Klein, "Marxism, Psychoanalysis, and Mother Nature," *Feminist Studies* 15, 2 (Summer 1989): 255–278; Domna Stanton, "Difference on Trial: A Critique of the Maternal Metaphor in Cixous, Irigaray and Kristeva," in *The Thinking Muse: Feminism and Modern French Philosophy*, edited by Jeffner Allen and Iris M. Young (Bloomington: Indiana University Press, 1989); Susan Suleiman, "Writing and Motherhood," in Garner, Kahane and Sprengnether, *The Mother Tongue*, (Ithaca: Cornell University Press, 1985).

4.   Dorothy Dinnerstein, *The Mermaid and the Minotaur: Sexual Arrangements and Human Malaise* (New York: Harper & Row, 1976).

5.   See Kristeva; and Iris Young, "Breasted Experience: The Look and the Feeling," in Iris Young, *Throwing Like a Girl and Other Essays in Feminist Philosophy and Social Theory* (Indianapolis: Indiana University Press, 1990).

6.   See especially Jessica Benjamin, *The Bonds of Love: Psychoanalysis, Feminism and the Problem of Domination* (New York: Pantheon, 1988); Dinnerstein, *The Mermaid and the Minotaur: Sexual Arrangements and Human Malaise* (New York: Harper & Row, 1976); Melaine Klein, *Love, Guilt and Reparation and Other Works 1921–1945* (New York: Delta, 1975); and D. W. Winnicott, *Through Paediatrics to Psycho-Analysis* (New York: Basic Books, 1975).

7.   Susan Bordo, "Anorexia Nervosa: Psychopathology as the Crystallization of Culture," in *Feminism & Foucault: Reflections on Resistance*, edited by Irene Diamond and Lee Quinby (Boston: Northeastern University Press, 1988); Hilda Bruch, *The Golden Cage: The Enigma of Anorexia Nervosa* (New York: Vintage, 1978); Kim Chernin, *The Hungry Self: Women, Eating and Identity* (New York: Harper, 1985); Patricia Moran, "Unholy Meanings: Maternity, Creativity and Orality in Katherine

Mansfield," *Feminist Studies, 17*, 1 (Spring 1991): 105–126; and Susi Orbach, *Hunger Strike: The Anorectic's Struggle as a Metaphor for Our Age* (New York: Avon, 1986).

8. See Sigmund Freud, *Civilization and Its Discontents* (New York: W. W. Norton, 1961); and for contrary arguments, Michel Foucault, *The History of Sexuality, Volume 1: An Introduction* (New York: Vintage, 1980); *Michel Foucault: Politics, Philosophy, Culture: Interviews and Other Writings 1977–1984*, edited by Lawrence D. Kritzman (New York: Routledge, 1988); Judith Butler, *Gender Trouble: Feminism and the Subversion of Identity* (New York: Routledge, 1990); and Biddy Martin, "Feminism, Criticism, and Foucault," in Diamond and Quinby, (Boston: Northeastern University Press, 1988).

9. Despite her protests, I believe Carol Gilligan's *In a Different Voice: Psychological Theory and Women's Development* (Cambridge: Harvard University Press, 1982) reads like this; as do the essays in *Women and Moral Theory*, edited by Eva Feder Kittay and Diana T. Meyers (Totowa: Rowman & Littlefield, 1987); and Jean Baker Miller, *Toward a New Psychology of Women* (Boston: Beacon, 1976).

10. For example, in Sara Ruddick's influential "Maternal Thinking," reprinted in *Mothering: Essays in Feminist Thinking*, edited by Joyce Trebilcot (Totowa: Rowman & Littlefield, 1984), sexuality is not discussed as an aspect of maternal practices.

11. Gayle Rubin, "The Traffic in Women: Notes on the 'Political Economy' of Sex," in *Toward an Anthropology of Women*, edited by Rayna Reiter (New York: Monthly Review Press, 1975); see also Shane Phelan, "Feminism and Individualism," *Women and Politics* 10, 4 (Summer 1991): 1–18.

12. Rosi Braidotti, *Patterns of Dissonance* (New York: Routledge, 1991), and the essays in *Gender/Body/Knowledge: Feminist Reconstructions of Being and Knowing*, edited by Alison M. Jaggar and Susan R. Bordo (Rutgers, NJ: Rutgers University Press, 1989) develop these themes.

13. Such fantasies play a part in the "sexuality debates" among feminists. See Carla Freccero, "Notes of a Post–Sex Wars Theorizer," and Teresa de Lauretis, "Upping the Anti *(sic)* in Feminist Theory," in Hirsch and Keller, eds., *Conflicts in Feminism*, (New York: Routledge, 1990) ; and Mariana Valverde, "Beyond Gender Dangers and Private Pleasure: Theory and Ethics in the Sex Debates," *Feminist Studies* 15, 2 (Summer 1989): 237–254.

14. Victimization is stressed by Catherine MacKinnon in *Feminism Unmodified: Discourse on Life and Law* (Cambridge: Harvard University Press, 1987); merger in Luce Irigaray, *This Sex Which Is Not One* (Ithaca: Cornell University Press, 1985).

15. Sara Ruddick, "Maternal Thinking," and "Preservative Love and Military Destruction: Some Reflections on Mothering and Peace," in Trebilcot, ed., *Mothering* (Totowa: Rowman & Littlefield). For a partial reconsideration, see Sara Ruddick, "Remarks on the Sexual Politics of Reason," in Kittay and Meyer, eds. *Women and Moral Theory* (Totowa: Rowman & Allenheld, 1987).

16.   Adrienne Rich, "Compulsory Heterosexuality and Lesbian Existence," *Signs* 5, 4 (Summer 1980): 515–544.

17.   But see Abel, "Race. Class amd Psychoanalysis?" in Hirsch and Keller, eds., *Conflicts in Feminism* (New York: Routledge, 1990); Audre Lordre, *Sister Outsider* (Trumansburg, NY: Crossing Press, 1984); *Third World Women and the Politics of Feminism*, edited by Chandra Talpade Mohanty, Ann Russo, and Lourdes Torres (Bloomington: Indiana University Press, 1991); Evelyn Brooks Higginbotham, "African-American Women's History and the Metalanguage of Race," *Signs* 17, 2(Winter 1992): 251–274; Barbara Smith, "Introduction," in *Home Girls: A Black Feminist Anthology*, edited by Barbara Smith (New York: Kitchen Table Press, 1983); and Patricia J. Williams, *The Alchemy of Race and Rights* (Cambridge: Harvard University Press, 1991).

18.   For more extensive critiques, see Deborah K. King, "Multiple Jeopardy, Multiple Consciousness: The Context of a Black Feminist Ideology," in *Black Women in America: Social Science Perspectives*, edited by Micheline R. Malson, et al. (Chicago: University of Chicago Press, 1990); and Elizabeth V. Spelman, *Inessential Woman: Problems of Exclusion in Feminist Thought* (Boston: Beacon, 1988).

19.   Patricia Hill Collins, *Black Feminist Thought* (New York: Routledge, 1991); Angela Y. Davis, *Women, Race & Class* (New York: Random House, 1981); Bonnie Thornton Dill, "The Dialectics of Black Womanhood," and Diane Lewis, "A Response to Inequality: Black Women, Racism and Sexism," in Malson, et al., eds., *Black Women in America* (Chicago: University of Chicago Press, 1990).

20.   Hazel V. Carby, "'On the Threshold of Women's Era': Lynching, Empire and Sexuality in Black Feminist Theory," in *"Race," Writing and Difference*, edited by Henry Louis Gates (Chicago: University of Chicago Press, 1985); and Jacquelyn Dowd Hall, "'The Mind That Burns in Each Body': Women, Rape and Racial Violence," Barbara Omolade, "Hearts of Darkness," and Rennie Simson, "The Afro-American Female: The Historical Context of the Construction of Sexual Identity," in Ann Snitow, Christine Stansell and Sharon Thompson, eds., *Powers of Desire: The Politics of Sexuality* (New York: Monthly Review Press, 1983).

21.   Carole Pateman, *The Sexual Contract* (Stanford: Stanford University Press, 1988).

22.   See also Eldridge Cleaver, *Soul on Ice* (New York: Dell, 1968); Bell Hooks, *Yearning: Race, Gender, and Cultural Politics* (Boston: South End Press, 1990); Alice Walker, *In Search of Our Mothers' Gardens: Womanist Prose* (New York: Harcourt Brace Jovanovich, 1983), especially pp. 271–338; and Michele Wallace, *Black Macho and the Myth of the Superwoman* (New York: Dial, 1978).

23.   Julia Kristeva,"Sabat Matter," in the *The Female Body in Western Culture: Contemporary Perspectives*, edited by Susan Rubin Suleiman (Cambridge: Harvard University Press, 1985), 117–118.

24.   Biddy Martin and Chandra Talpade Mohanty, "Feminist Politics: What's Home Got

To Do With It?" in *Feminist Studies/Critical Studies*, edited by Teresa de Lauretis (Bloomington: Indiana University Press, 1986).

Is Enlightenment Emancipatory?

1. The spectrum might include: Jurgen Habermas, *The Philosophical Discourse of Modernity* (Cambridge: MIT Press, 1987); Richard Bernstein, ed., *Habermas and Modernity* (Cambridge: MIT Press, 1985); Peter Dews, *Habermas: Autonomy & Solidarity* (London: verso, 1986); Nancy Fraser, *Unruly Practices: Power, Discourse and Gender in Contemporary Political Theory* (Minneapolis: University of Minnesota Press, 1989); Linda F. Nicolson, ed., *Feminism/Postmodernism* (New York: Routledge, 1990); Jean-Francois Lyotard, *The Postmodern Condition: A Report on Knowledge* (Minneapolis: University of Minnesota Press, 1984); Michel Foucault, *Power/Knowledge* (New York: Pantheon, 1980); and *The Foucault Effect: Studies in Governmentality*, edited by Graham Burchell, Colin Gordon, and Peter Miller (Chicago: University of Chicago Press, 1991).

2. Immanuel Kant, "What is Enlightenment?," with *Foundations of the Metaphysics of Morals* (Indianapolis: Bobbs Merrill, 1959), 85. My reading of Kant, especially the attention to its antinomies has been deeply influenced by Georg Lukacs, "Reification and the Consciousness of the Proletariat," in his *History and Class Consciousness* (Cambridge: MIT Press, 1968), even though my analysis of these splits is quite different from his.

3. Immanuel Kant, "What Is Enlightenment?" (Indianapolis: Bobbs Merrill, 1959), 85.

4. Sigmund Freud, *Civilization and Its Discontents* (New York: W. W. Norton, 1962); Jacques Lacan, *Four Fundamental Concepts of Psychoanalysis* (New York: W. W. Norton, 1978). Lacan differs from Kant and Freud in that his subject has almost no capacity or scope for autonomy or self-determination. However, his story is like theirs in positing a split between "precultural" maternal love and the demands of civilization (Law of the Father).

5. Immanuel Kant, "What Is Enlightenment?" (Indianapolis: Bobbs Merrill, 1959), 86.

6. Ibid., 85–86.

7. Ibid., 86.

8. Ibid., 86. This language is similar to the description of the Legislator in Jean Jacques Rousseau's *On the Social Contract* (New York: St. Martins, 1978), especially pp. 67–71. Tutelage and guardianship also play a central role in Rousseau's *Emile or On Education* (New York; Basic Books, 1979).

9. Immanuel Kant, "What Is Enlightenment?" (Indianapolis: Bobbs Merrill, 1959), 86. Likewise in Freud's account of the individual boy's oedipal crisis, the father is incorporated, not overthrown. In his story of the origin of the state, rule of the brothers replaces patriarchy (rule of a father). See Sigmund Freud, *Totem and Taboo* (New York: W. W. Norton, 1950).

10. Immanuel Kant, "What Is Enlightenment?" (Indianapolis: Bobbs Merrill, 1959), 86–87.

11. Sigmund Freud, *Civilization and Its Discontents* (New York: W. W. Norton, 1962), 50–51. Freud's story about the conflict between love and the demands of civilization is similar to Jean Jacques Rousseau's in his *Discourse On the Origins and Foundations of Inequality* (New York: St. Martins, 1964), especially 142–152.

12. Gayle Rubin, "The Traffic in Women: Notes on the 'Political Economy' of Sex," in *Toward an Anthropology of Women*, edited by Rayna Reiter (New York: Monthly Review Press, 1975); Carole Pateman, *The Sexual Contract* (Stanford: Stanford University Press, 1988).

13. Susan Moller Okin, *Gender, Justice and the Family* (New York; Basic Books, 1989); Joan Landes, *Women and the Public Sphere* (Ithaca: Cornell University Press, 1989).

14. Immanuel Kant, "What Is Enlightenment?" (Indianapolis: Bobbs Merrill, 1959), 87.

15. Jurgen Habermas, *Knowledge and Human Interests* (Boston: Beacon, 1971); and his *Philosophical Discourse of Modernity*.

16. As Sigmund Freud, in *The Ego and the Id* (New York: W. W. Norton, 1962), and Michel Foucault, in *Politics, Philosophy, Culture* (New York: Routledge, 1990) later point out.

17. Immanuel Kant, "What Is Enlightenment?" (Indianapolis: Bobbs Merrill, 1959), 87.

18. Ibid., p. 87.

19. Max Weber, "Politics as a Vocation," and "Science as a Vocation," in *From Max Weber*, edited by H.H. Gerth and C. Wright Mills (New York: Oxford University Press, 1958).

20. Immanuel Kant, "What Is Enlightenment?" (Indianapolis: Bobbs Merrill, 1959), 88.

21. Ibid., p.88.

22. Ibid., p.87.

23. Ibid., p.89.

24. Ibid., p. 91.

25. Ibid., p. 91.

26. Ibid., p. 92.

27. Ibid., p. 92.

28. Ibid., p. 92. Freud and Foucault later elaborate this point.

29. Ibid., p. 92.

30. I say "he" here, because in Kant's view women's reason is too deficient ever to develop in this way. As in Rousseau's account, the inclusion of women into citizenship would pollute public rationality and ultimately destroy it.

31. Jane Flax, *Thinking Fragments: Psychoanalysis, Feminism and Postmodernism in the Contemporary West* (Berkeley: University of California Press, 1990), part 2; Sigmund Freud, *The Ego and the Id* (New York: W.W. Norton, 1962); D. W. Winnicott, "Mind and Its Relation to the Psyche-Soma," in his *Through Paediatrics to Psycho-Analysis* (New York: Basic Books, 1975); and Daniel N. Stern, *The Interpersonal World of the Infant* (New York: Basic Books, 1985).

32. Julia Kristeva, "Women's Time," *Signs* 11, 4(Summer 1981); 13–35; Luce Irigaray, *This Sex Which Is Not One* (Ithaca: Cornell University Press, 1985); Alice A. Jardine, *Gynesis: Configurations of Women and Modernity* (Ithaca: Cornell University Press, 1985); Kathy E. Ferguson, *The Feminist Case Against Bureaucracy* (Philadelphia: Temple University Press, 1984); Agnes Heller and Ferenc Feher, *The Postmodern Political Condition* (New York: Columbia University Press, 1989); and Kathy E. Ferguson, "Interpretation and Genealogy in Feminism," *Signs* 16, 2 (Winter 1991); 322–339.

33. See the essays in *Gender/Body/Knowledge*, edited by Alison M. Jaggar and Susan R. Bordo (New Brunswick, NJ: Rutgers University Press, 1989); Luce Irigaray, *Speculum of the Other Woman* (Ithaca: Cornell University Press, 1985); and Michele Le Doeuff, "Women and Philosophy," in *French Feminist Thought: A Reader*, edited by Toril Moi (New York: Basil Blackwell, 1987).

34. Alison M. Jaggar and Susan R. Bordo, eds., *Gender/Body/Knowledge* (New Brunswick: Rutgers University Press, 1989); Carole Pateman and Elizabeth Gross, eds., *Feminist Challenges: Social and Political Theory* (Boston: Northeastern University Press, 1986); Irigaray, *Speculum of the Other Woman* (Ithaca: Cornell University Press, 1985); Helene Cixous and Catherine Clement, *The Newly Born Woman* (Minneapolis: University of Minnesota Press, 1986); Morwena Griffiths and Margaret Whitford, eds., *Feminist Perspectives in Philosophy* (Bloomington: Indiana University Press, 1988).

35. See Jurgen Habermas, "Neoconservative Culture Criticism in the United States and West Germany: An Intellectual Movement in Two Political Cultures," in Bernstein, ed., *Habermas and Modernity* (Cambridge: MIT Press, 1985); Michel Foucault, "Truth and Power," in *Power/Knowledge* (New York: Pantheon, 1980); and Michel Foucault, "Critical Theory/Intellectual History," in his *Politics/Philosophy/Culture* (New York: Routledge, 1990).

36. Stuart Hampshire, *Innocence and Experience* (Cambridge: Harvard University Press, 1989).

37. This is a position shared by liberals such as Okin and classical feminist socialists.

38. This is the position of Irigary, Kristeva, and other writers, including Audre Lordre, *Sister Outsider* (Trumansburg: Crossing Press, 1984).

39. John Rawls, *A Theory of Justice* (Cambridge: Harvard University Press, 1970); Jurgen Habermas, *Communication and the Evolution of Society* (Boston: Beacon, 1979); and Habermas' *The Theory of Communicative Action*, v.2 (Boston: Beacon, 1989). See my "The Play of Justice," in this volume for an elaboration of this claim.

40. On this point, see Reiner Grundman and Christos Mantziaris, "Fundamentalist Intolerance or Civil Disobedience? Strange Loops in Liberal Theory," *Political Theory* 19, 4(November 1991); 572–605; and Martha C. Nussbaum, "Human Functioning and Social Justice: In Defense of Aristotelian Essentialism," *Political Theory* 20, 2 (May 1992); 202–246.

41. Nancy Fraser, "Rethinking the Public Sphere: A Contribution to the Critique of Actually Existing Democracy," in *Postmodernism and the Re-Reading of Modernity*, edited by Francis Barker, Peter Hulme, and Margaret Iverson (Manchester: Manchester University Press, 1992).

42. I owe this line of thinking to Sarah M. Shumer, "Machiavelli's Republican Politics and its Corruption," *Political Theory* 7, 1(February 1979); 5–34; and J. Peter Euben, *The Tragedy of Political Theory: The Road Not Taken* (Princeton: Princeton University Press, 1990).

43. As Carole Pateman discusses in *The Disorder of Women: Democracy, Feminism and Political Theory* (Stanford: Stanford University Press, 1989).

44. Gila J. Hayim, "Naturalism and the Crisis of Rationalism in Habermas," *Social Theory and Practice* 18, 2 (Summer 1992); 187–209, traces some of the ecological consequences of Habermas' attachment to Enlightenment metanarrative. He accepts its characterization of the rationality and neutrality of the "system" (of technology, science, and instrumental rationality). Hence he cannot understand social movements like the Greens or some of the interactions between system and life world. He also is blind to some of the relations of domination and emancipatory possibilities within the system as well as within the life world.

45. Charles Taylor, *Sources of the Self: The Making of Modern Identity* (Cambridge: Harvard University Press, 1989).

Multiples

1. Participants in debates over subjectivity and emancipation include Nancy Hartsock, "Foucault on Power: A Theory for Women," in *Feminism/Postmodernism*, edited by

Linda Nicholson (New York: Routledge, 1990), and her "Rethinking Modernism: Minority vs. Majority Theories," in *The Nature and Context of Minority Discourse*, edited by Abdul R. JanMohamed and David Lloyd (New York: Oxford, 1990); Patricia Hill Collins, *Black Feminist Thought: Knowledge, Consciousness, and the Politics of Empowerment* (New York: Routledge, 1990); Judith Butler, *Gender Trouble: Feminism and the Subversion of Identity* (New York: Routledge, 1990); Diana Fuss, *Essentially Speaking: Feminism, Nature and Difference* (New York: Routledge, 1989); Nancy Fraser, *Unruly Practices* (Minneapolis: University of Minnesota Press, 1989); Patricia J. Williams, *The Alchemy of Race and Rights* (Cambridge; Harvard University Press, 1991); and Mary E. Hawkesworth, "Knowers, Knowing Known: Feminist Theory and the Claims of Truth," in *Feminist Theory in Practice and Process*, edited by Micheline R. Malson, et al. (Chicago: University of Chicago Press, 1989).

2.   Immanuel Kant, "What is Enlightenment?" printed with *Foundations of the Metaphysics of Morals* (Indianapolis: Bobbs-Merrill, 1959); Jurgen Habermas, *The Philosophical Discourse of Modernity* (Cambridge: MIT Press, 1987); John Rawls, "A Kantian Conception of Equality," in *Post-Analytic Philosophy*, edited by John Rajchman and Cornel West (New York: Columbia University Press, 1985); and Richard J. Bernstein, ed., *Habermas and Modernity* (Cambridge; MIT Press, 1985).

3.   This is a problem endemic to any "stage" theory of human psychological/moral development; for example, Lawrence Kohlberg, *The Philosophy of Moral Development* (San Francisco: Harper & Row, 1981).   Carol Gilligan, *In a Different Voice: Psychological Theory and Women's Development* (Cambridge: Harvard University Press, 1982), is correct to criticize the gender bias of Kohlberg's theory.   However, she and researchers inspired by her work do not question the assumptions intrinsic to the creation and plausibility of most developmental theories including their own. They do not confront the exclusions of many forms of difference (not limited to gender) they necessarily entail.

4.   The essay by Luce Irigary, "The 'Mechanics' of Fluids," in her *This Sex Which Is Not One* (Ithaca: Cornell University Press); and Helene Cixous and Catherine Clement, *The Newly Born Woman* (Minneapolis: University of Minnesota, 1986) have greatly influenced my thinking about subjectivity.

5.   Rene Descartes, *Discourse On Method and Other Writings* (Baltimore: Penguin Books, 1970).

6.   Immanuel Kant, *Critique of Pure Reason* (Garden City: Anchor Books, 1966).

7.   On the concept of metanarrative, see Jean-François Lyotard, *The Postmodern Condition* (Minneapolis: University of Minnesota Press, 1984).   I discuss this term and the complex relationships of psychoanalysis, feminism, postmodernism, and Enlightenment projects in *Thinking Fragments: Psychoanalysis, Feminism and Postmodernism in the Contemporary West* (Berkeley: University of California Press, 1990).

8. Variants of this view include Rene Descartes; *Discourse on Method* (Baltimore; Penquin Books, 1970); Immanuel Kant; *Critique of Pure Reason* (Garden City: Anchor Books, 1966); Karl R. Popper, *Conjectures and Refutations: The Growth of Scientific Knowledge* (New York: Harper and Row 1965), especially chapter 10; and Leo Strauss, *Natural Right and History* (Chicago: University of Chicago Press, 1953).

9. Examples of empiricism include David Hume, *An Inquiry Concerning Human Understanding* (Indianapolis: Bobbs-Merrill, 1955); Rudolf Carnap, *The Logical Structure of the World & Pseudoproblems in Philosophy* (Berkeley: University of California Press, 1967); Kenneth R. Hoover, *The Elements of Social Scientific Thinking* (New York: St. Martins, 1988); and Marshall Edelson, *Hypothesis and Evidence in Psychoanalysis* (Chicago: University of Chicago Press, 1984).

10. See Harold Morick, ed., *Challenges to Empiricism* (Indianapolis: Hackett Publishing, 1980); Donald W. Fiske and Richard A Shweder, eds., *Metatheory in Social Science* (Chicago: University of Chicago Press, 1986); and the essays in John Rajchman and Cornel West, eds., *Post-Analytic Philosophy* (New York: Columbia University Press, 1985).

11. Sigmund Freud, *The Ego and the Id* (New York: W. W. Norton, 1960), and his *An Outline of Psychoanalysis* (New York: W. W. Norton, 1969); Jacques Lacan, *The Four Fundamental Concepts of Psychoanalysis* (New York: W. W. Norton, 1981).

12. Michel Foucault, *Politics, Philosophy and Culture* (New York: Routledge, 1988); Luther H. Martin, Huck Gutman and Patrick H. Hutton, eds., *Technologies of the Self* (Amherst: University of Massachusetts Press, 1988); Judith Butler; *Gender Trouble* (New York: Routledge, 1990); and Teresa de Lauretis, *Technologies of Gender* (Bloomington: Indiana University Press, 1987).

13. Recent work includes Paula Giddings, *When and Where I Enter: The Impact of Race and Sex in America* (New York: Bantam, 1985); Andrea Nye, *Feminist Theory and the Philosophies of Man* (New York: Routledge, 1988); Patricia Hill Collins, "The Social Construction of Black Feminist Thought," *Signs* 14, 4 (Summer 1989); 745–773; Trinh T. Minh-ha, *Woman/Native/Other* (Bloomington: Indiana University Press, 1989); Carole Pateman and Elizabeth Gross, eds., *Feminist Challenges: Social and Political Theory* (Boston: Northeastern University Press, 1986); Elizabeth V. Spelman, *Inessential Woman: Problems of Exclusion in Feminist Thought* (Boston: Beacon Press, 1988); Alison M. Jaggar and Susan R. Bordo, eds., *Gender/Body/Knowledge* (New Brunswick: Rutgers University Press, 1989); and Carol Gilligan, *In a Different Voice* (Cambridge: Harvard University Press, 1982).

14. This may seem obvious but the centrality of gendering in the constitution of modern Western subjects is often completely ignored, even by some of our most influential modern theorists. See, for example, John Rawls, "Kantian Constructivism in Moral Theory: The Dewey Lectures 1980," *Journal of Philosophy* 77, 9(September 1980); 512–572; Charles Taylor, *Sources of the Self: The Making of Modern Identity*

(Cambridge: Harvard University Press, 1989); and Michel Foucault, *The History of Sexuality*, vol. 1 (New York: Vintage, 1980).

15. Feminists have our own forms of attachment to this sort of subjectivity. I discuss some of these forms and their consequences in other essays in this volume. See especially "Minerva's Owl," and "The End of Innocence."

16. Cf. Susan Rubin Suleiman, ed., *The Female Body in Western Culture* (Cambridge: Harvard University Press, 1985); Bryan S. Turner, *The Body & Society* (New York: Basil Blackwell, 1989); and Michel Foucault, *The History of Sexuality*, v.1.

17. A current form of this problem is the debate over the relation between mind and brain. Cf. Steven Rose, *The Conscious Brain* (New York: Vintage, 1976); Daniel C. Dennett, *Consciousness Explained* (Boston: Little, Brown, 1991); and Gerald M. Edelman and Vernon B. Mountcastle, *The Mindful Brain* (Cambridge: MIT Press, 1982). On the other hand, object relations theorists such as Harry Guntrip in *Personality Structure and Human Interaction* (New York: International Universities Press, 1961) or self-psychologists like Heinz Kohut in *The Restoration of the Self* (New York: International Universities Press, 1977) give up too much in their attempts to correct a simple drive theory approach. They end up separating embodiment from the person and in Guntrip's case assigning the "person" to psychoanalysis and the body to medicine. This is useless since neither physicians nor psychoanalysts work with disembodied persons. For a psychoanalytic attempt to overcome the mind/body split, see D. W. Winnicott, *Human Nature* (New York: Schocken, 1988).

18. Freud struggles with the problems this approach causes. For example, in his *Three Essays on Sexuality* (New York: Basic, 1962), the footnotes and textual interpolations reveal the slippery and indistinct nature of the material he keeps trying to contain within categories such as anal, masculine, or normal. A different and equally problematic "stage theory" is employed by those such as James F. Masterson, *The Narcissistic and Borderline Disorders* (New York: Brunner/Mazel, 1981), who attempt to ground their diagnostic and treatment categories in concepts of separation-individuation, especially as developed by Margaret Mahler, in her *The Psychological Birth of the Human Infant* (New York: Basic, 1975).

19. See Jean-François Lyotard; *The Postmodern Condition* (Minneapolis: University of Minnesota Press, 1984); Jacques Derrida, "Violence and Metaphysics: An Essay on the Thought of Emmanuel Levinas," in his *Writing and Difference* (Chicago: University of Chicago Press, 1978); Gilles Deleuze and Felix Guattari, *Anti-Oedipus: Capitalism and Schizophrenia* (Minneapolis: University of Minnesota Press, 1983); and Foucault, *The History of Sexuality*.

20. D. W. Winnicott, *Through Paediatrics to Psycho-analysis* (New York: Basic, 1975), part 3; W. Ronald D. Fairbairn, *Psychoanalytic Studies of the Personality* (Boston: Routledge & Kegan Paul, 1981); and Harry Guntrip, *Schzoid Phenomena, Object Relations and the Self* (New York: International Universities Press, 1969).

21.   I discuss a borderline patient in "Re-Membering the Selves: Is the Repressed Gendered?" *Michigan Review* XXVI, l(Winter 1987); 92–110; see also Michael Stone, ed., *Essential Papers on Borderline Disorders* (New York: New York University Press, 1986); and Harold F. Searles, *My Work with Borderline Patients* (Northvale: Jason Aronson, 1986).

22.   While such beliefs may be comforting, they can also be dangerous politically and personally. Cf. Stuart Hampshire, *Innocence and Experience* (Cambridge; Harvard University Press, 1989).

23.   The privileging of narrative is a major problem in hermeneutic approaches to psychoanalysis. See, for example, Donald P. Spence in *Narrative Truth and Historical Truth* (New York: W. W. Norton, 1982); and Roy Schafer, *The Analytic Attitude* (New York: Basic Books, 1983).

24.   Mary G. Dietz, "Context is All: Feminism and Theories of Citizenship," in *Learning About Women: Gender, Politics, & Power*, edited by Jill K. Conway, et al. (Ann Arbor: University of Michigan Press, 1989); and Kathleen B. Jones, "Citizenship in a Woman-friendly Polity," *Signs* 15, 4 (Summer 1990): 781–812.

The Play of Justice

1.   Defenders of (a historicized essentialism) do not confront these costs. Even someone as insightful as Martha C. Nussbaum seems to miss these points in her defense of "Aristotelian" essentialism. The example she employs to defend the utility of essentialism shows its limits. The group of international development planners she discusses already shared a high degree of ethical consensus. What effect would such ideas have if the goal was to change the behavior of a dictator opposed to the planners' commitments? See Martha C. Nussbaum, "Human Functioning and Social Justice: In Defense of Aristotelian Essentialism," *Political Theory* 20, 2 (May 1992); 202–246.

2.   D. W. Winnicott, "Transitional Objects and Transitional Phenomena," in his *Playing and Reality* (New York: Basic Books, 1971).

3.   This is true in classical Greek philosophy, for example, Plato, *The Republic* (New York: W. W. Norton, 1985); and Aristotle, *The Politics* (New York: Viking Penguin, 1981).

4.   John Locke, *The Second Treatise of Government* (New York: Mentor, 1963); Immanuel Kant, *Foundations of the Metaphysics of Morals* (Indianapolis: Bobbs-Merrill, 1959); and John Rawls, *A Theory of Justice* (Cambridge: Harvard University Press, 1971). See Carole Pateman, *The Disorder of Women* (Stanford: Stanford University Press, 1989), on the gender bias in Locke and Rawls' theories. On Kant, see my "What is Enlightenment," in this volume.

5. Seyla Benhabib, "The Generalized and Concrete Other," in *Feminism and Critique*, edited by Seyla Benhabib and Drucilla Cornell (Bloomington: Indiana University Press, 1987); Carole Pateman and Elizabeth Gross, eds., *Feminist Challenges: Social and Political Theory* (Boston: Northeastern University Press, 1987); Morwena Griffith and Margaret Whitford, eds., *Feminist Perpectives in Philosophy* (Bloomington: Indiana University Press, 1988); Eva Feder Kittay and Diana Meyer, eds., *Women and Moral Theory* (Totowa: Rowman and Littlefield, 1987); Iris Marion Young, "Impartiality and the Civic Public: Some Implications of Feminist Critiques of Moral and Political Theory," in her *Throwing Like a Girl and Other Essays in Feminist Philosophy and Social Theory* (Bloomington: Indiana University Press, 1990); and Iris Marion Young, *Justice and the Politics of Difference* (Princeton: Princeton University Press, 1990).

6. See Diana Fuss, *Essentially Speaking: Feminism, Nature and Difference* (New York: Routledge, 1989); and Alison M. Jaggar and Susan R. Bordo, eds., *Gender/Body/Knowledge* (New Brunswick: Rutgers University Press, 1989).

7. Wendy Brown, *Manhood and Politics* (Totowa: Rowman & Littlefield, 1988); Susan Moller Okin, *Gender, Justice, and the Family* (New York: Basic Books, 1989); and Joan Cocks, *The Oppositional Imagination: Feminism, Critique and Political Theory* (New York: Routledge, 1989).

8. Ellen Kennedy and Susan Mendus, eds., *Women in Western Political Philosophy* (New York: St. Martins, 1987); Carole Pateman, *The Sexual Contract* (Stanford: Stanford University Press, 1988); Carol Pateman and Elizabeth Gross, eds., *Feminist Challenges* (Boston: Northeastern University Press, 1987); Susan Moller Okin, *Women in Western Political Thought* (Princeton: Princeton University Press, 1979); Joan Landes, *Women and the Public Sphere in the Age of the French Revolution* (Ithaca: Cornell University Press, 1988); Mary L. Shanley and Carole Pateman, eds., *Feminist Interpretations of Political Theory* (University Park: Pennsylvania State University Press, 1991); and Nancy J. Hirschman, *A Feminist Method for Political Theory* (Ithaca: Cornell University Press, 1992).

9. Helene Cixous and Catherine Clement, *The Newly Born Woman* (Minneapolis: University of Minnesota Press, 1986); Luce Iriagaray, *This Sex Which Is Not One* (Ithaca: Cornell University Press, 1985).

10. Juliet Mitchell, "Women and Equality," in *Feminism and Equality*, edited by Anne Phillips (New York: New York University Press, 1987); Deborah Rhode, ed., *Theoretical Perspectives on Sexual Difference* (New Haven: Yale University Press, 1990); and Martha Minow, *Making all the Difference: Inclusion, Exclusion, and American Law* (Ithaca: Cornell University Press, 1990).

11. See Carol Pateman and Elizabeth Gross, eds., *Feminist Challenges* (Boston: Northeastern University Press, 1987); and Sandra Harding and Merrill Hintikka, eds., *Discovering Reality: Feminist Perspectives on Epistemology, Metaphysics, Methodology and Philosophy of Science* (Boston: D. Reidel, 1983).

12. See Christina Crosby, "Dealing with Differences," in *Feminists Theorize the Political*, edited by Judith Butler and Joan Scott (New York: Routledge, 1992); Chandra Talpade Mohanty, Ann Russo, and Lourdes Torres, eds., *Third World Women and the Politics of Feminism* (Bloomington: Indiana University Press, 1991); and my "Minerva's Owl?" in this volume.

13. Jane Flax, *Thinking Fragments: Psychoanalysis, Feminism and Postmodernism in the Contemporary West* (Berkeley: University of California Press, 1990); Julia Kristeva, "Women's Time," *Signs* 7, 1 (Autumn 1981); 13–35; Julia Kristeva, *Powers of Horror* (New York: Columbia University Press, 1982); Bell Hooks, *Yearning: Race, Gender and Cultural Politics* (Boston: South End Press, 1990); and Trinh Minh-ha, *Woman/Native/Other* (Bloomington: Indiana University Press, 1989).

14. See Luce Irigaray; *This Sex Which Is Not One* (Ithaca: Cornell University Press, 1985); and Jean-François Lyotard and Jean-Loup Thebaud, *Just Gaming* (Minneapolis: University of Minnesota Press, 1985).

15. Jacques Derrida, "Structure, Sign and Play in the Discourse of the Human Sciences," in his *Writing and Difference* (Chicago: University of Chicago Press, 1978); Jacques Derrida, *Positions* (Chicago: University of Chicago Press, 1981); Jean-François Lyotard and Jean-Lous Thebaud; *Just Gaming* (Minneapolis: University of Minnesota Press, 1985). Jean-François Lyotard, *The Postmodern Condition: A Report on Knowledge* (Minneapolis: University of Minnesota Press, 1984); and Michel Foucault, "Truth, Power, Self," in *Technologies of the Self*, edited by Luther H. Martin, Huck Gutman, and Patrick H. Hutton (Amherst: University of Massachusetts Press, 1988).

16. Foucault's analysis of the relations within our episteme between truth and power is particularly germane in untangling such beliefs. See especially Michel Foucault, "Politics and the Study of Discourse;" and his "Questions of Method," both in *The Foucault Effect: Studies in Governmentality*, edited by Graham Burschell, Colin Gordon, and Peter Miller (Chicago: University of Chicago Press, 1991).

17. Hanna Fenichel Pitkin, "Justice: On Relating Private and Public," *Political Theory* 9, 3 (August 1981); 348, states the problem particularly well. She says, "(i)n a way political theory has always been concerned with this transition from private to public and the relation between personal and political. . .the problem is always: How shall we understand ourselves as simultaneously private and public beings?"

18. Mary Dietz, "Citizenship with a Human Face: The Problem With Maternal Thinking," *Political Theory* 13, 1(February 1985); 19–38; but see Patricia Boling, "The Democratic Potential of Mothering," *Political Theory* 19, 4 (November 1991); 606–625 for a revaluation of Dietz's argument.

19. See Richard Rorty, *Consequences of Pragmatism* (Minneapolis: University of Minnesota Press, 1982); Michel Foucault, *Power/Knowledge* (New York: Pantheon, 1980); and Michel Foucault, *Politics, Philosophy, Culture* (New York: Routledge, 1990).

20. Judith Butler, *Gender Trouble: Feminism and the Subversion of Identity* (New York: Routledge, 1990); and Alison M. Jaggar and Susan R. Bordo, eds., *Gender/Body/Knowledge* (New Brunswick: Rutgers University Press, 1989).

21. D. W. Winnicott, "Mind and its Relation to the Psyche-Soma," in his *Through Paediatrics to Psycho-Analysis* (New York: Basic Books, 1975).

22. Sigmund Freud, *The Ego and the Id* (New York: W. W. Norton, 1960); and Jacques Lacan, *The Four Fundamental Concepts of Psycho-analysis* (New York: W. W. Norton, 1978).

23. Joan W. Scott, *Gender and the Politics of History* (New York: Columbia University Press, 1988); and Diana Fuss, *Essentially Speaking* (New York: Rutledge, 1989).

24. Linda Zerilli, "Machiavelli's Sisters: Women and 'the Conversation' of Political Theory," *Political Theory* 19, 2 (May 1992); 252–276; and Christine Di Stephano, *Configurations of Masculinity: A Feminist Perspective on Modern Political Theory* (Ithaca: Cornell University Press, 1991).

25. Jessica Benjamin, *The Bonds of Love* (New York: Pantheon, 1988); Dorothy Dinnerstein, *The Mermaid and the Minotaur* (New York: Harper & Row, 1975); and Nancy Chodorow, "Gender, Relation and Difference in Psychoanalytic Perspective," in her *Feminism and Psychoanalytic Theory* (New Haven: Yale University Press, 1989).

26. See Nancy J. Hirschman; *A Feminist Method for Political Theory* (Ithaca: Cornell University Press, 1992); Susan R. Bordo, *The Flight to Objectivity: Essays on Cartesianism & Culture* (Albany: SUNY Press, 1987); Christine Di Stephano; *Configurations of Masculinity* (Ithaca: Cornell University Press, 1991); and Hanna Fenichel Pitkin, *Fortune is a Woman: Gender & Politics in the Thought of Niccolo Machiavelli* (Berkeley: University of California Press, 1984).

27. D.W. Winnicott, "Mind and Its Relation to the Psyche-Soma," in *Through Paediatrics to Psycho-Analysis* (New York: Basic Books, 1975), 246–247.

28. D. W. Winnicott, "Anxiety Associated with Insecurity," in *Through Paediatrics to Psycho-Analysis*, (New York: Basic Books, 1975); 99. Psychoanalysts differ about the accuracy of Winnicott's claims concerning early merger. See, for example, Daniel N. Stern, *The Interpersonal World of the Infant* (New York: Basic Books, 1985). However, dissenters agree babies puzzle about difference and attachment and what is inside and outside.

29. D. W. Winnicott, "Primitive Emotional Development," in *Through Paediatrics to Psycho-Analysis*, (New York: Basic Books, 1975); 153.

30. D. W. Winnicott, "Creativity and Its Origins," in *Playing and Reality*, 71.

31. D.W. Winnicott, "Transitional Objects and Transitional Phenomena," in ibid., p. 11.

32. D. W. Winnicott, "The Location of Cultural Experience," in ibid., p. 97.

33. D. W. Winnicott, "Transitional Objects and Transitional Phenomena," in ibid., p. 13.

34. D.W. Winnicott, "Transitional Objects and Transitional Phenomena," in ibid. p. 12.

35. One of the problems with Lacan's account of subjectivity is that he misses the productive aspects of this gap. He focuses almost exclusively on its difficulties and terrors. See Jacques Lacan, "The Mirror Stage as Formative of the Function of the I as Revealed in Psychoanalytic Experience," in his *Ecrits: A Selection* (New York: W. W. Norton, 1977).

36. Deborah King, "Multiple Jeopardy, Multiple Consciousness: The Context of Black Feminist Ideology," in *Black Women in America: Social Science Perspectives*, edited by Micheline R. Malson, et al. (Chicago: University of Chicago Press, 1990); Evelyn Brooks Higginbotham, "African-American Women's History and the Metalanguage of Race," *Signs* 17, 2(Winter 1992); 252–274; and Elsa Barkley Brown, "'What Has Happened Here': The Politics of Difference in Women's History and Feminist Politics" *Feminist Studies*, 18, 2 (Summer 1992); 295–312.

37. Hazel Carby, *Reconstructing Womanhood: The Emergence of the Afro-American Woman Novelist* (New York: Oxford, 1987); and Angela Y. Davis, *Women, Race, and Class* (New York: Random House, 1981).

The End of Innocence

1. Recent attempts to grapple with this legacy include Joan Wallace Scott, "The Sears Case," in her *Gender and the Politics of History* (New York: Columbia University Press, 1988); and *Theoretical Perspectives on Sexual Difference*, edited by Deborah L. Rhode (New Haven: Yale University Press, 1990).

2. Examples of this double position of criticism and hope include Sandra Harding, *The Science Question in Feminism* (Ithaca: Cornell University Press, 1986); Carol Gilligan, *In a Different Voice* (Cambridge: Harvard University Press, 1892); Nancy Hartsock, "The Feminist Standpoint: Developing the Ground for a Specifically Feminist Materialism," and Catherine MacKinnon, "Feminism, Marxism and the State: Toward Feminist Jurisprudence," both reprinted in *Feminism & Methodology*, edited by Sandra Harding (Bloomington: Indiana University Press, 1987).

3. I have been deeply influenced in the development of this essay by Stuart Hampshire's recent book, *Innocence and Experience* (Cambridge: Harvard University Press, 1989).

4. Kant articulates this promise most clearly. See Immanuel Kant, "What is Enlightenment?" reprinted with his *Foundations of the Metaphysics of Morals* (Indianapolis: Bobbs-Merrill, l959).

5. On the state of nature, see John Locke, *The Second Treatise of Government* in *John Locke's Two Treatises of Government*, edited by Peter Laslett (New York: Cambridge University Press, 1960). On the veil of ignorance, see John Rawls, *A Theory of Justice* (Cambridge: Harvard University Press, 1971), ch. 24.

6. For more extensive critiques of a variety of Marxist theories, see Isaac D. Balbus, *Marxism and Domination* (Princeton: Princeton University Press, 1982); and Hilary Manette Klein, "Marxism, Psychoanalysis, and Mother Nature," *Feminist Studies* 12, 2 (Summer 1989); 255–278.

7. "The knell of capitalist private property sounds. The expropriators are expropriated. . .capitalist production begets, with the inexorability of a law of Nature, its own negation." See Karl Marx, *Capital*, v.1 (New York: International Publishers, 1967), 763.

8. Immanuel Kant, *Critique of Pure Reason* (Garden City: Doubleday, 1966), especially the introduction.

9. Many social scientists and philosophers of social science continue to write as if they are completely unaware of the implications of recent philosophic developments for their foundational notions. See, for example, Alexander Rosenberg, *Philosophy of Social Science* (Boulder: Westview Press, 1988); or *The Use and Abuse of Social Science*, edited by Frank Heller (London: Sage Publications, 1986). Feminist theories and postmodernism are either not mentioned or are acknowledged and then ignored in many of these texts.

10. Thomas Kuhn, in *The Structure of Scientific Revolutions* (Chicago: University of Chicago Press, 1962), is one of the first to question this set of assumptions. For further reflections, see the essays in *After Philosophy*, edited by Kenneth Baynes, James Bohman, and Thomas McCarthy (Cambridge; MIT Press, 1987); and *The Institution of Philosophy*, edited by Avner Cohen and Marcelo Dascal (LaSalle: Open Court, 1989).

11. David Ricci, *The Tragedy of Political Science* (New Haven: Yale University Press, 1984); and Raymond Seidelman with Edward J. Harpham, *Disenchanted Realists* (Albany: SUNY Press, 1985), discuss the recurrent power of this belief in American politics and political science.

12. Especially Michel Foucault, *Power/Knowledge* (New York: Pantheon, 1980); and his *Politics, Philosophy, Culture* (New York: Routledge, 1988).

13. See the essays in *Gender/Body/Knowledge*, edited by Alison M. Jaggar and Susan R. Bordo (New Brunswick, NJ: Rutgers University Press, 1989); and *Feminist Challenges: Social and Political Theory*, edited by Carole Pateman and Elizabeth Gross (Boston: Northeastern Press, 1986).

14. This phrase is from Jacques Derrida, "Violence and Metaphysics," in his *Writing and Difference* (Chicago: University of Chicago Press, 1978); see also Richard Rorty on

foundational illusions, in his *Philosophy and the Mirror of Nature* (Princeton: Princeton University Press, 1979), especially p. 6.

15.   On what a postmodernist philosopher might do, see the essays in Avner Cohen and Marcelo Dascal, eds., *The Institution of Philosophy* (LaSalle: Open Court, 1989); Kenneth Baynes, et al., eds., *After Philosophy* (Cambridge: MIT Press, 1987); Richard Rorty, *Philosophy and the Mirror of Nature* (Princeton: Princeton University Press); ch. 8; Richard Rorty, *Consequences of Pragmatism* (Minneapolis: University of Minnesota Press, 1982); Jacques Derrida, *Positions* (Chicago: University of Chicago Press, 1981); Michel Foucault, *Power/Knowledge*; and Nancy Fraser, *Unruly Practices: Power, Discourse and Gender in Contemporary Social Theory* (Minneapolis: University of Minnesota Press, 1989).

16.   The essays in Carole Pateman and Elizabeth Gross, eds., *Feminist Challenges* (Boston: Northeastern Press, 1986); and Alison M. Jaggar and Susan R. Bordo; eds., *Gender/Body/Knowledge* (New Brunswick: Rutgers University Press, 1989) discuss these questions. See also Luce Irigaray, *Speculum of the Other Woman* (Ithaca: Cornell University Press, 1985); Helene Cixous and Catherine Clement, *The Newly Born Woman* (Minneapolis: University of Minnesota Press, 1986); and the essays in *Feminist Perspectives in Philosophy*, edited by Morwenna Griffiths and Margaret Whitford (Bloomington: Indiana University Press, 1988).

17.   Cf. Jacques Derrida, *Spurs/Eperons* (Chicago: University of Chicago Press, 1978) and the sympathetic critiques of postmodernist positions by Naomi Schor, "Dreaming Dissymmetry: Barthes, Foucault and Sexual Difference," in *Men in Feminism*, edited by Alice Jardine and Paul Smith (New York: Methuen, 1987); Alice A. Jardine, *Gynesis: Configurations of Woman and Modernity* (Ithaca: Cornell University Press, 1985), especially ch. 9; Susan Bordo, "Feminism, Postmodernism and Gender-Skepticism," in *Feminism/Postmodernism*, edited by Linda J. Nicholson (New York: Routledge, 1990); and Judith Butler, *Gender Trouble: Feminism and the Subversion of Identity* (New York: Routledge, 1990).

18.   Such arguments have been made by Sandra Harding, "Feminism, Science, and the Anti-Enlightenment Critiques," and Christine Di Stefano, "Dilemmas of Difference: Feminism, Modernity, and Postmodernism," both in Linda J. Nicholson; ed., *Feminism/Posmodernism* (New York: Routledge, 1990); and by Mary E. Hawkesworth, Knowers, Knowing, Known: Feminist Theory and the Claims of Truth," in *Feminist Theory in Practice and Process*, edited by Micheline R. Malson, et al. (Chicago: University of Chicago Press, 1989).

19.   For strong statements of this position, see Nancy Hartsock, "Foucault on Power: A Theory for Women?," in Linda J. Nicholson, ed., *Feminism/Postmodernism* (New York: Routledge, 1990); and Mary E. Hawkesworth, "Knowers, Knowing, Known," in Micheline R. Malson, et al., eds., *Feminist Theory in Practice and Process* (Chicago: University of Chicago Press, 1989). Much of the feminist debate on postmodernism turns on a political question: whether the legitimacy and efficacy of

feminist practices and claims require an epistemological justification/grounding. On this debate see Nancy Fraser and Linda J. Nicholson, "Social Criticism without Philosophy: An Encounter between Feminism and Postmodernism." and Seyla Benhabib, "Epistemologies of Postmodernism: A Rejoinder to Jean-Francois Lyotard," both in Linda J. Nicholson, ed., *Feminism/Postmodernism* (New York: Routledge, 1990); Linda Alcoff, "Cultural Feminism versus Post-Structuralism: The Identity Crisis in Feminist Theory," in Micheline R. Malson, et al., eds., *Feminist Theory in Practice and Process* (Chicago: Univesity of Chicago Press, 1989); the essays in *Feminist Studies* 14, 1 (Spring 1988); Donna Haraway, "Situated Knowledges: The Science Question in Feminism and the Privilege of Partial Perspective," *Feminist Studies*, 14, 3 (Fall 1988); 575–599; Nancy Fraser, *Unruly Practices* (Minneapolis: University of Minnesota Press, 1989); and Kathy E. Ferguson, "Interpretation and Genealogy in Feminism," *Signs* 16, 2 (Winter 1991); 322–339.

20. Barbara Christian, "Race for Theory," *Feminist Studies* 14, 1(Summer 1988); 67–79; Audre Lorde, *Sister Outsider* (Trumansburg, NY: Crossing Press, 1984); Deborah K. King, "Multiple Jeopardy, Multiple Consciousness: The Context for a Black Feminist Ideology," in Micheline R. Malson, et al., eds., *Feminist Theory in Practice and Process* (Chicago: University of Chicago Press, 1989); Elizabeth V. Spelman, *Inessential Woman: Problems of Exclusion in Feminist Thought* (Boston: Beacon, 1988); Biddy Martin and Chandra Talpade Mohanty, "Feminist Politics: What's Home Got to Do with It?" in *Feminist Studies/Critical Studies*, edited by Teresa de Lauretis (Bloomington: Indiana University Press, 1986); and Bernice Johnson Reagon, "Coalition Politics: Turning the Century," in *Home Girls: A Black Feminist Anthology*, edited by Barbara Smith (New York: Kitchen Table: Women of Color Press, 1983).

21. As I argue in *Thinking Fragments: Psychoanalysis, Feminism and Postmodernism in the Contemporary West* (Berkeley: University of California Press, 1990). On postmodernism, race, and gender see Bell Hooks, *Yearning: Race, Gender and Cultural Politics* (Boston: South End Press, 1990).

22. See Stuart Hampshire, *Innocence and Experience* (Cambridge: Harvard University Press, 1989); Agnes Heller and Ferenc Feher, *The Postmodern Political Condition* (New York: Columbia University Press, 1989); and Judith N. Shklar, "Injustice, Injury and Inequality: An Introduction," in *Justice and Equality in the Here and Now*, edited by Frank S. Lucash (Ithaca: Cornell University Press, 1986).

23. Richard Rorty, "Method, Social Science, and Social Hope," in his *Consequences of Pragmatism* (Minneapolis: University of Minnesota Press, 1982), 208.

AUTHOR INDEX

SUBJECT INDEX